Creating a Successful Digital F

Increasingly graduates, and anyone who is entering employment, need an individual digital presence to stand out and showcase themselves to secure their first professional role. This book takes an employability approach to encourage those currently studying, or about to enter the world of work, to develop a set of skills that enables them to recognise and deliver an effective digital presence, firstly for themselves and then for the organisations that would employ them. It does not assume any prior technical knowledge and emphasises the value and benefits of creating a presence to actively participate in the digital economy.

By structuring the chapters incrementally, the reader is guided through the development of their own presence while also being given the concepts and tools that will enable them in the future to scale this activity to suit the needs of a startup, an SME or a social business. By using well-established business principles to design a strategy, the reader is guided through the creation of a personal Theory of Change that will enable them to turn an abstract goal into an individual digital presence through a defined series of stages and intermediate change objectives. The book then proposes a series of tactics to draw out concrete actions. A range of examples and case studies from around the world feature in each chapter to showcase the range of different types of digital presence that can be created.

By using a strategic and systematic process, this book draws together academic thinking with tangible and highly practical outcomes. It is essential reading for advanced undergraduate and postgraduate students studying any discipline related to the digital world, particularly digital marketing and digital business, entrepreneurship and strategy, as well as those taking employability and personal professional development programmes.

Gordon Fletcher is Director of Business 4.0 at Salford Business School, UK. His interests relate to the intersections of digital with business and culture. These interests have resulted in previous publications about digital transformation and digital marketing as well as work around the impact of digital on the UK High Street, science fiction prototyping and the concept of visual management.

Noel Adolphus is a web support analyst with Red Valley Technology in Manchester, UK. He helps his clients with solutions involving the WordPress platform and has helped numerous businesses connect with their customers online, amplifying visibility and profit. Noel has a BS in Electrical Engineering Technology from Michigan Technological University, US, and an MSc in Managing IT from the University of Salford, UK.

Creating a Successful Digital Presence

Objectives, Strategies and Tactics

Gordon Fletcher and Noel Adolphus

Routledge
Taylor & Francis Group

LONDON AND NEW YORK

First published 2022
by Routledge
2 Park Square, Milton Park, Abingdon, Oxon OX14 4RN

and by Routledge
605 Third Avenue, New York, NY 10158

Routledge is an imprint of the Taylor & Francis Group, an informa business

British Library Cataloguing-in-Publication Data
A catalogue record for this book is available from the British Library

Library of Congress Cataloging-in-Publication Data
Names: Fletcher, Gordon, author. | Adolphus, Noel, 1975– author.
Title: Creating a successful digital presence : objectives, strategies and tactics / Gordon Fletcher and Noel Adolphus.
Description: Abingdon, Oxon ; New York, NY : Routledge, 2021. | Includes bibliographical references and index.
Identifiers: LCCN 2021005254 (print) | LCCN 2021005255 (ebook) (paperback) | ISBN 9781003026587 (ebook)
Subjects: LCSH: Public relations. | Social media. | Branding (Marketing) | Internet in public relations. | Internet marketing.
Classification: LCC HM1221 .F63 2021 (print) | LCC HM1221 (ebook) | DDC 659.20285/4678—dc23
LC record available at https://lccn.loc.gov/2021005254
LC ebook record available at https://lccn.loc.gov/2021005255

ISBN: 978-0-367-46034-1 (hbk)
ISBN: 978-0-367-46037-2 (pbk)
ISBN: 978-1-003-02658-7 (ebk)

DOI: 10.4324/9781003026587

Typeset in Bembo
by Apex CoVantage, LLC

Contents

4 Personas – understanding your audience 43

5 Ethical and legal issues 52

**PART II
Planning** 65

6 What is a Theory of Change? 67

7 Tactics for building your presence 79

Figures

Preface

This book is unique. It takes a strategic perspective towards the creation of your digital presence and uses the theory of change to get there. It also avoids casually using hundreds of technical acronyms and abbreviations assuming your prior knowledge. Throughout the book, there is a conscious recognition that a successful digital presence can only be the outcome of a cyclic strategic process that cannot simply be reduced to a single sequence of technical operations. Taking a strategic approach also differs from many solely digital marketing perspectives that focus narrowly on a set of specific techniques or the most currently available tools. As a result, there is no suggestion being made in this preface to just dive in with any of the chapters and read on. This book is consciously intended to be read in the regular, "old-fashioned" way from the first chapter through to the end. This will be a challenge for a reader who has already created some form of digital presence. However it is a challenge worth accepting. Adopting a strategic view for the creation of your digital presence brings long-term benefits that definitely include saving you time in the long run. Another key difference in this book is the attention given to your personal digital presence rather than to that of a more detached or theoretical organisation. By starting with a personal presence, there are immediate benefits to be gained from reading and using this book. Not least is that, by defining and deploying a Theory of Change (Chapter 6) as an integral aspect of creating your digital presence, you can bridge the gap between where you are currently and where you want to be as a direct result of the change process that you are initiating.

This book uses the Theory of Change as a useful framework to manage the complex combination of social and technical challenges – and pitfalls – for creating a successful digital presence. Being strategic in creating your digital presence and using the Theory of Change has wider benefits too. Once you have successfully created your own digital presence, the same approach can be revisited again and again. You can support your own employer's digital presence, build your own entrepreneurial startup, enhance your local community or improve the impact of a charitable organisation.

Why we created this book

This book is written by an academic and a practitioner. As an academic, Gordon has seen how students – in their transformation to graduate roles – struggle with the application of theory in their new workplaces. Students on internships are also often asked to create or improve their organisation's digital presence as one of the first tasks they are allocated. The majority of these students immediately recognise the limitations of their current training and limited resources that they have access to in order to complete the task.

Gordon found that the available training resources could be generally clustered into three broad and sometimes overlapping categories.

1   Theoretical material with disjointed technical examples. For example, books on HTML and CSS that never reveal how to create a website or that "connect the dots" through the building up of a single case study.
2   "How to" guides such as "3 steps to success with Twitter". Materials that were too basic and offered little value beyond the immediate specifics of the task being described.
3   Practical resources presented without any overarching theoretical framework that leads to an often piecemeal approach to the task.

What became clear was that Gordon's students needed a richer and integrated combination of guidance, technical skills and a systematic (or theoried) way to approach the task itself that lies at the intersection of these challenges (Figure 0.1)

As a practitioner, Noel was tasked with the development of a digital agency within an already established small firm. It was a daunting task. Seemingly small operational decisions, such as whether to manually hardcode a new website or use an existing content management system (CMS), proved to be of enormous significance in the long run. A few years after commencing the project, Noel found himself with about 25 ongoing website developments that had been created with the WordPress CMS system. The most frustrating realisation that came out of these years of work was that many of the sites were underperforming and unsuccessful. The learning from this experience was the hard-won realisation that an organisation does not solely need a well-designed website (even if that is all they are asking for in the design brief or initial scoping conversation). Their requirements are inevitably rather more complex and expansive and are much better expressed as the overall requirements for a successful digital presence. This was a paradigm shift in

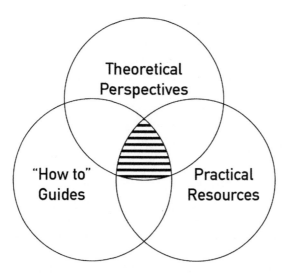

Figure 0.1 Categories of the resources to support the creation of a digital presence

Noel's own thinking that had been gained through a steep learning curve and painful experience.

In sharing their personal experiences, Noel and Gordon recognised that no book existed that tackled these intersecting challenges in a consciously systematic or even useful way. The majority of these books started with the viewpoint of a traditional academic discipline (computer science or marketing) rather than focusing on the combined set of skills that an individual would need to create their own digital presence. Together, Noel and Gordon then spent many hours framing their combination of awareness, reflection and knowledge into what eventually evolved into the book that you are now reading.

The objectives of this book

The intended audience for this book is primarily a student completing a programme of studies and preparing to enter the world of work. The book is not targeted at students in any specific discipline as the need for a digital presence is now effectively universal in order to gain the attention of suitable prospective employers. Some graduates may plan to take an entrepreneurial route with their entrance to professional life. The challenge of creating a startup is also heavily reliant on building a successful digital presence even if the specific need for this presence will differ from more traditional graduate employment pathways.

In this book we demonstrate how a successful digital presence is the consequence of achieving defined objectives through a strategic approach. This observation can be applied equally to an individual or an organisation. We see the project of creating your personal digital presence as an important stepping stone to presenting yourself as a professional and building a pathway to a career with suitable roles. Building your personal presence is the "living lab" for similar activities that you will very likely be asked to undertake for a future employer. The lab gives you the opportunity and flexibility to test different approaches, to learn from the results and to act upon these results in ways that continuously improve and enhance your digital presence. At the heart of this work is the goal of personal or professional success through your newly created digital presence.

Achieving your objectives is the desired end state. However, by employing a strategic approach, you also learn about the wider generic applicability of your own skills and understanding. Creating one successful digital presence enables you to create (or direct the creation of) a presence for other individuals or organisations. This is not about the narrower set of actions connected with becoming a web developer but rather reflects the wider set of skills that are an integral part of becoming an analyst, an innovator and a strategist. Creating a digital presence does require the interpretation of circumstances, planning techniques and the implementation of change. These actions, and many others associated with creating a digital presence, all represent the application of valuable "generic soft skills" that are needed across many roles in business and government and within communities.

To manage the creation of a digital presence, this book shows how to use tools and models that will simplify many of the processes by breaking down this one big challenge into its smaller parts. From its top level of challenge, the creation of a digital presence is broken down into three core tactics: engaging with channels, building visibility and generating a positive reputation (Figure 0.2).

This book goes beyond introducing a single preferred strategic framework and aims to more deeply instill strategic thinking and perspectives into you as the reader. Strategic

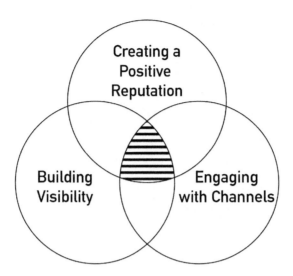

Figure 0.2 The combined challenges of creating a digital presence

thinking is an invaluable skill that enables you to understand the consequences of imme-diate actions within a long-term perspective. A strategic perspective also brings the capa-bility to integrate and manage different (sometimes competing) resources and actions to achieve a defined objective. This approach reflects our belief that it is more important to create a pipeline of individuals who are strategic thinkers than "filling these individuals up" with content that fits a specific discipline's current perspective. In short, we see build-ing a digital presence as being the successful result of applying a combination of many key management skills.

This is also a "how to" project book. Each chapter steps through a case study that shows how to create a successful digital presence. Knowledge is reinforced by experience, and experience assists in making knowledge real. The purpose of the case study is to parallel the stages in the development of your own digital presence. The case study demonstrates the concepts being applied and reinforces the emphasis on maintaining a strategic long-term perspective on the project.

Structure

The five parts of this book represent the stages that create a successful digital presence. The parts also represent a continuous cycle of development (Figure 0.3) and should be read in this iterative manner. This provides a form of safety net in the creation of your own presence. If the outcomes are not quite what is expected at the end of a cycle of development, there is an opportunity to return to earlier parts and repeat, with the additional benefit of having learned from failure (or just poor performance). The order-ing of the book's parts also consciously sets out to develop strategic and systems thinking skills alongside more specific knowledge. Each chapter starts with its intended learning objectives so you can commence with an awareness of the end objectives and what you are aiming to achieve. Each chapter also ends with a brief summation of the ground that has been covered. This approach echoes the act of reading the last page of a thriller but

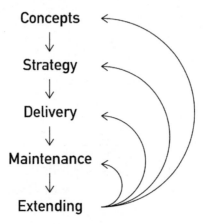

Figure 0.3 The cycle of development represented by the book's sections

is an attempt to overcome the often significant cognitive barrier of trying to learn about something when "you don't know what you don't know".

At the end of this book you will have learned

- How to create your own digital presence
- How combining the actions of engaging channels, building visibility and generating positive reputation creates a digital presence
- How to define strategic objectives and formulate specific actions to achieve these objectives
- How to use a Theory of Change as a project management tool to support the creation of a digital presence (or any other strategic objective)
- The relationship and ways of integrating your online and offline presences

A key feature of this book is the use of a real-world running case study indeboraskitchen, which is developed to illustrate each of the five sections of the book. The dynamic nature of demonstrating a real-world case study and fast-changing technology presents unique opportunities and challenges. The journey to creating a successful digital presence for indeboraskitchen will be captured on the accompanying digital presence of this book (https://digitalonespace.com/).

We hope you find the journey enriching and worthwhile.

Acknowledgements

Alfie Showman and Earnest McQueen for their many case study suggestions.

Dr Simon Brown, Director of Red Valley Technology for patience in accommodating Noel to work on the book and for contributing to the term "Masked Marketing".

Subrahmaniam of the Greater Manchester Chamber of Commerce for contributing personal knowledge and insight to Chapter 16.

Debora Capeleti and Gustavo Andrade for allowing us to intrude on them at a complex time in their lives.

Ameera Fletcher for her patience as we realised that writing a book during a pandemic turned out to be onerous and complex.

All the royalties from the sale of this book assigned to Noel Adolphus will be donated to the Lighthouse Church (lighthousecc.co.uk), North Manchester, to support its humanitarian work in the local community.

All the royalties from the sale of this book assigned to Gordon Fletcher will be donated to Cre8 Macclesfield (Cre8Macclesfield.org) to support its education work with young people and their families among the Moss Rose community in Macclesfield.

Part I

Concepts

1 What is a digital presence?

What you will learn

- What does digital mean?
- Your value proposition
- The key elements of a digital presence

1.1 What does digital mean?

Digital is a broad term. It is sometimes uncritically used as a badge to represent anything "new". Often it is applied to distinguish from other practices, behaviours or products that are simply older. Most people personally have some sort of broad understanding of what digital means. But in amongst the details of each of these individual definitions there can be significant variations. This is the key explanation for why book authors on topics such as digital presence devote time to explaining their own perspective on the meaning of the term "digital". A definition left unspoken for what might be a seemingly obvious term leads to later confusion. That ongoing need for clarity and consistency is no different in this book.

The label for the consequences of using digital technologies, "digitalisation", is a coverall for all aspects of the economy and society affected. Digitalisation has now created vast and automated parts of the economy that function invisibly, although the consequences and outcomes can be highly visible. The impact of digital on society and the economy can be regarded as the biggest shift in behaviour and practice since the Industrial Revolution and the current culmination of the changes achieved over that previous 250 years (Arthur 2011; Hilali and Manouar 2019). An appreciation of the increasing scale and wide-ranging impact of digital technology in contemporary economic and social activity leads directly on to an acknowledgement of the importance for developing and maintaining a digital presence. In this context, a digital presence can also be seen as a specific personal requirement within the wider processes that are moving us towards ubiquitous digitalisation.

Dorner and Edelman (2015) argue for digital to be seen less as a thing and more as a way of *doing* things. In this way, "digital" is an enabler for action, not a goal in itself. We build on this core idea to make the understanding of the digital more concrete. The challenge is that the word "digital" is used as an adjective that describes and conditions a previous situation but at the same time marks it as being in some ways distinct. The examples of "digital marketing", "digital business", "ecommerce" or even "email" all evidence the prevalence of this thinking. In each of the examples substituting the adjective "digital"

DOI: 10.4324/9781003026587-1

with the phrase, "the digitalisation of" is the wordier but arguably more appropriate way of expressing the significance of the change and enabling of each of these functions. The oldest of these example processes particularly highlights the scale of the impact with "the digitalisation of mail".

Breaking the understanding of digital down into its constituent attributes (Dorner and Edelman 2015) also assists in better representing the impact and meaning of digital on individuals and organisations. The effective application of the "digital" creates new value for organisations and for individuals. Our own focus on creating a digital presence is instructive. In the current example, a key impact of digitalisation is that anyone can create a highly visible profile that is directed to and accessible by a clearly defined and targeted audience.

However, the need to create a personal or organisational presence has not emerged with the rising popularity of digital. As with so many practices that we now consider largely or solely in a digital context, the need to build and manage a presence has been evolving, accelerating and extending since the Industrial Revolution. Prior to digital technology's integration into mass consumption practice (the digitalisation of commerce), the availability of the tools to create a presence were largely restricted to public figures and large enterprises. The idea that a presence was even needed was largely restricted to Hollywood icons, national politicians and multinational corporations. Technology that permits digitalisation is a significant leveller with anyone now enabled to construct and promote their presence. However, the consequences of digital being an economic and social leveller also increases the need for everyone to create a presence. As the volume, velocity and variety of the information now available about anyone has also increased, it is not just Hollywood icons who must be seen, heard and recognised. With everyone able to build a strong digital presence, anyone else attempting to secure a professional role, find a life partner or present their organisation to a local audience must also build a strong digital presence or risk being shut out.

The value of creating a successful digital presence can be measured at its most base level through the financial rewards associated with the rise of the new and digitally enabled role of "influencer". Successful influencers now enjoy the lifestyle of a 1950s Hollywood icon and the recognition of an international sports star. Value is being generated individually through the digital presence of the influencers and for the businesses that work with and sponsor them.

Digital also enables closer alignment of perspectives and values. For a business seeking to increase its market share, this is re-interpreted directly and becomes central to its marketing efforts. For charities and community organisations, this is about representing the common purpose they share with donors and supporters while also communicating their services to the intended beneficiaries. The importance of making connections and building relationships through digital channels as part of the purpose of creating a presence also emphasises a mindset of sharing, openness and transparency. A mutual alignment of values is reinforced by continuous forms of contact that are appropriate for the audience and the values being expressed. This might be expressed through, for example, the sharing of lifestyle experience images, high levels of data visibility or opportunities to have feedback channels from the intended audience. Maintaining a close alignment of values and perspectives with an intended audience is a key pathway to success. Social media channels, as part of their own processes to monetise audience engagement, emphasise likeness and tend to push away those with different values by demoting or not showing their presence. This situation described the key concept of the social media "echo chamber" that came under increased scrutiny during the Trump presidency and subsequently (Bruns 2017). The positive aspect of social media channels and their capability to target a like-minded audience is simultaneously negative as it limits diversity of experience, opinion and perspectives.

The pivotal digital technology for all this opportunity is the internet. Without this well-established, open and global network of computing working under the same protocols and processes, what we now label "digital" would simply not work. Increasingly the purpose of computers, laptops, tablets and mobile phones is as physical touchpoints into the internet. Exploiting the unique characteristics of the internet is at the heart of understanding how to create and capture value through a digital presence.

Building on the works of Afuah and Tucci (2003) and Laudon and Laudon (2021), we identify 11 interdependent characteristics of the internet that can be applied directly to the development of a digital presence and explain the value of creating this presence (Figure 1.1). These characteristics can also be the basis for shaping entirely new businesses, defining new ways of socialising and working together, building communities and addressing global issues. Taken entirely uncritically as having solely positive features presents the libertarian view of the digital and a type of emancipatory capacity. Through this and subsequent chapters, we encourage a more critical and nuanced perspective on shaping your presence within a digital context. This is a position that does encourage exploration of the many social and economic opportunities provided by the "digital" while still being situated within the acknowledged constraints of existing channels and practices. In other words, creating a digital presence is primarily seen as being for an individual to make themselves more attractive to prospective employers or make their products more visible to potential customers. But we acknowledge that a digital presence can also focus on the purpose of building a social movement and advocating change. While the influences of libertarian perspective can sometimes be clearly identified in social media channels, websites or other apps, there are other philosophies that equally influence our experience of the "digital", including traditional capitalism and populism.

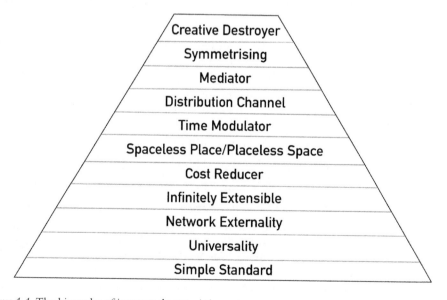

Figure 1.1 The hierarchy of internet characteristics

The 11 characteristics of the internet – and more broadly of the "digital" – shape how we will approach the creation of a digital presence. These 11 characteristics represent an accumulated assemblage with the result that the latter characteristics need some or all of the previous characteristics to function. Although there are many examples of different simple technical standards that provide ways of doing things (in the lower-numbered characteristics), there are very few examples of social or economic practice that enable symmetrising practices or can bring creative destruction (Figure 1.1).

1   Simple standard: The internet is built on simple technical standards that are well documented and open. The initial cost of development was underwritten by the US government, removing its conceptualisation and establishment from immediate direct commercial pressures.
2   Universality: By being based on a simple standard that can be accessed through easily reproduced processes and technologies, the internet is a global system.
3   Network externality: The network is better whenever more people use it. This characteristic benefits from the universality of the internet but can also be evidenced at more sophisticated levels such as individual social media channels or within a specific online community of practice.
4   Infinitely extensible: As a global network built on relatively simple standards and a global universality, the internet enables any channel to grow and expand to become as large as it requires. This can be considered in terms of its technical requirements as well as the size of a channel's community.
5   Cost reducer: The initial non-commercial development of the internet removes any need now to recoup these establishment costs. The universality of the internet also enables the ongoing costs of delivering the technical infrastructure to be spread across a number of services such as electricity suppliers, services providers and specific channel subscriptions. Network externality and being infinitely extensible also bring costs benefits to individuals who share the costs of delivering a service with a far larger base of consumers than may have been the case traditionally. In combination these characteristics reduce the transaction costs of all types overall and for any individual.
6   Spaceless place/placeless space: The internet has the capacity to present digital twins of physical equivalents, a quality already well utilised for video and music distribution, while also being an entirely different place in its own right that is separate and distinctive as any other places separate by time or space. This twinned ability to echo traditional services while enabling entirely new types of experiences drives popular acceptance at the same time as encouraging innovation.
7   Time modulator: One consequence of being a spaceless place is the internet's characteristic of modulating time. The time frames for actions can be varied, in contrast to those conducted in other spaces. Retail activities can be automated and are continuously available. Entertainment activities, particularly games, can pace out the achievement of goals over many days if not weeks.
8   Distribution channel: Anything that can now be offered as a digital asset can be distributed through the internet, including images, audio and video. The metadata of any physical asset can be distributed through the internet including its schematic, availability, location and price.
9   Mediator: Through network externality and by being a spaceless place, the internet creates new connections and associations. The mediator characteristic of the internet

enables these connections to be two way. Some channels are actively engineered to restrict this interaction and instead are delivered as analogs of more traditional broadcast media.

10 Symmetrising: In any form of exchange, one party will often have more information than the other party. The internet acts to level out the differences in information held by separate parties and enables different forms of reciprocation between them.

11 Creative destroyer: The advantages of being a simple standard, having universality and being infinitely extensible, coupled with its role as a distribution channel, make the internet an "obvious" replacement to old ways of doing things. This has already been shown with music and video business models, with further substitutions emerging continuously. The cost reducer characteristic of the internet also means the previous channels that use the internet can be rapidly changed and substituted by newer versions.

In combination these 11 characteristics represent the internet's core values. The same characteristics can also be recognised in different combinations within many of the most iconic, significant and valuable digital channels, apps and websites. Creating your own digital presence will also take advantage of some or all of these characteristics either directly or indirectly.

1.2 Your value proposition

The value proposition is core to any business model and by extension to any organisation. A value proposition can be described most simply as the benefit that someone else gets from you. For an organisation, defining and amplifying the value proposition is at the heart of their business models. From the perspective of an individual, the same principle also applies. In the majority of cases, the value proposition that an individual provides to an organisation is traditionally compensated directly through payment of wages. Individuals also gain value from other individuals through actions such as building a sense of association or connection (with influencers and other public figures), learning something new or just by being entertained.

At the core of the value proposition is a reliance on the fundamental human concept of reciprocation. The value gained by one person from another is reciprocated in a different form in the opposite direction at a later time (Figure 1.2). Reciprocation is not necessarily immediately received, nor is its value necessarily directly equivalent from the point of view of the recipient. Reciprocation may also be achieved through a chain of intermediaries over longer periods of time.

The act of directly paying for a service or goods is the most familiar and direct form of reciprocation. This recognition is because payment is the most obvious and most transactional form of reciprocation and an integral part of market-based economies. However, many other forms of reciprocation are not based on giving or receiving a direct payment.

The symmetrising and mediator characteristics of the internet (and of digital generally) increase the opportunity for a wider range of non-transactional forms of reciprocation. It is through these opportunities that your personal digital presence can develop and flourish. For a successful presence, the principle of reciprocation is needed to build visibility and reputation through multiple channels (Figure 1.2). The indirect monetisation of this reciprocation – and the key measure of success for your digital presence – is realised with obtaining suitable employment (or achieving whatever goal you choose to define). The

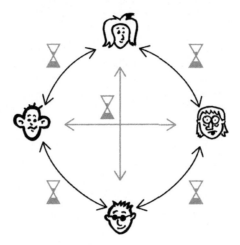

Figure 1.2 The principle of reciprocation

digital value proposition is about exploring and exploiting the opportunities for reciprocation that can only be enabled through the combined 11 characteristics of the internet.

The benefits of a digital value proposition also apply at an organisational level, and the learning that comes from creating your own digital presence translates well into this larger scale. The digital value proposition is not transactional in its purpose or focus. An organisation working to improve their value proposition involves a dynamic and iterative cycle in which communications, processes and capabilities are constantly being evolved based on feedback from customers and consumers. This cycle of improvement encourages loyalty, keeps pace with competitors and ensures clear alignment with organisational vision and mission (Figure 1.3 and compare with Figure 0.3).

The characteristics of the internet and being digital enable a critical rethinking of how the value proposition can be made real for consumers through the organisation's products and services as well as how these are delivered. Acknowledging the impact of digital can be a significant challenge in some organisations. Beyond the use of social media channels for marketing, the digital value proposition may provoke a fundamental review of what and how a product is provided. The digital value proposition may even be a prompt for changes in the business model with the identification that different forms of reciprocation are possible and that long-term generation of value can be achieved more effectively.

The value proposition for an organisation also assists in better understanding its role for your own personal digital presence. The value proposition – what benefit you offer to others – is simultaneously top-down and bottom-up. The top-down component is the mission and vision of the organisation itself. It is what makes the organisation distinctive and defines its purpose and ongoing reason for existence. From the opposite direction come the specific details about the organisation's products and services and how these are delivered. The specific products and services should be a reflection of, and align with, the mission of the organisation. The symmetrising characteristic of the internet crucially makes it easier for consumers to recognise misalignment and mismatches between a product and the organisation making the offer (Figure 1.4).

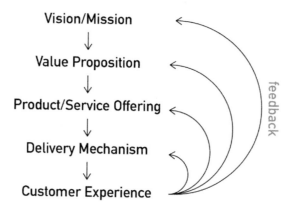

Figure 1.3 Continuous improvement as part of an organisation's digital value proposition

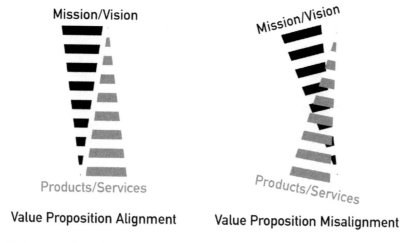

Figure 1.4 Value proposition alignment and misalignments

For your own digital presence, having alignment between what you believe and what you offer is equally important. The symmetrising characteristic of the internet also applies to personal presence. There are many documented cases of companies choosing not to employ a well-qualified candidate because of what is revealed about the individual through open accounts on social media channels. For these organisations, an individual being able to personally offer the right qualifications and work experience is not sufficient if the behaviours documented through social media do not align with their own expectations of professional behaviour. The reverse situation also holds true. If the actions of your own that are revealed through social media are actions that you stand by and truly reflect your worldview and beliefs but do not align with those of a potential employer, then you may seriously want to reflect on whether the role that they are offering is right for you.

The role of digital is regularly cited as being about change and disruption. However, this is not unfocused or random change for the sake of change. Change activities are guided by a vision and mission. It is about delivering a value proposition in more effective and efficient ways. The eventual reciprocation – the benefits that flow back to you (or to an organisation) – will be improved through the more effective and efficient delivery of a value proposition.

1.3 The key elements of a digital presence

Having now developed a working understanding of the digital value proposition, a definition of "digital presence", in turn, presents itself after some negotiation of its intersecting elements. When the "digital presence" of an organisation is mentioned, it is invariably the website and social media channels that come to mind. These are the most visible and obvious elements of any digital presence. But even this observation belies a degree of complexity and variability. Despite the volume of academic research around the topic of digital, there is remarkably little consistency on what defines a "digital presence". Academic debate is invariably founded upon debate and the synthesis of contrasting positions, but it is more important to acknowledge that the lack of precision also comes from the rapidly evolving nature of the field. Nonetheless, this is not an excuse to avoid definition. It is important to have a concrete starting definition of a digital presence in order to build and extend your own working knowledge and understanding.

One view is that a "digital presence" is how a person or organisation presents themselves online. However, this can just as easily be reversed to argue that a "digital presence" is how a person or organisation is received by its audience online. Although clearly connected, these two different perspectives highlight the complexity of the debate – and of finding a single consistent definition (compare this with §1.2). It is also important to stress that both these views take a more traditional direct communications–based view, emphasising the differentiated roles of the producer and the consumer. However, a critical perspective is required before accepting these definitions.

Despite the many ways of producing content to be presented online, the mere fact that content exists does not guarantee that it will find an audience. The astronaut.io website reveals an endless stream of YouTube videos that have had no audience attention (until you visit them through astronaut.io). Many of the videos are object lessons in the wrong ways to build content with default file names such as "DSC 0214", no clear purpose, no sense of story and no understanding of the intended audience. The COVID-19 pandemic period has only further contributed to this unfocused creation of content with increased levels of spare time, material being made unintentionally public and the assessment regimes brought about by remote schooling.

The same caution is needed in viewing a digital presence as being defined purely by the audience. The potential scale of any internet-based audience should itself be a warning against unsophisticated definitions of audience – and especially those that simply describe "the public" or "everyone". Similarly audience reception is itself variable and can differ from the purpose envisaged by its creator. The Reddit subchannel Accidental Comedy (reddit.com/r/AccidentalComedy/) is a continuous stream of content that is consumed ironically. The UK magazine *Private Eye* has a regular "Malgorithms" column that highlights online content that has been juxtaposed with contradictory or contrasting advertisements. The column is intended to be read satirically. Sometimes, unintentionally humorous content brings a big audience that contains within it the emerging core of a loyal consumer base. The work of Blendtec and the 140 "Will it blend?" infomercial-style YouTube videos are a seminal example of the value of virality for gaining audiences (Miller 2015). More recently, the FlexTape infomercials present a specific product – a flexible rubberised tape that can perform under extreme conditions (youtube.com/watch?v=nDeSODQ_hCo). The content itself is compelling viewing and has been the focus of a US television consumer watchdog programme where it received positive reviews (youtube.com/watch?v=Kp_gsxHmwCE) and online reviewers who examined more outlandish claims – that were not made by the retailer – about FlexTape to a generally positive outcome (youtube.com/watch?v=uaG56S3lqkE). For global internet audiences, FlexTape only became available outside the US a number of years after the infomercials appeared.

The lesson of these examples is that, as with the digital value proposition, digital presence is a combined consideration of both creator and audience. With creator and audience in alignment, the benefits of the digital presence can be fully realised (Figure 1.5).

The creator/audience relationship is the top-level view onto the elements of a digital presence. Without breaking these elements down further, there is the risk of creating the impression that a successful digital presence is "simply" a case of saying the "right" things to the "right" people. This does answer "what" and "who" questions of creating a digital presence. The preface and the initial parts of this chapter have already outlined "why" a digital presence is important. The "why" question is returned to throughout subsequent chapters. But in order to be able to do anything yourself, these questions all fall short of offering any advice as to "how" or "when" your actions for creating a digital presence should happen. How a successful digital presence is created can be discovered in the specific individual qualities of visibility and reputation being delivered through the right channels (Figure 1.6). These are elements of a digital presence that, when brought together in the right mix, can bring success.

The visibility element is the breadth of your presence. This does not necessarily correlate with being present on many different channels but rather having a recognised and differentiated presence across the key channels that are relevant to your objectives. This means that your name (or your online equivalent) is recognised widely within specific online communities. Communities can be of varying size, with "influencers" being the label for the most recognisable people in the largest and most general communities or even across entire channels. The premium examples of this whole channel visibility is represented with the rise of the role of "YouTuber" and the "Instafamous" (Callout 18.1).

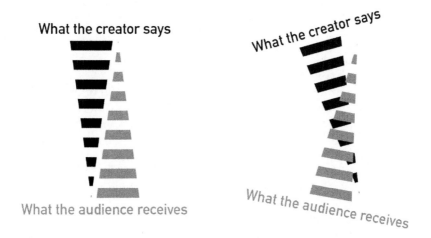

Figure 1.5 Aligning (or misaligning) the creator's message to reception by a defined audience

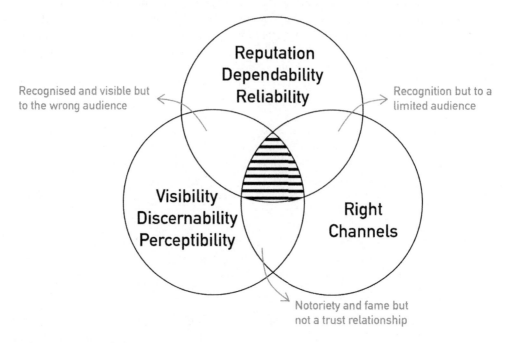

Figure 1.6 Balancing channels, trust and visibility in a digital presence

The reputation element is the trust associated with your presence. Without trust your presence is not sustainable or professional. Building a reputation and gaining the trust of your audience are specific challenges that are considered in detail in the next chapter. Inevitably, these are built through the content that you create and use to represent yourself. It does not have to be unique. A number of lifestyle-based online businesses initially built their reputations and audience trust around the curation of consistently appropriate content. The LadBible(.com), 9gag(.com) and TheDodo(.com) have all built their reputations – and significant audiences – around the targeted curation of content. These businesses are sometimes described as "viral publishers" or good news channels. These labels describe what they are, but our focus here is on how they do their business. Being a reliable source of content for a well-defined audience can become a significant business. Since being founded in 2012, the LadBible is the 860th most visited site in the UK (www.similarweb.com/website/ladbible.com/) and reported income in 2018 of over £20 million, with a profit of £3.8 million. This is in sharp contrast to five years earlier when the company reported current liabilities of £7,500 (Companies House n.d.). These accounts provide some evidence of the (financial) value of providing trusted and reliable content for the right audience.

The right channels are the selected mechanism for sharing your presence. A lot of attention is paid to the many different channels that are available. Many of the channels are their own examples of successful online businesses and of the power of the combined characteristics of the internet. But high levels of popular familiarity are not necessarily the primary criteria for deciding which channels are the right ones for your own presence. Using the right channels is also a separate consideration to the element of visibility. Having visibility on the wrong channels is as obstructive to achieving your objectives as having no visibility on the right channels. The difference is that being visible on the wrong channels has taken personal effort and resources for no tangible benefits.

The right channels will be a combination of different channels that are described in the forms of paid, owned and earned media (POEM). The combination of multiple channels will create the most effective platform for building your reputation and visibility.

There is a further element to your successful digital presence that may initially appear to be incongruous. Creating a presence has a strategic purpose with clear goals. Achieving these goals may not solely come through the creation of digital content or its distribution through digital channels. Other opportunities for building your reputation and visibility will come through direct face-to-face contact. As a student these types of opportunities come through co-curricular and extracurricular activities at college or university as well as at a local community level. Clubs and societies all provide potential routes to building a presence. While many face-to-face opportunities exist, the key paradigm shift is that any activity or action is closely tied to your online presence. Your digital presence is your comprehensive "business card" for what you do face to face. This is a "digital first" perspective on the purpose of your face-to-face activity, which is primarily to reinforce the strategic objectives of your presence online.

In many respects the distinction between direct face-to-face interactions and those online is becoming increasingly blurred. Mobile phones are one form of bridge between these experiences. Smartphones are devices that combine the complexity of internet access with the more mundane function of "calling" someone. Even the relatively rare opportunity (for the vast majority of people) of being on a broadcast media like radio and TV competes with the ability to appear live on YouTube with relative ease (through another capability of smartphones). As fewer and fewer people consume live broadcast media and more and more prefer to use software such as WhatsApp to make video calls rather than the mobile phone network, the primary driver for building a presence tilts ever more toward the digital.

The final element of a successful digital presence is quality. High quality is at the core of any strong presence. Quality has many meanings, and it applies to all the other elements of the presence. Although well-produced content is an aspect of this quality element, it is also expressed as well-researched, correct and verifiable content. The role of quality also translates to the element of visibility as being well positioned, well timed, relevant and applicable to its intended audience. Using the right channel has the same type of considerations when the channel itself offers credibility, simplicity and accessibility.

In the next section, we consider how all these elements are balanced. You have limited time and resources to create your digital presence, and doing "everything" is not an option. We will consider how to deliver high-quality content that builds visibility and reputation through the right mix of channels. A further consideration will be how different combinations of content delivered to different channels helps build your overall presence (Sudhakar 2018).

Throughout the book, case studies of individuals are presented to capture the different journeys that people take to create their digital presence and the many different reasons why someone might create that digital presence. The selection covers a mix of individuals from around the world who will be of varying degrees of familiarity. Some of the case studies chart the story of self-described influencers while others use their digital presence to convey a specific message, whether it is commercial, political, social or a mix of all three. The first case study looks at Greta Thunberg's evolution from Swedish school student to an international climate change activist who is unafraid to take on world leaders about their own lack of response to the climate emergency.

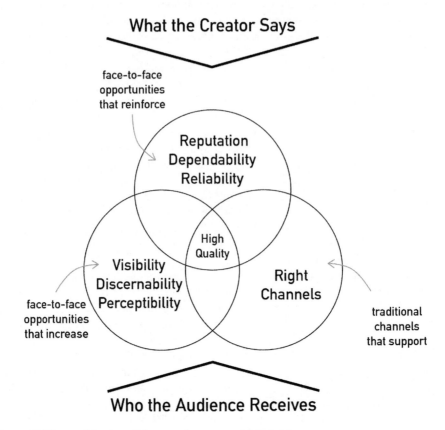

Figure 1.7 The combination of elements for a successful digital presence

The second case study through the book documents the development of a single digital presence for an individual creating a startup. This case study works through their steps in parallel with the content of each chapter. The case study joins up the discussions through each chapter while, at the same time, being an aspirational journey for anyone considering building their own startup based around a digital presence.

TL;DR (too long; didn't read)

In each chapter we conclude with a quick primer. If you are attempting to skim read the chapter, then these are your signposts. Hopefully, on occasion, the TL;DR will prompt you to back up and read in more detail. If you are reading this book through the eyes of a startup, a small organisation, a corporation or a charity, you may choose to read the chapters in a different sequence, particularly if you already have an established presence. The TL;DR will help guide your reading in the right order to suit your own needs.

The message from this chapter is to take a long view on the creation of your digital presence. You will need a clear goal, and you will need to use a mixture of channels with high-quality content that builds visibility and reputation with a well-defined audience.

Callout 1.1: Case Study – Greta Thunberg

Aligning values with presence

Greta Thunberg's digital presence is significant for someone who has gone from being a Swedish school student to an international climate activist in the space of two years. Greta was born in 2003 or, as their Twitter account says, at 375 ppm (or parts per million of CO2 in the atmosphere). Attention to Greta's concerns and that of climate activism more broadly came after they regularly appeared outside the Swedish parliament with a placard calling for students to strike for climate action. These actions attracted an increasingly wide audience and supported the establishment of an ongoing school climate strike internationally. Greta's age and openness about having Asperger's syndrome also helped raise awareness of the climate crisis in a wider audience. While some media reported Greta's mental health as a vulnerability, they describe the condition as a superpower and respond to their critics and troll robustly through Twitter. Donald Trump's criticism of Greta's recognition as *Time* magazine's Person of the Year in 2019 helped further promote recognition of their personality and of the concerns that they represent. The President's tweet made reference to the need for anger management and offered the advice to "chill". Greta's use of Twitter as the primary channel for their presence reveals an individual prepared to take on critics, address world leaders directly and framed with wit. Almost one year on from Donald Trump's response to *Time* magazine's announcement, Greta advised the outgoing president to work on their anger management and chill – simply recycling the former president's words from 12 months earlier.

Channel	Link	Followers	Views	Content
Twitter	https://twitter.com/GretaThunberg	4.4m		8.5k tweets
YouTube	www.youtube.com/channel/ UCAgIfWgzZ6QtvB_Oj1SBNnA	22.5k	788k views	6 videos

Callout 1.2: Your action – defining your goal

At the end of each chapter, there is an action that will help develop your digital presence as you read through this book. You are encouraged to work through these actions as you finish each chapter (and you may want to skip back to earlier actions as you read later chapters. That is OK. This process is iterative, and you will benefit in returning to earlier actions after reading later chapters.)

Having read the first chapter, now is the opportunity to pause and reflect. Do not get caught up in or weighted down by how a particular digital feature works.

Do not get burdened by speculating how this first action will connect with the ones in later chapters.

Before the next chapters develop the concept in more detail, give some thought to the following question: *What is your goal?*

This is not a question about using digital technology, using a particular social media channel or having a website. This is about defining a goal for yourself (or an organisation if you are reading from that perspective – in this case you may hopefully already have a vision statement to work with). Some secondary questions might help pin your answer down more precisely. What do you want to have achieved in the next five years? What would you like to be known for in the next five years? Who would you hope knows about you in five years' time?

To help your task further, your reflection could involve some research. Consider what parts of the web you visit. If there are particular people and sites that you return to repeatedly, these are useful sites to start your reflection. What is the attraction? What do you find appealing? How do these sites link to you (and, potentially, your goal).

If you need a technical solution to help you, a browser history analyser may focus your reflections. For example, Web Historian (webhistorian.org/education/) provides tools to examine your web history in visual ways (Figures 1.8 and 1.9) over a selected period of time.

Your answer doesn't need to be an essay – and it is better to be a sentence or less.

(If you are still not sure about your goal, jump to §6.3 for a quick look at some workable suggestions.)

Figure 1.8 Web Historian word cloud view of search terms for a three-week period (for one of the authors)

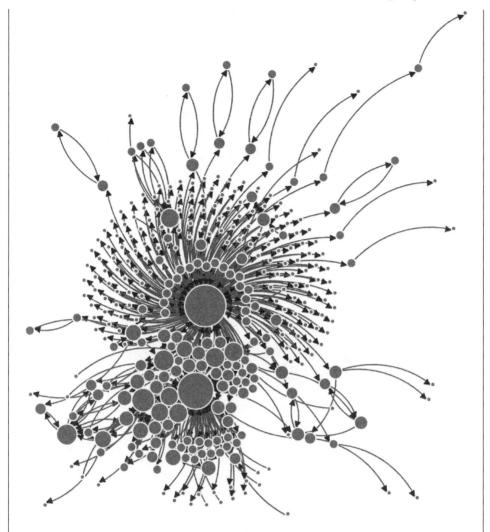

Figure 1.9 Web Historian network map of websites visited over a five-week period (for one of the authors)

Callout 1.3: "In Debora's Kitchen" – motivation and rationale

Debora Capeleti (Figure 1.10) is a 27-year-old Brazilian teacher of English and lives with their husband in Belo Horizonte, the sixth-largest city in Brazil. Debora is of Italian descent and also holds Italian citizenship. Debora will be migrating to the UK in February of 2021 with husband Gustavo.

Debora's grandmother is preparing a cookbook of the family recipes as a gift before they leave Brazil next year. As a result of the massive transition in their lives, Debora has been thinking of starting a side business to pursue a

Figure 1.10 Debora Capeleti

long-held passion for cooking as well as potentially boosting and hedging their income. Debora already has a personal YouTube channel (youtube.com/channel/UCHr9aTpGSBijxT3VfsoiC3g) with an infrequent posting of several videos about the experience of migrating to the UK. Debora's channel has nine subscribers and 197 views. The significant life-changing decision to migrate from Brazil to the UK presents the perfect opportunity to finally fully commit to the digital world and a coherent presence. Debora's husband, Gustavo, is a helicopter mechanic, is technically skilled and uses an iPhone for recording Debora's videos and then edits them using DaVinci Resolve software.

Debora had been thinking of creating a YouTube channel and blog to share Latin cooking to a global audience. The current channels by top Brazilian bloggers are all in Portuguese and primarily serve Brazil, which is a large, rapidly developing and populous country.

The task of creating video and text content as part of building a successful presence seems daunting.

Debora found out about this book in 2020 and asked if we could help build a successful online presence called "In Debora's Kitchen". Like their grandmother, Debora has a passion for cooking. While living in the UK as a student, Debora was regularly asked about Brazilian and Latin cuisine more generally. Debora's initial intention was to translate and publish the recipes received from their grandmother into a cookbook. However, Debora has now decided to first build an online presence that will also serve as a platform for the recipe book. The recipes from the book now have to be turned into video and text content. This is also a good example of how content can be repurposed for different channels to gain a multiplier effect (§2.2). A physically printed book will also be an additional "offline" channel.

Debora has already created a few recipe videos and resolved to post one a week alongside text and photographic content from 2021 on to her newly established channels. (Debora's journey is also documented on the accompanying website for this book: https://digitalonespace.com/.)

Current Channels

YouTube (www.youtube.com/channel/UCElpUNo1_5QXdtKHLCel4tw)
Facebook (www.facebook.com/indeboraskitchen/)
Instagram (www.instagram.com/indeboraskitchen/)
Website (https://indeboraskitchen.com/)

References cited

Afuah, A. and Tucci, C. (2003) *Internet Business Models and Strategies: Text and Cases*, Boston: McGraw-Hill.

Arthur, B. (2011) "The second economy", *McKinsey Quarterly*, 1st Oct., www.mckinsey.com/business-functions/strategy-and-corporate-finance/our-insights/the-second-economy

Bruns, A. (2017) "Echo chamber? What echo chamber? Reviewing the evidence", *6th Biennial Future of Journalism Conference (FOJ17)*, https://eprints.qut.edu.au/113937/

Companies House (n.d.) "LADBible", https://find-and-update.company-information.service.gov.uk/company/08018627/filing-history

Dorner, K. and Edelman, D. (2015) "What digital really means?", *McKinsey & Company*, www.mckinsey.com/industries/technology-media-and-telecommunications/our-insights/what-digital-really-means

Hilali, W. and Manouar, A. (2019) "Digital business models: Definitions, drivers and new trends", *SCA '19: Proceedings of the 4th International Conference on Smart City Applications*, ACM International Conference Proceeding Series, Oct., https://dl.acm.org/doi/10.1145/3368756.3368964

Laudon, K. and Laudon, J. (2021) *Essentials of Management Information Systems*, Harlow: Pearson Education.

Miller, J. (2015) "Astonishing tales of content marketing: Blendtec", *LinkedIn Marketing Solutions*, 24th Nov., https://business.linkedin.com/marketing-solutions/blog/a/astonishing-tales-of-content-marketing-blendtec

Sudhakar, G. (2018) "Categorization of media vehicles in the digital world", *SCMS Journal of Indian Management*, Aug., pp. 57–64, https://ssrn.com/abstract=3726242

Further reading

Fenton, A., Fletcher, G. and Griffiths, M. (2020) *Strategic Digital Transformation*, Abingdon: Routledge.

2 You need a digital presence

What you will learn

- How digital empowers the consumer and the audience
- The multiplier effect of digital
- Six objectives that a digital presence can fulfill

2.1 Digital empowers the consumer and audience

You need a digital presence. Having read the first chapter of this book, you will hopefully already recognise the importance of this statement. So many people create a digital presence unwittingly – by signing up for Instagram or interacting with an online community; even playing some games will contribute to your ever-expanding digital footprint and, by extension, your presence. Without consciously managing this accidental digital presence, the presentation of yourself will be genuinely expressed, but it will also be lacking any purpose or direction. Those initial first footprints online will inevitably be done for many reasons, including the pursuit of friendship and entertainment. It is not a case of condemning this earlier activity but consciously building upon this existing base to have a digital presence that presents a professional, self-aware and consistent representation of yourself.

The best way to recognise the power of digital is to use a search engine to search for yourself. This piece of research is also the first step in creating a better digital presence. The extent to which links appear relating directly to you in the first set of results is a simplistic metric of your current overall visibility and a measure of the extent of the work that will need to be done to create a successful presence. A complete lack of any presence in the search results should not discourage you. If you do have the luxury of a complete blank sheet as a starting point, then the opportunities are broad.

A digital presence is not just an extension of your identity; it is part of your identity. As an externalised part of your identity, presenting yourself online requires some self-reflection and awareness. This will guide the definition of your objectives and what you want as an outcome from a successful presence. This is a mark of your ambition. At the very least you should be defining an objective that overcomes a challenge or blocker in your current situation. Greater ambition may be to obtain a new job or start a new business through your presence. An even more expansive ambition – with the aspiration to gain an even wider audience – may be to influence government policy or change social norms. Many of the case studies presented through the chapters present individuals with this scale of ambition.

DOI: 10.4324/9781003026587-2

To return to the first statement in this section, there is a need for some modification. You need a digital presence because everyone is constantly creating a presence whether they realise it or not, and it is through their digital presence that people are increasingly judged and compared. These comparisons are being made to support so many decisions being made by others – including university applications, job interviews and supporting a crowdfunding project. In the first chapter we presented 11 characteristics of the internet. Your digital presence intersects particularly with the internet's role as a distribution channel, a mediator and a symmetriser. These characteristics all place power in the hands of the consumer and the audience. By implying that the internet can reveal details about anybody, this statement could be seen as menacing. However, this reinforces the need to actively manage a presence rather than letting it grow organically out of (and away from) your digital footprint. It is a question of managing your online reputation. You cannot necessarily make existing "bad stuff" (or just "silly stuff", "naive stuff") go away, but if you work to develop a positive, trusted and curated presence, the volume of right material will bubble up to the top of people's attention.

A key factor to recognise at this point is that there are many different types of channels that can contribute to the creation of your presence. These different channels can be clustered in a typology defined by how they are used to present your own presence.

All the channels that shape your presence can be classed as being paid, owned or earned media (POEM) (Figure 2.1). The categories are defined by who owns the channel and who creates the message. In some situations – and particularly where there is a more experimental business model being used – the channel sits in more than one category (Burcher 2012). The value of understanding the channels used in a presence is not to neatly allocate each to a single category but to recognise the general ways to interact and gain visibility and reputation through a channel.

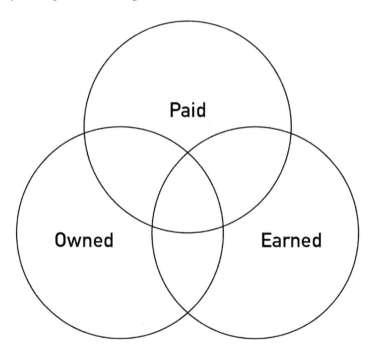

Figure 2.1 Paid, owned and earned media

Paid media refers to paying for media space or for a third party to undertake a promotion. This category includes advertising. From this point of view, there is also a close link between paid digital media and older ways of conveying a commercial message. Traditional paid media includes television commercials and magazine and newspaper ads. Digital paid media includes web-banner advertising, in-app product placement and paid search engine listings. Paid media is very rarely used for a personal digital presence and is still largely a type of channel used primarily by businesses. Even for a business establishing its own presence, the use of paid media will tend to come later in their planning, after they have established a presence through owned media.

Owned media covers all the online activities done on channels that you control yourself. Although you may pay for access to the service, what you put onto these channels is entirely controlled by you. These include your own website, blog, email newsletter and/ or customised app. Owned media is generally the starting point for taking active control of your digital presence exactly because it is entirely controlled by you. During the COVID-19 pandemic, and beyond, there has been increasing recognition that considering how a channel is controlled should be a factor in deciding which channels to prioritise and use. People have been moving away from systems where the control is divided between the user and the system itself, including Facebook and Twitter (Pierce 2020).

Earned media are communications that are about you but are generated by someone else on their own channel or through another owned channel. Earned media is unprompted communication. These communications can come through positive word of mouth, supportive viral videos or a news article. When you speak to your neighbour about a new product that excites you, when you buy a book from Amazon that prompts you to write a good review or when you forward a popular commercial to your friends through WhatsApp, that is earned word of mouth (WOM) media. Earned media can become part of your presence, but it is outside your direct control – you earn this media attention with visibility and reputation. Importantly, earned media crosses between digital and offline as well as personal and corporate communications; it is another way that these types of distinctions become so readily blurred.

Some academic research and industry publications add the fourth media category of social media. The addition creates an unnecessary complexity as the categorisation is based primarily on the underlying delivery mechanism. Instead, social media channels can be positioned as a hybrid that sits in the overlap between paid and owned media (Figure 2.2). Setting up a YouTube channel, a Facebook page, a TikTok account or a LinkedIn profile provides many of the tools associated with the control of an owned channel. At the same time, because the channel is free to set up and to access by an audience, there are recognisable elements of a paid media channel also present.

POEM reinforces how the audience and consumers are being empowered. POEM also highlights the importance of using the "right" channels to build a digital presence that reaches out to the audience you are targeting. For example, using purely paid media to reach an audience may create the wrong impression and be misaligned with your values or those of your audience. Similarly, relying solely on owned media, such as a personal website, may hamper your attempts at creating visibility and building reputation.

The POEM model also encourages a strategic perspective about your presence. Reflecting upon and understanding the role and value of earned media to build trust with your audience will also shape some of your most immediate actions with owned or social media. Positive earned media can be among the hardest types of media to obtain, largely because it is created outside your direct control, but this is also why it can be the

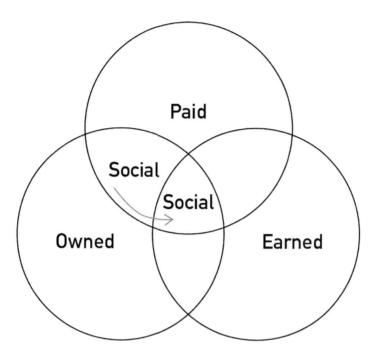

Figure 2.2 POEM categories including social media channels

most powerful. The role of earned media further reinforces the power of the audience. It is the audience's interactive communications with you that become some of the important positive third-party commentary that you are seeking.

With all these categories, there is also the consequence that digital media is "always on" and immediate to its audience and their power. On a day-to-day basis, this realisation may be a minor consideration, but it does impact on issues of reputation management. Challenges to your reputation or reactions to your visibility can appear at any time and be rapidly amplified by an audience. In a social media–connected world, every action creates a reaction. Creating a mixed usage of media categories supports a successful presence. While personal presence may not require purely paid media (such as banner advertising), there is a need to engage with this category through social media channels and to aspire to gain earned media. The key learning is that a single media channel is not sufficient to create a successful presence. You need to engage your intended audience in different ways, and this requirement alone necessitates going to the channels that they use and engaging in the ways that they expect.

2.2 The multiplier effect of digital

The environment into which you will offer your presence is dynamic. There is constant activity on social media, and increasingly, journalists report what is happening in newspapers that are now printed traditionally as well as being owned digital media, further blurring the boundaries between digital and physical media. Communicating through multiple channels produces a synergy effect in which one activity enhances another.

A benefit of having multiple channels across the POEM categories is the "multiplier effect" (Bao et al. 2014). This occurs when earned media activity increases the amplification of another aspect of your presence by becoming a "sounding board" that reinforces the positive messages of your presence. The autonomy of earned media and its trusted status increase the value of this amplification. Your personal challenge is to realise the opportunity through the other parts of your presence, which can, in turn, bring further earned media. This cycle of activity assists in increasing your visibility and reputation. Receiving earned media can be regarded as light confirmation that your presence is finding its intended audience through the right channels. This confirmation is a stronger signal if you can also recognise that the reasons for the earned media closely reflect the intention and purpose you have defined for your own presence.

A clear example of the multiplier effect comes from the early development of Amazon's business (Bao et al. 2014). In 1999, Amazon began using the *New York Times* bestseller list (a traditional form of earned media) on its website in conjunction with customer reviews (social earned media). The result was that when both forms of earned media were used, there was a multiplier effect on book sales for Amazon. The skills and insight from Amazon were to direct the power of earned media being achieved by the books and their authors into its own sales. The complexity of the relationship that can exist between categories of media is also revealed by this example. Amazon's use of the bestseller list is a form of reverse earned media for the *New York Times* as it acknowledges a level of quality and trust for this specific list over that of other outlets. The use of its own customer reviews by Amazon is also recognition of the power of its own customers over, for example, journalists and professional reviewers. The alignment created by Amazon emphasises how the elements of a digital presence bring success when they are consciously made to work together.

Creating your own presence may not appear to have much connection to Amazon's journey as a company. But substitute yourself for Amazon and replace the books they want to sell with your own purpose for creating a presence and the goal that you want to come out of this presence. Earned media will probably not be a bestseller list, but positive comments are definitely something to seek out. Getting endorsements and recommendations on a LinkedIn profile is a good example of a form of personal review that you can foster and encourage for a professional presence. Just like Amazon's reciprocation of earned media with the *New York Times*, you can gain earned media through reciprocating activities with other people on the same or different channels. Benefitting from the multiplier effect is not a solely passive outcome that is a result of luck. Getting the full potential from earned media and its multiplier effect comes from reciprocating and networking through digital channels as well as in face–to–face events.

The power to create a successful digital presence lies heavily with your intended audience. But you are personally part of the audience for others who are also attempting to create their own presence. Rather than seeing every other personal presence as a competitor, there is greater, longer–term value in reaching out, collaborating and reciprocating activities (§1.2). This is not advocating a blanket positive response to the actions of others. Your own reputation is also built around what you recommend and highlight to your own audience. Consideration to the quality and relevance of anything you "like", "recommend", or comment on should be your initial filter to these types of actions.

Ultimately, your presence is part of your identity and is distinct from anyone else's for different reasons. This is your value proposition to your intended audience. The challenge is to emphasise and bring out this distinctiveness within your own digital presence and to encourage the same in others who are on the same journey to build their reputation and visibility (because, in the end, they have different goals to your own).

Callout 2.1: Case Study – Kelvin Doe (aka DJ Focus)

Bringing an international audience to a local project

Born in Sierra Leone in 1996, Kelvin was a self-taught engineer at the age of 13. Using these skills, Kelvin built a battery system for the local neighbours to overcome the intermittent power supply in the local area. Encouraged by the success of this project, Kelvin then created a radio station, including everything from the transmitter to the mixing desk, built from components salvaged from waste found around the local community. The radio station then broadcast music by their alter ego DJ Focus.

A 2012 YouTube video on the THINKR channel about Kelvin's life and skills brought this work to an international audience and has had over 16.5 million views. Kelvin's relatively low-key digital presence is itself an inspirational example of achieving a goal. Kelvin is primarily focused on completing a degree in North America but remains a proud Sierra Leonian supporting a range of projects and causes that are evidenced through a range of TEDx talks and other engagements. The impact of the original THINKR video has been significant, propelling Kelvin to study at MIT through the mentorship of an academic who saw the video. Without this initiation into the wider media attention, Kelvin would have struggled to achieve this goal. Recent reconfiguration of the YouTube channel into the "Kelvin Doe Foundation" provides a small indication of future plans after Kelvin finishes graduate studies.

The Kelvin Doe website uses WordPress as its content management system and has the MailChimp plugin installed.

Channel	Link	Followers	Views	Content
YouTube	www.youtube.com/channel/ UCC3iJ4tASwwzfRYRyBzFddw	657 subscribers		5 videos
Twitter	https://twitter.com/kelvinbdoe	993 followers		319 tweets
LinkedIn	www.linkedin.com/in/ kelvin-doe-1765aa61/	27 followers		
Website	https://kelvindoe.com/		Ranked 3,640,000th website globally	

2.3 Six objectives that a digital presence can fulfill

The importance of a strategic perspective in creating your own digital presence has already been highlighted. What strategy means does require some unpicking (Chapter 3), but at this stage, if nothing else, it tells you that this is a long-term and ongoing project. Strategy works best if you can answer the "why" question first. Chapter 1 laid out the elements of the presence and focused on the "how" and "what" questions. So far, our assumption is that why you are creating a digital presence is to give you some type of advantage. For many new graduates, this advantage is straightforward – it is about standing out in the job market. For some leaving full-time education, the purpose may be to create a vehicle for their own startup business. Others may have their sights set on a bigger, more altruistic purpose, whether it be to bring some change in their local community or one of the grand global challenges facing society, such as the climate emergency, uneven development or the aging population. Your purpose may be to improve your organisation's digital presence (and we have already acknowledged that this work parallels the personal journey to a successful presence). In this case your thinking is still drawn to the same "why" question but should be informed by the current or planned business models, the mission and the vision as well as the current internal reality in terms of staff capacity and skills to embark on a strategic project.

But this perspective of finding the answer to "why create a digital presence?" is the wrong way around. Creating your digital presence **may** be the way to solve your challenge. If you have read this far, you will have intuitively recognised that a new or improved digital presence is likely part of the solution that you require. What we are doing is now checking that intuition and encouraging your own reflection by clearly defining the answer to that "why" question by asking "what are you trying to change?" Answering this question defines your purpose and your goal. Your digital presence **may** then be the way that your goal can be realised.

To assist your own reflection, it is possible to identify the general types of objectives that a digital presence can satisfy (Afuah and Tucci 2003). Your digital presence may fulfill some or all of these purposes as they can overlap and are not mutually exclusive (Figure 2.3).

Coordination

Q: "What are you trying to change?"

A: To provide a consistent representation of myself, my work and/or my ideas online.
A: To work with others to improve my community of interest.

A digital presence can take on a coordinating role. With a combination of the right channels, the digital presence can be the outlet for all your activities. This approach

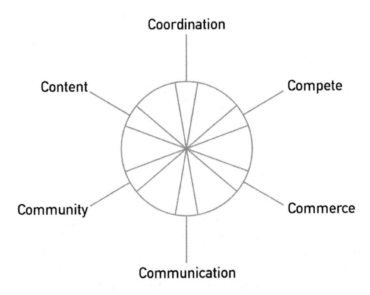

Figure 2.3 Six types of objectives that a digital presence can fulfill

encourages authenticity and transparency as well as alignment with your underlying purpose. The coordination objective is about bringing activities and content together and keeping these clearly interlocked. The coordination objective is also about becoming increasingly digitally mature as all your activities move towards being online. Coordination can also become an integrated aspect of a community objective as you contribute to a wider community of interest.

Community

Q: "What are you trying to change?"

A: Participating in the online community because I want to be recognised as part of the wider (professional/social/local) community.

(Tentatively) A: Building a community because one does not currently exist (or the existing one does not satisfy my objectives).

The community uses many of the characteristics of the internet to succeed. The ability to contact people with similar interests and mindsets is not constrained by geography or time (zones) as a result of its universality. Your own presence can become embedded within a community of interest with the use of the right channels. Being a positive aspect of a community contributes to your own reputation while also creating wider good.

Content

Q: "What are you trying to change?"

A: To share my (writing/images/videos/music/skills/other) to an interested audience wider than my own friends.

Content – in some way – will figure as an aspect in the overall objective of any digital presence. It is about what you do to represent yourself and your identity digitally. For a sports person, such as Fabio Wibmer (Callout 3.2), it will be video material of their best performances. For an activist, such as Greta Thunberg (Callout 1.2), it will be her observations, her interactions with world leaders and calls to action to address the climate emergency. For a gamer, such as Pokimane (Callout 4.2), it will be sharing her Twitch stream and the highlights and commentary from different games.

Commerce

Q: "What are you trying to change?"

A: To present my (self/products/services) to a receptive audience wider than my own immediate friends.

If you have ambitions towards creating a startup (or you are already part of a business), there must be a commerce element to your objective. Defining the market for your products or services will shape your objective as well as determining the right channels for your presence. Different commerce platforms are defined by this identification. Etsy would be the right channel for handcrafted items, eBay would be more suited to trading second-hand items and an Amazon store would be a consideration for new items. If you are introducing a new product or delivering a professional service, a standalone website combined with the use of paid media will figure in your solution. You can also see this as the objective that incorporates a goal to obtain a professional role.

Communication

Q: "What are you trying to change?"

A: To interact with an audience who wants to talk about my (self, content and/or commerce).

Communication complements an objective that features community, content or commerce. Communication also returns to the original purpose of the internet and can utilise some of its oldest services, including email. A communication objective is focused on two-way communications with your audience. This is a dialog that is initiated through other actions but one that forms and maintains relationships. Social media makes it possible to directly interact with an audience in order to mitigate negative opinions and motivate the creation of positive earned media (Vahanvaty 2013). If your objective is to gain graduate-level employment, then your digital presence includes a communication aspect to your objective as you want to interact with potential employers. If you have more of a commerce aspect to your objective, then communication is about building loyal and passionate customers who will take your message to their own friends and family.

Compete

Q: "What are you trying to change?"

A: To highlight to a receptive audience how my (self, content and/or commerce) is different and a reflection of my own values and purpose.

Competing is about creating differentiation of what you do from that of others. Differentiation can come through a range of actions that includes many overlaps with the other objectives. From a commerce perspective, the social communications that take place on Booking.com have the capacity to guide potential consumers by differentiating between the services offered by different accommodation providers (Rodríguez-Díaz et al. 2018). Even now in some sectors, a digital presence is still seen as a hallmark of being contemporary or even of being able to deliver a higher quality of service (AbuGhazaleh et al. 2012).

The six types of objectives will help you craft your own response to the "what are you trying to change?" question. While it may appear that these are obvious considerations, it is still relatively rare for a recent graduate to have a well-coordinated presence that consciously speaks to an audience and prospective community of practice (or interest) in a way that differentiates them clearly. Many organisations also suffer from a lack of collective conscious reflection and awareness. For example, asking directors from medium-size businesses about details of their business model will invariably produce responses ranging from a pregnant silence to an elaborate explanation about how the response is self-evident without ever producing an actual answer (McKenna et al. 2019).

TL;DR

Use a mixture of channels to define your digital presence. Using a network of these channels, aim to obtain an amplifying multiplier effect in order to obtain earned media from people sharing your content, saying good things about you or just generally supporting your reputation. Your audience holds all the power in this process.

Callout 2.2: Your action – defining your value proposition

With your goal defined – what you are aiming for in the next five year – your next step is tackling the challenge from the other end of the equation. *What is your value proposition?*

Your value proposition is a work in progress and will change over time. It may even evolve as you are reading this book. Defining your personal value proposition will take further reflection. What is it that you offer personally? This is not just a list of skills, a reiteration of your qualifications or a description of some projects you might have worked on. These attributes may inform the definition of your value proposition, but it is not just the sum of these lists. As an individual the combination of experience, knowledge, perspective and situation create a unique offering that is different from those of others around you. Greta Thunberg's (Callout 1.1) visibility and reputation for a strong and consistent perspective on the climate crisis means that she engages with world leaders (Cockburn 2020) through her preferred social media channel of Twitter.

What makes you different? Your combination of experience and circumstances is the place to start. Consider how this combination will offer benefits to others. Kelvin Doe's (Callout 2.1) experience of the poverty of Sierra Leone and homebrew making as well as a postgraduate qualification in engineering make his value proposition attractive in developing economies for this hybrid combination of knowledge. His visibility outside Sierra Leone also gives him opportunities to do fundraising and support his home country in other ways.

You should be able to define your value proposition in a single sentence. Label your value proposition as an "Enabler 1".

Callout 2.3: "In Debora's Kitchen" – building a value proposition

Debora's initial goal:

To create a "go to" online presence for busy people to learn how to make simple and healthy Latin cuisine.

Debora's initial objectives (to support the goal):

- To consistently create and publish content that is fun to watch and easy for beginners to understand
- To grow in subscribers and organic viewers over the next three to five years
- To create a blog to support the YouTube channel
- To build a community (using WhatsApp Business) where it is possible to leave feedback and request recipes
- Within the next three to five years, "InDeborasKitchen" should be in a position to draw in revenue that is sufficiently strong and consistent to become Debora's day job

Debora's has also jumped ahead and believes that a WordPress-based video-oriented website will become the focal point of the digital presence.

Enabler 1: Debora's Brazilian–Italian heritage provides credibility for presenting simple family homestyle recipes.
Enabler 2: Consistent identity for the presence "InDeborasKitchen".
Enabler 3: Debora's move to the UK from Brazil provides impetus to do something different.

References cited

AbuGhazaleh, N., Qasim, A. and Haddad, A. (2012) "Perceptions and attitudes towards corporate website presence and its use in investor relations in the Jordanian context", *Advances in Accounting, Incorporating Advances in International Accounting*, 28, pp. 1–10, https://doi.org/10.1016/j.adiac.2012.02.004

Afuah, A. and Tucci, C. (2003) *Internet Business Models and Strategies: Text and Cases*, Boston: McGraw-Hill.

Bao, T. and Chang, S. (2014) "Why Amazon uses both *New York Times* Best Sellers List and customer reviews: An empirical study of multiplier effects on product sales from multiple earned media", *Decision Support Systems*, 67, pp. 1–8, https://doi.org/10.1016/j.dss.2014.07.004

Burcher, N. (2012) *Paid Owned Earned: Maximizing Marketing Returns in a Socially Connected World*, Oxford: Kogan Page.

Cockburn, H. (2020) "Jacinda Ardern defends environment policies after Greta Thunberg criticises New Zealand's 'so-called climate emergency declaration'", *The Independent*, 14th Dec., www.independent.co.uk/environment/jacinda-ardern-greta-thunberg-climate-emergency-b1773097.htm

McKenna, S., Fletcher, G. and Griffiths, M. (2019) "Hiding in the light: Recognising UK mid-size businesses as a distinct category and their economic and social value to the nation", *MSB Leaders*, Manchester, www.msbleaders.com/the-report

Pierce, D. (2020) "Building your own website is cool again, and it's changing the whole internet", *Protocol*, 28th Nov., www.protocol.com/blogging-is-back

Rodríguez-Díaz, M., Rodríguez-Díaz, R. and Espino-Rodríguez, T. (2018) "Analysis of the online reputation based on customer ratings of lodgings in tourism destinations", *Administrative Sciences*, 8(3), Sept., pp. 1–18, https://doi.org/10.3390/admsci8030051

Vahanvaty, M. (2013) "Social media in online reputation management", *SocialMediaToday*, www.socialmediatoday.com/news/social-media-in-online-reputation-management/462540/

Further reading

Osterwalder, A., Pigneur, Y., Bernarda, G. and Smith, A. (2014) *Value Proposition Design: How to Create Products and Services*, Hoboken, NJ: Wiley & Sons Ltd.

3 You need a strategic digital presence

What you will learn

- Understanding strategy and its five elements
- Creating differentiation in your digital presence

3.1 What is strategy?

Graduates need to succeed in an increasingly competitive world. Irrespective of whether you are seeking a role in a multinational company, starting a job in your family's business, seeking a life partner or launching your own startup, the challenges are multifaceted. Expectations can run high, and there is a sense that it is all too easy to fail. However, there are some straightforward ways that you can prepare yourself and help you go in the direction you want and be successful in the role. As a student you will have focused heavily on the content of your course of study. That is, you will have concentrated heavily on primarily learning about the knowledge and understanding related to the specialism of the course that you enrolled into. In some courses taking even a slight deviation from this core body of knowledge to study related subjects will have been presented as risky or a lack of focus. This chapter is a provocation against this narrow thinking and stresses the value of having a wider set of skills that are sometimes described as "soft" or "generic".

Strategy – or, more precisely, strategic thinking – is one these soft skills. Strategy may be a term that you have only encountered casually in gaming, in movies, on *Dragon's Den* (or *Shark Tank* or *Lion's Den*) or something that you hear being mentioned in news reports. This vast array of references hints at the term being used very loosely, but the intended meaning is consistent. Strategic thinking is about taking a long-term perspective that is measured in years, rather than days or weeks. Even in the gaming world, this long view can be recognised when conventional time frames are heavily condensed to introduce an entertainment element. A strategy is the top-level direction for achieving specific objectives that takes into consideration what is realistic, given the resources and time available. The strategy leads to more detailed planning that creates project(s) and leads to specific actions on a day-to-day basis. Strategic success is what happens when these objectives are achieved. Learning to think strategically is a critical skill and mindset to cultivate. The strategic approach that you will use to create your own digital presence also translates into creating a startup, reinvigorating a family business or developing (or improving) the presence of an existing organisation.

A good strategy tends to have a consistent set of elements, irrespective of whether the vision relates to an individual or a larger organisation. With your focus on creating a

DOI: 10.4324/9781003026587-3

digital presence, some considerations should play into the development of your strategy (Figure 3.1).

1   The role of digital is as an enabler and an aspect of the overall strategy. The consideration of digital within a strategy should not be fragmented into isolated systems. This is usually more of a challenge in larger organisations when the priorities of departmental structures can fall out of alignment with the overall direction of a strategy.
2   There is no such thing as a "digital strategy". Taking this perspective introduces an unnecessary separation of actions and perspective. There are many examples of organisations taking this path for creating a digital presence. While some short-term progress could always be evidenced, the inevitable longer-term result was a disjuncture between the digital presence and the overall organisational vision.
3   There is no benefit in making distinctions between what is presented online and what is presented offline at a strategic level. The channels through which a strategy is realised in practice are at a level of detail below the strategy itself.

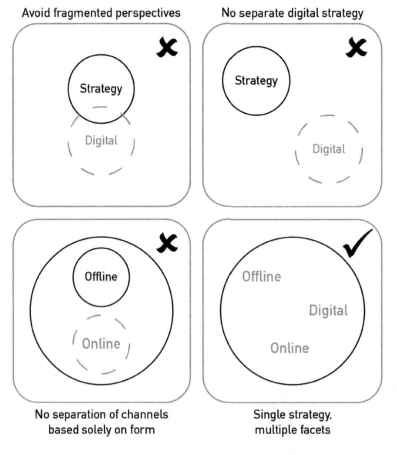

Figure 3.1 The place of digital within your strategy

The history of the term "digital strategy" is grounded in a misunderstanding of the role of digital within a strategy and a misunderstanding of the purpose of a strategy. As with so many usages of the term "digital", it should be read as a verb rather than as a noun (or part of a noun phrase). In this way "digital" is inevitably part of any contemporary strategy.

Viewed retrospectively, strategy represents a repeated pattern of actions that has produced consistent success. Looking prospectively, a strategy is the combination of available choices most likely to produce the intended positive outcome. The real power and role of strategy are realised by looking forward.

Strategy is an integrated, externalised concept of how you – or an organisation – will achieve defined objectives (Hambrick and Fredickson 2001). Without a clear, unambiguous strategy, time and resources will be wasted on piecemeal, disparate activities that may counteract one another or push attention in the wrong direction for long-term benefits. In larger organisations that do not have a clear strategy, middle managers will tend to shape their own direction in this uncertainty. The result will be a mixture of disjointed, ineffective localised actions. In a wider organisational context, "every business organisation, every subunit of an organisation, and even every individual [must] have a clearly defined set of purposes or goals which keeps it moving in a deliberately chosen direction and prevents it drifting in undesired directions" (Andrews 1971). This is the version of strategy that businesses and consulting firms have used for the last 50 years. The outcomes of strategic thinking are often associated with high levels of visible external success; however, a strategy can support a much wider range of objectives from survival at worst to thriving at best.

There are many examples of established organisations and promising startups that have floundered as a result of not having a clear strategy. The global COVID-19 pandemic attenuated the lack of any suitable strategy among many traditional face-to-face retailers, who failed through the pressures of the short-term necessity of lockdowns and an unexpected halt to their trading. An externally focused strategy would have been built around objectives that prioritised a shift to ecommerce coupled with a reduction in leased real estate long before the pandemic arrived. Far less clearly documented are the many personal aspirations that have not succeeded for a similar lack of a strategic perspective.

Strategy is about the integration of the pivotal choices that need to be made—to move in one direction or another when faced with the need to make crucial decisions. However, a strategy should not become a catchall documentation of every choice that needs to be made as a decision maker (Hambrick and Fredickson 2001). Well-articulated objectives and strategy provide the guiding compass when more specific choices must be made.

As a strategy addresses how to engage with the volatility, uncertainty, complexity and ambiguity of the external environment, how to specifically do this – the internal organisational arrangements – are not directly part of the strategy. Instead, these internal organisational arrangements, including who does what, any training that might be required and any required software and hardware, all reinforce and enable the strategy. The apparent contradiction of describing software and hardware as internal enablers for the strategy while categorically stating that digital is a facet of strategy requires further elaboration (Figure 3.1). Digital provides a variety of mechanisms for external engagement, and it is these elements that figure in your strategic thinking. The importance of digital is significant for the scale, variety and cost effectiveness that it can deliver to a strategy (irrespective of the objectives of the strategy). From the perspective of building a strategy for a successful digital presence, it is a case of focusing on the goal. Embedded in this thinking is the *a priori* acknowledgement that success can only be delivered primarily through digital means.

These statements remain constant throughout your strategy to build a successful digital presence. They continue to hold true for any projects that require you to apply strategic thinking.

What can make this situation appear confusing is when a single digital system is used for multiple purposes that cover both internal enablers and facets of the strategy itself. The Google productivity suite is an exemplar of this increasing blurring of boundaries (not envisaged by Andrews in 1971). Through this suite of tools, it is possible to create your own documents and spreadsheets and access other, less well-known apps. Once you are logged into Google, a waffle icon (the tiny 3x3 grid of dots) in the top right-hand corner of the browser provides immediate unimpeded access to all these apps. The majority of these apps provide very easy mechanisms for sharing your work – not just with friends and family but to an entire internet-wide audience.

Janelle Shane's blog – aiweirdness.com – provides an example of how these personal (internal) productivity tools can easily become part of a strategy to build a wider presence. The blog itself is hosted on the Tumblr platform and encourages visitors to subscribe to a (usually) weekly emailed newsletter alerting them to new posts. A further element of this presence is the incentive for subscribers to get access to the extra weird (and sometimes NSFW) results from the experiments in artificial intelligence (AI) that Shane conducts. This extra content is shared through a simple loosely formatted Google document – which generally includes publicity for Shane's book about AI and also follows the same theme of documenting the unexpected results that AI can produce. These documents are clearly part of the strategy for building Shane's digital presence.

This example evidences in a positive way the potential for blurring what could be regarded as internal or external to your strategy. This persistent lack of clarity provokes a need for some further underpinnings to understand what forms the key elements of a strategy. A set of five *V*s provides guidance to the "big" strategic questions that need to be asked.

- **Value** (proposition): What do (or can) I/we offer that is different/interesting? Who benefits from my/our offer?
- **Venue**: Where do (or will) I/we show and deliver this difference?
- **Vehicle**: How do (or can) I/we communicate and deliver this difference?
- **Velocity**: What pace (or when) will I/we deliver this difference?
- **Victory**: How do I/we assess when I/we have been successful?

Value (proposition)

Combining the "what" and "who" questions, the value proposition is the core starting point for your strategy (§1.3). Knowing what you offer that is valuable to your intended audience is the cornerstone of your strategy and filters down into specific actions and activities that enable a successful achievement of objectives (victory). The questions around what you offer and who you offer it to are not answered easily. An externally focused method of analysis described as PLOT may help you answer this question as well as those of the other four *V*s. (Cousins 2020). In this analysis, you focus on people, learning, opportunities and transformation. The people element is about understanding your value and its potential audience who will recognise this value. It is the "dream" stage of the analysis. Think about the external world, who is in it and how you can make a contribution. It does not have to be a Nobel Prize–winning contribution but could be focused on your ability to entertain, to explain complex ideas in simple ways or to provide reassurance in uncertain times. Learning then brings you to the "discovery" phase of the analysis as you better understand your audience, including the other people's voices that have trust and influence with them. You then design your opportunity and deliver the transformation that your value proposition gives to your audience, and these aspects of the PLOT analysis are picked up through your other four *V*s (Figure 3.2).

Venue

The venue for your strategy is wide ranging. It is not solely a physical or online location. Venue is also a consideration as to what part of the economy you are presenting yourself, your products or your organisation. Traditionally these discussions are described as the segmentation of the market that you choose to occupy. However, the importance of digital and the rising use of artificial intelligence challenge rigid notions of categorisation in the push for ever more personalised engagement (Retail Dive 2020). Invariably the claim that segmentation is dead is somewhat premature as some degree of anchorage is still required to give your strategy focus. But a degree of caution is also required not to

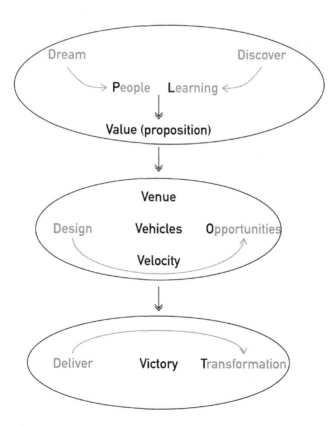

Figure 3.2 PLOT analysis and the five *V*s of strategy

become driven by your categorisations. So many traditional categories are being challenged as the boundaries of disciplines and industries are being blurred (Howells 2018), precisely because consumers and the audience are in control (§2.1). In creating your own presence, the message is not to feel bound to the sectors defined by the courses you have studied. Your value proposition defines you and who you want to engage with, and this helps define the venue(s) for your presence.

Vehicle

Once you have determined your venues, you can move to the vehicles that will enable you to deliver on your value proposition. Vehicles also cover a range of elements for inclusion in your strategy. It is not solely how the value proposition will be packaged up – for your digital presence, this might be thinking about whether you plan to use video, audio, images or text. You may also consider the type of relationship you have with your defined venues and the types of organisational arrangements. So, for your digital presence, the vehicle for your strategy is the content you create. You might want to collaborate with others to reduce the personal pressure on delivering content or seek a sponsorship arrangement for your digital presence. Vehicles also highlight the need to communicate your value proposition as well as actually delivering it. It may be that a combination of different vehicles is required to cover the messaging and delivery. Weighing up the benefits of different vehicles will also reinforce the characteristics of the internet and digital as a distribution channel.

Velocity

Strategies have a time frame, and the velocity question asks you to define starting points as well as the pace of what you are delivering. High velocity for either of these considerations may not be possible as a result of restricted time and resources. However, as the PLOT analysis recommends, if your audience demands or expects high velocity, then your immediate need is to look at ways of overcoming this internal limitation rather than being defined and constrained by it.

Victory

Irrespective of the purposes of your strategy, you need to set objectives, define what success will look like and ensure that this definition can be measured. Your victory conditions may experience some shift during the delivery of the strategy, but they should remain defined and measurable.

3.2 Highlighting differentiation within your digital presence

The importance of knowing when you have achieved victory justifies the use of SMART objectives from the beginning. SMART is an acronym for specific, measurable, achievable, relevant and time-bound. Any objective should clearly have all five of these attributes in order to be regarded as SMART. A SMART objective can then be assessed for victory with relative ease. Objectives that fail to have any one of these five attributes will be more difficult to evaluate for victory. A SMART objective for a digital presence may seek to "Double the number of Twitter followers in three months" (O'Connor 2018).

Presuming that the existing number of Twitter followers is relatively small and Twitter is one of the "right" channels for you, without the quantity, the specified channel or the time frame, this objective would be difficult to assess. The objective also clearly helps define the venue and velocity elements of the strategy and points to individual actions that will be required to deliver the value proposition and even the specific vehicles – in terms of appropriate content that might be delivered. Without additional information, it is clear that this objective is a commitment to a planned series of relevant tweets as well as supporting and linked material through other channels that will be needed to expand the audience at this velocity.

With a focus on creating a successful digital presence, the beginnings of your strategy are already taking shape. A successful digital presence is a key outcome of your ultimate goal and ambition that you will need to define. By utilising the first half of the PLOT analysis, you can define your value proposition. With a focused value proposition, the other four *V*s also become clearer. Clarifying all five *V*s confirms how what you offer is of value to others – and encourages you to define your differentiation.

Returning focus to your digital presence (Figure 1.7), the five *V*s of strategy (Figure 3.2) can be more precisely aligned to this specific goal. The starting point for this alignment is to focus on the big questions provoked by the five *V*s.

- **Value** (proposition): What do I say or do that is interesting, engaging or different? Who is my audience?
- **Venue**: Which high-quality social media channels will deliver my content in a way that maximises visibility?
- **Vehicle**: In what form and format will I present content to best develop my reputation? Will I collaborate with others?
- **Velocity**: When and how regularly do I need to present my content to ensure the highest quality that gains and retains my intended audience?
- **Victory**: What measure of visibility, reputation and quality will be used to assess whether my presence has become successful?

The varying conceptualisations of digital visibility offers different routes for shaping your own visibility and the victory conditions that will determine your success.

1   "The extent to which a user is likely to come across a reference to a company's Web site in his or her online . . . environment" (Dreze and Zufryden 2004)
2   "[A]s the probability, for firms, to be included in the consideration set of a random user" (Lappas et al. 2016)
3   "The firm's familiarity in the eyes of its online stakeholders, relative to that of its rivals" (Reuber and Fischer 2011)
4   "As a differentiating factor to produce superior organisational performance through the capture of new clients" (Smithson et al. 2011)

The first version focuses on the visibility of a single channel, the website, the inherent assumption of this statement being that a website is one of the right channels for the digital presence. The reference to users in both the first and second versions assumes an undifferentiated internet audience with the implication that any user is a suitable audience for your digital presence. The third view presents a traditional view of business defined around competitors, although the power of the audience is recognised by referencing stakeholders. The fourth perspective does focus on the importance of differentiation but narrows its view and success factors around client acquisition.

How you determine the priorities for your own visibility and how these can be measured also shapes the SMART objectives for this element of your digital presence.

- References, or links back to, your own content. This could be, for example, links to a website, retweets or likes. This is a measure of how your own content is generating earned media and, as a result, is measuring the volume of independent positive responses to your presence.
- Presence quality measurements. Many channels that can be used as part of your digital presence can be assessed for what can loosely be described as their quality. The scores vary in purpose and meaning from channel to channel. For example, LinkedIn offers the social selling index (linkedin.com/sales/ssi), and Google presents a quality score (support.google.com/google-ads/answer/140351). These quality scores are a proxy measure of visibility.
- Engagement activities. Greater levels of participation in relevant social media and communities of interest directly relate to higher levels of visibility within the intended audience.

(Otero et al. 2014)

Reputation is also built on a set of related but subtly different definitions. These definitions can be broadly grouped around three different perspectives: quality, aggregate and objective (Cioppi et al. 2019).

The quality perspective for reputation positions its role as a performance indicator. Measured through its quality, reputation is then presented as a hallmark of the extent to which you are different from others around you. The perspective is that higher reputation is a result of the higher quality in comparison to others. The quality perspective focuses on the generation of a positive reputation.

The aggregate perspective calculates reputation as the sum of your audience's positive and negative perceptions of you. Negative or positive perceptions may be derived from comparisons that are made by your audience with others, but these perceptions are generally outside your direct control. More important are the positive or negative experiences that you generate in your engagement with your audience. There is an emerging industry that specialises in generating reputation scores for companies and individuals. The scores are generated by measuring various visible attributes such as the sentiment analysis of web or social media channels and earned social media comments.

In the objective perspective, reputation is conceptualised as one of the key mechanisms that encourages and generates actions from your audience. This may come about within your digital presence as offers for direct cooperation and collaboration, suggestions for working with others outside your current audience, generating earned media and increasing the conversations across your channels between you and your audience as well as between your audience members. All these actions reflect increasing trust in you and your presence.

Creating SMART objectives around the development of your reputation will draw on a combination of these three perspectives to ensure that there is a useful quality of measurability. The use of reputation scores provides the most clearly measurable aspect of reputation. The decision about which objectives to define for your presence will be determined by overall goals.

TL;DR

You need to build a pathway from your current situation to your planned goal (victory). Your digital presence is about delivering value to your audience. This is done through the strategic combination of vehicles (content) and venues (channels). There is also consideration of how quickly you deliver your content (velocity). In combination, these are the five *V*s of strategy.

Callout 3.1: Your action – reviewing your existing presence

Your digital presence is based on the visibility of your identity. At this point it is worth reviewing the situation that already exists online regarding your identity. Document the social media channels where you already have an account and note which are active or inactive. This action picks up on the development of your strategic thinking – and particularly the venues for your presence (the channels) and the vehicles (your content in these venues). You have already worked on the value (Callout 2.1) and victory (Callout 1.1) elements of your strategy.

If you cannot remember what you have signed up to in the past, there are a few ways to track down your digital footprint. Signing in to Google and visiting your permissions list (myaccount.google.com/permissions) will show you which services you have used your Google ID to log in to. It is also worth checking back through your primary email account and searching for the phrase "verify your". This will highlight channels that have asked you to verify your email before letting you access the account.

Finally, using a username name-checking service (e.g. namechk.com) will show you the overall situation for your own name (Figure 3.3). This final check will confirm not only your current social channels but also whether other people with the same name are active online. You do not need to occupy every social media channel, but you need to ensure that your identity is consistent on the most popular channels and that specialist channels relevant to your value proposition can also be obtained. Namechk highlights the many channels that are currently available, and you can use this service to identify potentially relevant services that you will need to consider based on your value proposition. For example, if your value proposition incorporates music, you need to check the availability of your name on Sound-Cloud, Bandcamp and Patreon.

If your name is common or you share your name with someone who is very active online, then now is the time to consider a consistent ID that incorporates an additional initial from your name, a nickname that plays on a combination of your name and interests (e.g. Callout 4.2 and Callout 6.2) or a description that emphasises your value proposition (e.g. Callout 5.2).

Label your chosen consistent personal identification for your digital presence as "Enabler 2".

If you have identified any social media channels that appear to be relevant to your value proposition, identify the creation of personal accounts for each of these as "Action 1a, 1b, 1c, etc.".

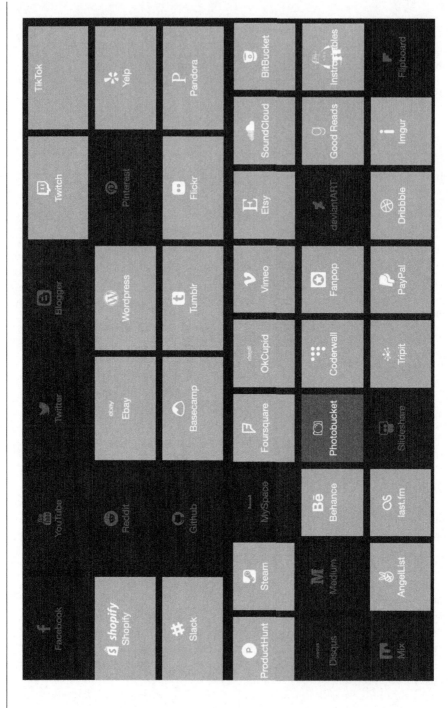

Figure 3.3 Name availability report (partial) from NameChk with the shaded services already taken and unshaded available (for one of the authors)

Callout 3.2: Case Study – Fabio Wibmer

Sharing your sporting skills with others

Born in 1995, Fabio Wibmer is a mountain trail bike (MTB) champion from Austria. Fabio first started posting videos online when they were 13. The first of these short videos focuses on Fabio doing backflips into the snow. However, through the next year, the number of videos increased rapidly to focus on their MTB or motocross action. Three years after posting their first video, Fabio was invited to the Red Bull Wings Academy at the age of 16.

Fabio has become an increasingly well-known figure through their YouTube videos that focus on high-adrenaline downhill trails and urban shoots with the use of a head camera. The 2014 production "Paris is my playground" won a German Web Video Award. This was one year before Fabio won an award for their bicycling skills. More recent videos have explored more creative filming options as part of their sponsorship by Red Bull since 2017. Fabio's current views on YouTube are nearly one billion in total.

There is also an Instagram channel with just under 1,500 posts and 1.9 million followers. The Twitter account is less popular, with only 11,600 followers. The lower numbers are because this channel is primarily a vehicle for sharing Facebook videos and has been inactive since December 2019. On Facebook there are over 600k followers with a more personal account of Fabio's life. Fabio broke a leg in two places on a motocross bike in November 2019 and shared the accident, the surgery and the recovery on this channel. Facebook is also a vehicle for promoting another sponsor, Canyon Bicycles. However, the Facebook videos and posts are generally more immediate and less polished than the material that appears on YouTube. The linkage with bikes, motocross, adventure and an international range of activities is evident throughout all the channels, but the hierarchy of content is also visible. The mix of polished videos and personal photos builds trust while maintaining a quality appropriate for each of the channels being used.

Channel	Address	Followers	Likes	Content
YouTube	www.youtube.com/channel/ UCHOtaAJCOBDUWIcL4372D9A	5.85m		250 videos
Instagram	www.instagram.com/wibmerfabio/	1.9m		1500 posts
TikTok	www.tiktok.com/@wibmerfabio	785.5k	10.1m	
Facebook	www.facebook.com/wibmerfabio/	610k	404k	699 timeline images
Twitter	https://twitter.com/wibmerfabio	11.6k		
Website	www.redbull.com/gb-en/athlete/ fabio-wibmer			

Callout 3.3: "In Debora's Kitchen" – existing presence and identification

Personal identification:
Enabler 2: InDeborasKitchen

Current channels:
Action 1a: YouTube (youtube.com/channel/UCElpUNo1_5QXdtKHLCel4tw)
Action 1b: Facebook (.facebook.com/indeboraskitchen/)
Action 1c: Instagram (instagram.com/indeboraskitchen/)
Action 1d: Website (indeboraskitchen.com)

Future channels:
Action 1e: TikTok

Type of Content: Videos, text-based blog post content
Frequency: At least one video on YouTube which will be reposted on Facebook weekly. A text (blog post) recipe will be written to accompany each video that will be placed on the website. Pictures will also be posted on Instagram with links to the recipe.
Metrics used to gauge early success: subscribers, views, Facebook likes, followers, social shares.

References cited

Andrews, K.R. (1971) *The Concept of Corporate Strategy*, Homewood: Richard D. Irwin.

Cioppi, M., Curina, L., Forlani, F. and Pencarelli, T. (2019) "Online presence, visibility and reputation: A systematic literature review in management studies", *Journal of Research in Interactive Marketing*, 13(4), pp. 547–577, https://doi.org/10.1108/JRIM-11-2018-0139

Cousins, B. (2020) "Abandon the SWOT: Instead, PLOT a new strategy to deal with uncertainty", *Forbes*, 1st Dec., www.forbes.com/sites/forbescoachescouncil/2020/12/01/abandon-the-swot-instead-plot-a-new-strategy-to-deal-with-uncertainty/

Dreze, X. and Zufryden, F. (2004) "Measurement of online visibility and its impact on internet traffic", *Journal of Interactive Marketing*, 18(1), pp. 20–37.

Hambrick, D. and Fredickson, J. (2001) "Are you sure you have a strategy?", *Academy of Management Executive*, 15(4), pp. 48–59, https://doi.org/10.1002/dir.10072

Howells, R. (2018) "How the digital economy is blurring industry boundaries", *Digitalist*, 2nd Apr., www.digitalistmag.com/digital-supply-networks/2018/04/02/how-digital-economy-is-blurring-industry-boundaries-06034431/

Lappas, T., Sabnis, G. and Valkanas, G. (2016) "The impact of fake reviews on online visibility: A vulnerability assessment of the hotel industry", *Information Systems Research*, 27(4), pp. 940–961, https://doi.org/10.1287/isre.2016.0674

O'Connor, M. (2018) "How to set SMART social media marketing goals for your business", 18th Jan., https://marieennisoconnor.medium.com/how-to-set-smart-social-media-marketing-goals-for-2018-862d1002a172

Otero, E., Gallego, P. and Pratt, R. (2014) "Click-and-mortar SMEs: Attracting customers to your website", *Business Horizons*, 57(6), pp. 729–736.

Retail Dive (2020) "Segmentation is dead!", 17th Jan., www.retaildive.com/spons/segmentation-is-dead/570237/

Reuber, A. and Fischer, E. (2011) "Signalling reputation in international online markets", *Strategic Entrepreneurship Journal*, 3(4), pp. 436–386, https://doi.org/10.1002/sej.79

Smithson, S., Devece, C. and Lapiedra, R. (2011) "Online visibility as a source of competitive advantage for small and medium-sized tourism accommodation enterprises", *The Service Industries Journal*, 31(10), pp. 1573–1587, https://doi.org/10.1080/02642069.2010.485640

4 Personas – understanding your audience

What you will learn

- What a persona is and how this is important
- How to define a persona
- How to frame your digital presence for a persona

4.1 What is a persona?

A persona is a profile that describes your ideal target audience in categorical terms. Putting this in another way, your persona describes a group of people with similar attributes as if they were an individual. The key advantage of describing a combination of attributes that are associated with a group of people in the singular is that they become more accessible, more real and more comprehensible. The effect is further reinforced by giving the persona a name, such as "Lena the Lawyer" and a profile photograph. You can even find specific advice about what to name your persona to make them seem even more appropriate (Schall 2020). All this work means that the persona you craft is easier to speak with and hold a conversation with through different channels over time (Figure 4.1).

A persona is based on research and may include information like the age, income, education level, the products they like or buy, employment or their marital status. These hard demographic facts can be mixed with more creative flourishes that further help make the persona seem more real. What information is included in the persona is heavily directed by your objectives and your strategy, but the key is to think strategically. If your value proposition is orientated around sport, then your persona should be described in relation to their own interests around sport. Your persona does not have to mirror the depth of your own interest, but it should define clearly how they enjoy and engage with sport. A persona with a more casual interest in sport may eventually point you towards presenting less, shorter and more spectacular material in preference to more technical material. In other words, the persona needs to be "fleshed out" fully and not moulded too narrowly around your short-term assumptions of what may or may not be relevant. It is a truism of all research that information discarded at an early stage of gathering regularly turns out to be the very information that provides the most crucial insights.

The reason for using a persona is to understand who you want to speak to. If you understand who your persona is with some degree of insight and detail, you can then speak to them in a meaningful way. A persona helps to optimise your efforts to match the needs and wants of your audience (Chapter 1) with your own goals and skills. Defining your audience through your persona is the key first step. Your own objectives should

DOI: 10.4324/9781003026587-4

Figure 4.1 Your persona in relation to your audience

speak to your persona. If you were to share your strategic objectives, they would resonate with your persona in clear ways. This relationship between objectives and a persona is a checkpoint when you have all the elements of your thinking lined up. If you would not want to share your objectives in this way – or the persona would not recognise them – this points to a misaligned perspective. What you say and do should always be relatable to your persona. Concerns for authenticity and transparency are wider considerations that are discussed in further detail in Chapter 5.

To explore this concept in more depth, another way of describing and understanding personas is the earlier but parallel concept of psychological masks. This link is thoroughly unsurprising as the term "persona" is itself simply the Latin word for "mask". You can think of the persona that you have defined as the mask that many members of your audience wear when they are engaging with you. Reversing this perspective slightly, the psychiatrist Carl Jung originally spoke of a persona as the mask that you present to the social world. We now appreciate that this statement has multiple contexts and nuances. We wear different masks in different social circumstances that consider the particular situation with greater finesse. Digital has a role in shaping the masks we wear by providing different *social* channels where entirely different personas can be developed. Without considering the benefits of creating and curating a consistent digital presence, it is possible to be both an angry contrarian and an empathetic counsellor. The 1993 *New Yorker* magazine cartoon "On the Internet, nobody knows you're a dog" is the pivotal exemplar of how digital channels enable and extend the opportunities to explore and present a fluidity of identity and personas. In creating your own digital presence, a key premise is to create a coherent core identity across channels. What changes between channels will be how you address a persona in a way that meets their social expectations. Your development of a digital presence is precisely to confirm to your persona that you are not a dog. A more recent example of poor identity alignment came in the wake of the 2020 US presidential elections. A Republican representative from Pennsylvania was identified as the source of a tweet stating "I'm a Black Gay Guy" who argued support for Donald Trump (Chang 2020). Unfortunately the White Republican representative had not correctly logged into another Twitter "burner" account, where he had intended to make the statement under an alias. This example of sock puppet activity – masquerading under a different identity to boost the impact of a statement – being called out for bad behaviour and poor ethics points to the extreme antithesis of what a strong digital presence should become.

Thinking of the persona as the mask we wear when we engage with particular content reinforces the purpose of the persona from the point of view of creating a digital presence (or engaging with an audience for any reason). We cannot address an entire audience on a one-by-one basis. The persona is a way of managing the complexity of addressing a large number of people at the same time in a way. By combining the key attributes of your core audience into the persona that you are addressing, you are speaking genuinely to a group with knowledge of their general tendencies, perspectives and preferences.

There is an additional dimension to working with personas. You can create more than one. In most cases, identifying multiple personas is even preferable as it helps to more clearly determine which channels and what content are right to engage with each persona. The majority of the individual case studies in this book reveal how the use of different channels reflects a conversation with various personas and their varying interests. Businesses use personas in the same way. In most cases, the business will define one or more personas for each product or service. Occasionally, a business will go further and define a separate persona around each of their points of contact – however, the value of using personas does diminish as the number of them grows unless there is a very specific purpose for this intricate level of examination. For your own personal presence, start with the definition of a single persona. As you come to understand your audience better, the number of personas you have and use will increase. The increase in personas may also be loosely connected with (but not a direct correlation to) your own use of an increasing number of channels.

4.2 How to define a persona

Many companies specialise in creating personas. These are normally done for other companies building their own digital presence. A better understanding of what individual personas look like can be found through a quick image search for a "persona card". This will not give you your own persona – unfortunately, there is no shortcut to that task – but it will show you how you can frame the final outcome for your own personas.

The starting point for any persona is research. The research that you do will take a range of forms. You can learn a lot from observing others through different channels before even creating a presence. Most social media channels let you investigate the profile of the person making a post. Who you research will be determined by your strategic goal. If you are building a community of shared interest, identifying members whose contributions you agree with and can readily associate with will heavily guide the development of your persona. If your goal is to gain a professional role, your research will focus on people (not organisations) who are involved in employment decision-making. This professional persona will be identified with activity around specific channels, such as LinkedIn, and will incorporate a role within an organisation as part of its definition. Other goals that might be achieved through your digital presence, such as founding a startup, will lead you to develop your research around different personas – such as funders and future customers.

A more direct form of research is to talk to people. Your initial observations will guide you to the people you want to speak to in more depth. A conversation with even a small number of people will really help get some depth – and realism – into your persona. Speaking directly to people will also give insights that are not easily discovered solely through observation of their online activities. The personal twists that you discover will help you think about crafting a biography for your persona that is plausible. You won't simply be adopting someone's story for your own persona, but the twists and turns of the stories from the people you speak to will help you craft your own persona's unique history. After having a few conversations, you may also begin to discover common themes in their experiences, themes that your persona, too, should reflect. Some people will be reluctant to be recorded while they are speaking – and this will have an effect on the answers they give you (the Hawthorne Effect) – so it is better to record notes of your conversation immediately afterwards. Irrespective of how you record or remember your conversations, you should be clear and transparent about the nature of the conversation with the people you speak with. If they are not comfortable having the conversation once you have explained your purpose, you should abandon this intention immediately. On a positive note, starting the conversation with key people may sometimes also lead to longer-term opportunities, either directly or through a "friend of a friend" as a collaboration or a recommendation and contribute to achieving your goal.

Other sources of secondary research data may also be useful. Summaries of demographic profiles from your national statistics agency will help you frame your persona with terms and categories that are recognisable and comparable against national trends. Groupings such as job titles, industrial sectors and geographic regions all help position your persona with more realism.

With a broad picture of your persona's demographic attributes and background story, you need to identify their goals. These are your persona's goals, not your own – perspective that is sometimes missed by people who create personas. Your persona's goals will be personal, reflect their background story and provide an insight into the persona's psychology. The goals will reflect their outlook on life, their ambition and their long-term plans. Their goals will also generally echo the focus of the persona. For example, a persona that describes a potential decision maker in terms of them employing you will be confined to professional goals as it is primarily a professional persona. A persona describing a participant in a shared community of interest will be more likely to include personal goals. Defining the goals of your persona may also lead to the identification of a broad label such as "optimist", "realist" or "open". There are also a wide range of personality traits (Diener and Lucas n.d.) that can be deployed individually or in combination as a short list to describe your persona.

Irrespective of how positive or negative a light the persona is being presented in overall, there is also value in defining the things that motivate and frustrate the persona. The interactions in their life that bring joy and bring pain. The persona's increasingly articulated personality will lead you to specific examples of joy and pain that are customised to them personally but reflect the broader types of issues you may have already seen or heard about when you spoke to people during your research.

Many personas will also include additional details such as skills, a personal quote, a list of their key (technological) possessions or a list of the social media channels they prefer. All these additional details help create realism. If this description of the persona is beginning to sound very similar to a dating or employment agency website profile, you are getting the idea. Many online services ask the same questions of their clients that you need to answer to create your persona. The purpose is very similar; they are building a profile that will have the best chance of matching with someone compatible.

We also created a form of persona for this book. The audience for a book is never "everybody". Narrowing the defined audience assists in focusing the message of the writing and creates a better book as a result. In order to explain to the publisher who this book was intended to be read by, it was necessary to outline their situation − the intended audience for this book is primarily a student completing a programme of studies and preparing to enter the world of work − and the reasons they would need a book of this type − to stand out among other graduates seeking employment and to support them through their first work task of developing their new employer's digital presence. We also recognised there was a secondary persona in the form of the recent graduate with aspirations to found a new startup. The categorisation of our intended audience did not go into as much precision about some demographic aspects as might normally be expected in a persona. However, we do write for an audience that we describe as trans-European. As a result, our examples and perspectives consciously try to avoid solely a UK or US focus, and we recognise that the audience may be multilingual, with English having been learnt as an additional language.

4.3 Framing your digital presence for personas

The majority of the strategic components that shape your digital presence have now been introduced (Figure 4.2). We have started with the big picture. Setting your goal is about the big change or improvement that you are seeking (and this is developed further in Chapter 6). We have presented two parallel threads that set out to achieve your goal. Understanding and defining what your value proposition is forces some internal self-reflection and consideration of what you are good at, what you enjoy doing and what you do differently from those around you. However, the value proposition is really an external presentation of yourself; it is really about what you offer others. This is an extremely difficult task if you do not understand who your value proposition is being presented to in the first place. This is why up until now we have focused on the internal aspects of defining your value proposition.

The second parallel thread has been to define and set out objectives for achieving your goals. We have emphasised the importance of objectives that are SMART (specific, measurable, achievable, relevant and time-bound). Understanding and being able to phrase SMART objectives so that they are SMART is a skill in its own right. An important step in understanding objectives is being able to place them in terms of scale and pace within your bigger strategic project. It is within the definition of the objectives, too, that your digital presence is starting to emerge. This comes back to the role and meaning of digital as an enabler. Digital is a doing word or a verb. The emergence of your digital presence within your objectives makes sense when we consider the point that strategy is about the external and overall project − which, in this book, is you. The five *V*s of strategy (value, venue, vehicles, velocity and victory) reach down into the widest description of your digital presence, but they are doing this to consciously link aspects of the solution − your digital presence − with your goals.

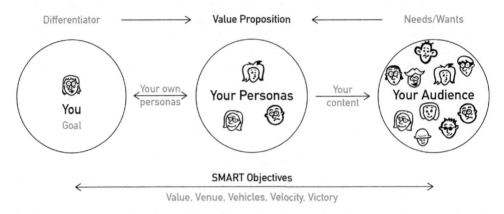

Figure 4.2 The interrelated components that shape your digital presence

This brings us to the role of personas. Previously (in Chapters 1–3) we have been loosely using the term "audience" as a familiar term with a broadly similar meaning. At this point, with an appreciation of the value and greater level of precision that the concept of personas provides you, it is a valuable exercise to go back and substitute the word "personas" for "audience". This substitution will highlight the importance of understanding the personas that you want to engage with. Your persona research will also gain renewed importance. Fundamentally, your key research question is "What do you want to hear from me?" (Figure 1.7), rather than "How do you want to hear from me?" This latter question is a subsidiary that is often largely answered by the response to the first and more urgent question.

The perspective that is being shaped here places your digital presence at the heart of the solution for achieving your goals. The solution being proposed makes your digital presence the conduit between you and your personas. If the focus here was to develop an organisation – for example, to grow its business or expand its territories – this statement could be put coldly and moved on without further consideration. Organisations are often considered as people legally, and they do have their own identity and cultures, but these attributes are shared and generally not specifically owned by any one person. In other words, the statement that a digital presence is the conduit between a business and its personas (Heinze et al. 2020) can be made dispassionately.

However, our earlier statement that your digital presence is part of your own identity requires some deeper consideration. Your digital presence is part of a solution for realising your goals. But in a strategic perspective and by defining SMART objectives, your digital presence is shaped and informed by the personas that you are attempting to reach. Your strategic digital presence, then, is necessarily a negotiated identity. It is the combination of your own expression of yourself with the expectations and (potentially) the needs of your personas. Extending this observation still further, it becomes clear that your digital presence is also a form of persona. It is your online mask that you wear for these other personas. Evidence for this can be spotted throughout the personal case studies presented across the book. The individuals we highlight all have more than a single channel to present themselves, and across the many examples, there is a clear theme that different channels present different masks to slightly different personas.

Some channels carry a more personal thread by documenting events in their lives (in traditional media terms, this is the "behind the scenes" view), and the presentation is often consciously more intimate and less polished. The contrasting view can then be found in the "official" professional channel, where their persona shifts to address what is generally a more broadly defined persona (and consequently a larger audience). The personas you define and then focus your attention on become so important in this light. At the same time, recognising your digital presence as being personas of yourself is an important step forward in terms of understanding how to achieve your goals.

TL;DR

Defining who you are speaking to with your digital presence is an essential part of its development. This audience will be clustered into smaller groups that can be defined with their own specific interests and needs. Understanding these differences will help you better shape your content and build your visibility and reputation among these groups.

Callout 4.1: Your action – defining your personas

Your personas will be heavily defined by your goal. If your goal is to become a high-reputation influencer, blogger or vlogger, you might identify your personas as persons who find appeal in what you are saying and would be entertained by your material. Other types of goals effectively come down to the same point of view; your personas will identify with your value proposition and the value that it offers to them directly. If you want to gain employment, your persona will be shaped around the archetype profile of an employer in the types of companies that you are setting your sights on. If you are founding a startup, then your personas are the types of people who would be interested in purchasing and using (that might be two separate personas to define) your product or service.

There are number of toolkits freely available for creating personas (sometimes called an audience persona, a buyer persona or a consumer persona), such as the Diytoolkit (diytoolkit.org/tools/personas/) and Hubspot (hubspot.com/make-my-persona). These tools give you a neat and consistently formatted page for each of the personas that you identify. These are a useful artefact to have in front of you when you are developing your presence. You can be looking directly at your personas when you are creating content. You are directly looking at the person you are engaging with.

Engaging your personas positively and over time will be essential in achieving your goal. Once you have defined your personas, you now identify what you want to happen to them. Frame the description in the past tense and with some form of quantification (TSIP 2019). For example, drawing on the earlier examples, you might say, "Increased positive conversations with potential employers to five per month", "Improved pre-orders from [Persona 1] from social media recommendations" or a shorter-term statement might "Increased subscriptions from [Persona 2] to email newsletter by 100 by the end of the calendar year".

Label each of your personas as "Persona 1, 2, 3 etc.".

Label each of these description that you create as "Outcome 1a, 1b, 1c etc.".

Callout 4.2: Case Study – Imane Anys (aka Pokimane)

Pokimane is a gamer best known for streaming Fortnite and League of Legends games. Their online handle is based on a combination of their first name and Pokémon – one of their favourite games – because of what they believe, perhaps somewhat tongue-in-cheek, is an unfortunate combination of given and family name if it is said too quickly. Born in Morocco in 1996, Pokimane started streaming games in 2013. A relaxed and accessible style took their following from 1,000 viewers per stream in 2015 to 12,000 three year later. After studying chemical engineering, Pokimane focused on streaming activities to take it to a professional footing. In 2017 they were recognised as one of the 100 most followed on Twitch and the most followed woman on that channel. Pokimane has worked directly with the channel since then as one of its ambassadors. Pokimane has since expanded their digital presence into other channels that present other interests and activities. Perhaps the most unexpected of these interests, but very much in keeping with a relaxed gaming style, is an autonomous sensory meridian response (ASMR) channel on YouTube. Effectively, this is a form of presentation that involves whispering and low levels of other relaxing sounds. Pokimane's expansion into new activities has included founding OfflineTV, supporting a campaign for US voters to participate in the 2020 presidential election, appearing in a film and partnering in creating a fashion brand.

Channel	Link	Followers	Views	Content
YouTube	www.youtube.com/ pokimane	6.1m	142.2m views	468 videos
TikTok	www.tiktok.com/@poki	3.9m	32.4m likes	
Twitch	www.twitch.tv/pokimane	6.5m	523.5m views	
Twitter	https://twitter.com/ pokimanelol	2.7m		20.1k
Facebook	www.facebook.com/ pokimane/	477.6k	360k likes	
Instagram	www.instagram.com/ pokimanelol/	5.5m		735 posts
Website	https://poki.uwu.ai/		Ranked 2,319,000th website	

Callout 4.3: "In Debora's Kitchen" – defining personas

> **Persona 1**
> **Persona Name:** Nigel
> **Age:** 25–45
> **Country:** UK
> **Occupation:** Stock control manager
> **Languages known:** English, A-Level (high school) French
> **Interests:** cooking, foodie, travel, fitness

Needs

- To keep fit by cooking more meals at home
- To learn to cook all their favourite Latin meals to spend less money and time eating at restaurants
- Looking for a channel where they can share and request Latin American recipes in English

Frustrations/Struggles

- Too much time at work means less time to cook
- Doesn't have time to watch long, drawn-out cooking videos; looking for quick and simple videos that get straight to the point
- YouTube videos do not have the recipes in a written form
- Too many websites and channels to choose; most are not in English Seeking one channel that can satisfy their Latin American cooking needs
- Difficult to find Latin American recipes that are easy to make with ingredients found in UK supermarkets

Favourite Cuisines: South American/Latin, South Indian, Italian, Arabian, Chinese

Channels they follow:

- AmigoFoods
- Tasty
- Palins Kitchen
- Homecooking Show
- Your Food Lab

Channels they use: YouTube, Facebook, WhatsApp

Outcome 1a: Organically attract and retain 100 YouTube subscriptions by March 2021.

References cited

Chang, D. (2020) "'I'm a Black Gay Guy', viral tweet from Pa. GOP candidate leads to social media mystery", *NBC Philadelphia*, 10th Nov., www.nbcphiladelphia.com/news/politics/im-a-black-gay-guy-viral-tweet-from-pa-gop-candidate-leads-to-social-media-mystery/2591767/

Diener, E. and Lucas, R. (n.d.) "Personality traits", *NOBA*, https://nobaproject.com/modules/personality-traits

Heinze, A., Fletcher, G., Rashid, T. and Cruz, A. (eds) (2020) *Digital and Social Media Marketing: A Results-Driven Approach*, London: Routledge.

Schall, A. (2020) "What's in a name? How to select a name for your personas", *UX Booth*, 21st Apr., www.uxbooth.com/articles/whats-in-a-name-how-to-select-a-name-for-your-persona/

TSIP (2019) "Theory of change: Eight common mistakes", www.tsip.co.uk/blog/2019/7/18/theory-of-change-eight-common-mistakes

Further reading

Pruitt, J. and Adlin, T. (2005) *The Persona Lifecycle: Keeping People in Mind Throughout Product Design*, San Francisco: Morgan Kaufmann.

5   Ethical and legal issues

What you will learn

- Being ethical at your core
- Who owns your data
- Privacy, consent and trust
- Using the General Data Protection Regulation (GDPR) in a positive way

5.1 Being ethical

Ethical behaviour is the final core concept of your digital presence. The piecing together of the concepts of your strategy in the previous chapter (Figure 4.2) does not include ethical behaviour as a separate category because, put most bluntly, it should be a part of everything you do. If the goal you have defined for yourself is based around a social cause or change, then this statement unnecessarily belabours the point. However, even when your goal is focused on your own improvement or a business opportunity, there is still the underlying need to be ethical in what you do and how you behave through your own digital presence.

Ethical behaviour is a reflection of your own identity. The decisions you make on what are generally regarded as ethical or unethical actions are shaped by the same processes that shape your own identity, including your age, education, gender, religiosity, ethnicity, where you live and the views of your parents (Ford and Richardson 1994). This combination of factors confirms that ethical decisions are personal and can vary depending on circumstances. What is regarded as ethical when you are a child, a teenager or more mature may also change over time. The separation of ethical and unethical behaviour cannot (and should not) be reduced to a question of whether an action is legal or illegal. Being ethical is more closely related to being authentic and empathetic in your decisions and actions.

It may be helpful to take a more systematic approach by using a process for ethical decision-making (Figure 5.1). Discussing ethical decision-making in general terms can be quite difficult and disconnected because each ethical issue and decision is personal, with each situation requiring separate consideration. Within most frameworks, there is an initial fact-gathering stage, consideration of the different people affected, identification of the consequence and obligations contained in the decision and thought to your own character and integrity. A reflection of the complexity and subjective nature of ethical practice is that many documented frameworks conclude with reference to your own

DOI: 10.4324/9781003026587-5

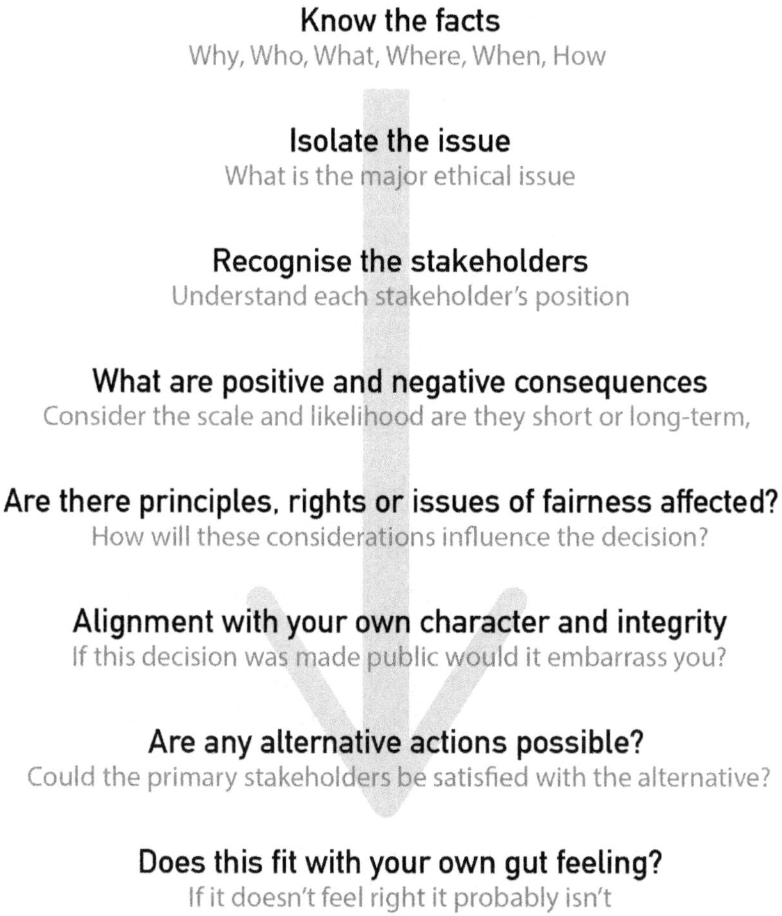

Know the facts
Why, Who, What, Where, When, How

Isolate the issue
What is the major ethical issue

Recognise the stakeholders
Understand each stakeholder's position

What are positive and negative consequences
Consider the scale and likelihood are they short or long-term,

Are there principles, rights or issues of fairness affected?
How will these considerations influence the decision?

Alignment with your own character and integrity
If this decision was made public would it embarrass you?

Are any alternative actions possible?
Could the primary stakeholders be satisfied with the alternative?

Does this fit with your own gut feeling?
If it doesn't feel right it probably isn't

Figure 5.1 An ethical decision-making framework (after Kansas University 2006)

"gut feeling". In other words, if it doesn't feel right to you, then it probably is not ethical (Kansas University 2006).

It is around the consideration of your integrity and character that the relationship of the action of being ethical to your digital presence is particularly relevant. In considering your character and integrity, you can reposition the question as "What would my personas do in this situation?" The way your defined personas would act in relation to an ethical dilemma can help further guide your own actions. Similarly, what you have done in the past through your digital presence should guide your actions in the future (while acknowledging that prevailing attitudes change over time and that you may – through increased self-awareness – want to move away from some of these previous actions). Having consistency in your actions is one rationale for doing this. As part of your identity, the actions of your digital presence reflect directly on you.

A core ethical behaviour is acknowledgement that a digital presence can never be a veil to your "real" self. The opportunity for anonymity online is an illusion, is not ethical and is not sustainable.

> Not too long ago, theorists fretted that the Internet was a place where anonymity thrived. Now, it seems, it is the place where anonymity dies.
>
> (Stetler 2011)

On 7 December 2019, a female reporter for an NBC affiliate, Alex Boarjian, was covering a marathon when she was slapped on her bum by a male runner. The man was quickly identified by social media users and was later charged with assault. One of the first acts by the man after he was identified was to shut down his social media accounts. His accounts still remain closed (Mettler 2019).

During the COVID-19 pandemic, an oncology nurse in Oregon posted a TikTok video of herself, revealing that she has not been using a mask, had been letting her children interact with others and had been travelling freely with restriction. The video itself appeared to mock her colleagues with references to Dr Seuss's character the Grinch. The video attracted widespread attention after it was criticised by other users, and after being identified by officials from the hospital where she worked, the nurse was suspended from her duties. The video itself was also removed from TikTok. However, it remains accessible through the other users who had posted it as part of their criticism of her actions (Vallejo 2020).

While these stories are arguably high-profile extreme examples, they do confirm Stetler's observation regarding anonymity, the internet and, by extension, ethical behaviours. Your digital presence should reflect you, and you cannot hide your true self behind this presence. In these examples, the lack of anonymity has been used to call out outmoded and unacceptable individual behaviours.

It is not uncommon for a potential employer to search for a candidate through the web or social media channels. These actions could also be questioned. Whether this vetting of a candidate is itself ethical, or if aspects of someone's digital presence undertaken in the past should prohibit them from obtaining a job now, is debatable. These employers are not just seeking out information that will provide confirmation of details in a CV (they are doing this as well); they are looking for more general patterns of behaviour and interactions. Social media channels will reveal your tendencies over time. Some graduates choose to delete some of their social media channels upon graduation. But increasingly, a gap in your digital presence is becoming as much a cause for concern to employers as a gap in your employment experience. Instead of completely deleting poor content or an account from a social media channel, it is worth considering how the negative content can be overcome with a programme of structured and thoughtful positive content. This maintains your presence on a channel – but as with the creation of all elements of your digital presence, it should be considered strategically.

The ethical issues specifically relating to your digital presence and the representation of your identity online connect with issues of privacy, consent and, in Europe, the GDPR legislation (and its broad equivalents elsewhere). The origins of the consideration towards digital privacy can be traced to the US Department of Health, Education and Welfare's 1976 Code of Fair Information Practices. The code is based on two core principles (Pence 2015) that still remain relevant nearly 50 years later. This longevity should not appear too surprising despite predating the web and social media channels (other than email). The two principles are the outcome of ethical decision-making processes and recognise that information relating to an individual is an aspect of their core identity. The two principles are:

1   Fair notice: No secret data collection. The use of information should not bring subsequent surprises to those who have chosen to share.
2   Specific consent: Data collected for one purpose cannot be used for another purpose.

These principles come from considering the expected rights of an individual sharing information. The General Data Protection Regulation (GDPR) captures similar sentiments with its enshrinement in the law of the European Union in 2018.

5.2 Who owns your data?

A frequently asked question is "Who owns my social media accounts?" The ownership of data and how it is used are among the most persistent ethical questions in the digital age. Data is the fundamental building block of the digital economy and of everyone's digital presence. Social media channels sit in a particularly complex relationship in terms of the ethical issues of data ownership (Figure 2.2). Because the channels are effectively free to use the infrastructure, it is designed to produce an income for the owners of the channels. In 2010 Tim O'Reilly retweeted a user named blue_bettle that summarised the situation: "If you are not paying for it, you're not the customer; you're the product being sold" (www.metafilter.com/95152/Userdriven-discontent#3256046). The origins of this statement, however, go back earlier, relating to free-to-air television and its business model. Irrespective of this realisation, the majority of social media users believe they own the content that they add to each channel. However, as with so much related to digital technology, there are layers of unseen data that sit beneath the content itself. For social media channels, the more important data lies hidden underneath the content. These are the layers of demographic and behavioural data that parallel the information that helps shape the construction of your own personas except on a vast scale. Knowing the relationships between demographic attributes and tendencies for certain actions is highly valuable for each channel as these insights can be sold to advertisers for highly targeted campaigns. Facebook's Pixel technology (facebook.com/business/learn/facebook-ads-pixel) lets the company track people after they have left the ecosystem of this one social media channel.

The benefits, the thinking goes, should be mutual. The more targeted a campaign, the better return the advertiser gets in terms of increased sales. The prospect of better targeting means the channels can sell advertising at higher rates than less-precise campaigns, therefore also increasing their own profitability. A targeted campaign means that the right people receive the right campaigns and are exposed to products and services that are most likely to interest them while keeping campaigns irrelevant to the individual out of sight.

To deal with the ethical question of data ownership, we look specifically at Facebook. Although the demographic of Facebook (Noyes 2020) may not be the right channel for your own digital presence, its ownership of the younger-orientated Instagram and its relative maturity provide more general learning about the ownership of data in social media channels. Extending the same type of analysis to other platforms is relatively straightforward but is left as an exercise for the reader to focus on the key channels of their own interests. There are many social media channels; some have a near-global reach while others are presented to a specific country or a specific interest group or designed for a single profession. Each channel has its own terms and services and nuances. When you include a channel as part of your digital presence, you should be aware of the commitments that you are making in terms of the data that is generated through its use.

The starting point for understanding any social media channel is the terms of service. This is the basis of the contract between you and the channel. Facebook's terms of service (www.facebook.com/terms.php) says that

> You own the intellectual property rights (things such as copyright or trademarks) in any such content that you create and share on Facebook and the other Facebook Company Products you use.

This statement reinforces that Facebook is owned media in the sense that you have control over how you present yourself. The fact that the terms of service make this statement does, however, point to the hybrid mode of social media channels as there is the production of value for Facebook rather than you. Facebook is a data-driven organisation. This means that its income and its focus are driven by the collection and analysis of all forms of data. The insights that Facebook gains from this aggregation of massive volumes of data is then translated into income by selling the aggregation and insight from this data to other companies, including advertisers – this is how it monetises the free service that is given to its users.

The Cambridge Analytica-Facebook partnership from 2013 onwards highlighted that data ownership and privacy issues can become far more complex ethical issues. The Cambridge Analytica situation became controversial after it was revealed that Facebook had agreed to share personal data with a specific political research company whose targeting techniques were being used to influence voters (Wong 2019). The relationship became public on 17 March 2018, when media reports revealed that the data of an estimated 87 million Facebook users had been exploited for psychographic profiling. A data scientist and psychologist, Aleksandr Kogan, developed a personality quiz app that circulated on Facebook under the title "thisisyourdigitallife". Users answered questions about themselves but also granted access to parts of their profiles including their "likes" and "contact lists". Kogan developed the app under the guise of academic research, and Cambridge Analytica obtained the entire contents of the data set that was generated.

The actions of Kogan, Cambridge Analytica and Facebook became a discussion about the sharing of personal data and the rights (and expectations) of those who use the platform to have this data kept private. Facebook's decision to share data fell down on a number of points in terms of an ethical decision-making framework (Figure 5.1) but particularly with the consideration of character and integrity and the likely perception of these actions if they were to become public, as well as the straightforward gut-feeling test.

How such an ethically sensitive issue could have become so controversial reflects the sometimes complex interrelationship of an organisation doing business, behaving in an ethical way and adhering to the laws and regulations of the countries it operates in. The starting point for Facebook's woes is revealed in its data policy under "Sharing with third-party partners" in the subsection labelled "Researchers and academics" (facebook.com/about/privacy/).

> We also provide information and content to research partners and academics to conduct research that advances scholarship and innovation that supports our business or

mission and enhances discovery and innovation on topics of general social welfare, technological advancement, public interest, health and well-being.

This was the type of access that Aleksandr Kogan utilised. His subsequent actions and his relationship with Cambridge Analytica have been well investigated and reach well beyond being a question of ethical behaviour.

The key issue with this example is its implications for the creation of your own digital presence. All social media channels are in a continuous process of evolving their policies. For Facebook, the result of the Cambridge Analytica leak was to publicly state that it is a privacy-oriented company. Other channels will change policies when they identify systematic and continuous behaviours that they consider unethical or inappropriate and detrimental to their business. A search of the web will reveal many cases in which accounts on social media channels have been closed down for breaches of the terms of service. Regaining an account can be a time-consuming process and is often unsuccessful.

There are four principles for planning and creating an ethical digital presence. Applying these principles will avoid any current or future breach of a channel's terms of service.

1   Behave ethically, everywhere. If your content and actions do not pass the ethical decision-making framework (Figure 5.1), you may be facing issues now or in the near future.
2   Social media channels are for-profit businesses. Your data is being used to make money for them. Treat your social media channels as paid media channels that are temporarily lending you space to create your own presence.
3   Back up your data. This is particularly true of the content you have created for social media channels (see 2 in this list). Having a backup in multiple locations will enable you to rebuild your presence rapidly if something goes wrong.
4   Loosely "owned" media should direct your personas to more tightly "owned" media. For example, use social media channels to encourage visits and conversations on your own website.

Facebook's data policy mentioned "sharing with third-party partners". The viewpoint of the data you will encounter in creating your digital presence will shape how and what you choose to do – particularly with the overriding principle of behaving ethically. The distinctions between different data viewpoints are particularly relevant for understanding GDPR, as well as taking advantage of your analytics data.

First-party data is what you have collected directly through your digital presence. In this viewpoint, you own and control the data and can use it in accordance with the terms and conditions that you set and specify on owned media such as a website. First-party data includes emails as well as registration information that you might collect when someone signs up to receive blog updates from you. First-party data is your most valuable data viewpoint as it directly relates to you and the people most interested in you.

Second-party data is the viewpoint of data collected by someone else (a person or an organisation) and shared with you. Sharing data can help both parties grow their audiences. You can see this viewpoint in practice when you use a travel site to book a flight, and the site then lets you book a restaurant or a rental car at the destination.

From the viewpoint of third-party data providers, they do not collect data directly but have agreements with others to provide it with their first-party data. Third-party data aggregators take the data from multiple sources to build a more comprehensive profile of a person.

Liveramp is a third-party data aggregator with a 50-year history. It is "one of the biggest companies you've never heard of". Liveramp has information on about 500 million active consumers worldwide that includes 1,500 separate pieces of data (data points) per person. Their strategy is to collect everything about a person's offline and online activities in order to build a "360-degree view" of every consumer in the USA and other countries, often without the consumer being entirely aware of this collection process (Singer 2012). Following consumer privacy concerns and calls for the ability to opt out, Liveramp introduced "Security Manager" and an opt-out option for consumers (liveramp. com/opt_out/).

Creating your digital presence will involve dealing with different data viewpoints. This awareness of different data viewpoints should also influence how you handle your own data and that of the people who visit your channels (§16.2).

5.3 Privacy, consent and trust

Building trust with your personas is a core element of a successful digital presence. The foundation of any ongoing relationship is based on building and maintaining trust. This trust then translates into reputation. While trust is a very wide subject, we will initially focus on the ethical building blocks of trust in the form of providing an assurance of privacy and obtaining clear consent. While people may casually share information through websites and social media channels without directly considering the privacy of this information, any perceived misuse may break their trust and prevent the development of a longer-term relationship.

With control and power shifting into the hands of the consumer (§2.1), an ethical and trust-based relationship is built on the evidence of this intention even if an individual's specific concerns for these issues are more casual. One of the most surprising outcomes of privacy violations such as the Cambridge Analytica-Facebook scandal was how little it affected the overall active daily users of Facebook. Many of these regular users did not rush to delete their Facebook accounts or alter their privacy settings despite the significant coverage, the campaigns by concerned individuals and potential risks to their own data (Lazarus 2018). There could be many possible reasons, and one study (Reczek et al. 2016) uncovered the fact that individuals considered themselves immune to psychographic tailored advertisements and did not understand how automated approaches or targeting algorithms worked on social media channels.

Examples of data-driven organisations – including Facebook – collecting large quantities of personal data without the full knowledge or understanding of the data subject (you and every other individual) can be described as "masked marketing". The role of "masked marketing" has emerged as a result of complex terms of service statements, obscure statements regarding sharing data with third parties and the use of a default opt-in approach to gaining consent. In combination, this means it is simply easier to accept everything rather than to actively opt out. The data-driven business model of social media channels means that each incomplete profile represents a lost opportunity and ultimately a (tiny) loss of income. In this sense "permission marketing" is a misnomer. "Masked marketing" better describes the experience a user has when they engage with social media channels and elsewhere.

From the perspective of your own digital presence, it is important to work with your audience through your personas. Gaining and respecting their consent is only the first step in developing a two-way trust relationship. Even if your own presence does eventually

Digital content and devices	Email alerts, messages, ads, and cookies
Amazon Drive	Cookie preferences
Apps and more	Advertising preferences
Audible settings	Communication preferences
Content and devices	Message centre
Games and software	Alexa shopping notifications
Music settings	Deals Notifications
Video settings	
Digital and device forum	

Figure 5.2 All privacy setting are easily accessible and configurable

grow substantially and become monetised (§17.2), your own ethical position should focus consideration on your original audience in terms of what they were promised. The majority of audiences do not mind some data being collected as long as there is a recipro-cated and trusted relationship, and the consent process is clear and transparent.

Amazon consistently receives high customer satisfaction results in surveys. But simul-taneously, Amazon tracks a significant amount of data about its visitors and customers. Much of this data is aggregated to feed back to individual visitors with new product recommendations and reminders. This assists in showing returning customers the value in the data they share – even when it is also used for other purposes. Amazon balances the transparent and discreet capture of user information with high levels of consent and disclosure (Figure 5.2). This level of transparency around consent translates into ongo-ing trust between Amazon and its customers. While your own digital presence will not have the resources or capabilities of Amazon, gaining explicit consent and showing clear sensitivity to privacy can be positively combined for even the least sophisticated presence.

5.4 Using the General Data Protection Regulation (GDPR) in a positive way

The General Data Protection Regulation (GDPR) covers the personal data of all EU residents, regardless of the location of processing. Personal data is data that, directly or indirectly, can identify an individual and specifically includes online identifiers such as IP addresses, cookies and other digital footprints, as well as physical location data that identi-fies the individual. GDPR is founded on six general data protection principles (Goddard 2017):

1   Fairness and lawfulness
2   Purpose limitation
3   Data minimisation
4   Accuracy
5   Storage limitation
6   Integrity and confidentiality

This purpose of this section is not to belabour the legal obligations introduced by the GDPR but instead to emphasise its value as a framework for ethical behaviour in any digital environment. This means that while the GDPR is only an EU regulation, its value is far more universal and a template for action in any jurisdiction. From this perspective, the GDPR should not be seen as a regulation that necessarily has to be followed but rather as a set of base principles for you to match and then exceed in terms of your own ethical online behaviour.

At the core of the GDPR is data protection. More specifically, it is about the handling of personal data in ways that would generally satisfy the person that the data relates to. In this way, the GDPR is also a tacit acknowledgement that our personal data is an extension of our own identity. The GDPR balances accountability with transparency. Organisations have to take responsibility for the personal data they hold and must ensure that this data can be accessed by individuals in a readable manner. But even this obligation can be regarded as setting a standard for ethical behaviour in organisations as it forces reflection on what types of data are held, why they are held and how long they are held. The introduction of the GDPR provoked organisations to take a more active role in managing personal data and closed a loop in that records should be as willingly discarded as they were obtained.

The thinking behind the GDPR encourages you to create your digital presence with trust built in from the outset. If you are collecting personal data – and you will – what you tell your audience you want to do with the data should be clear. The GDPR is people centred, and this has encouraged movement away from tick-box compliance to indicate your privacy policy has been read (even when it hasn't been) to clearer statements and forms of engagement. Privacy policies are traditionally long and written in legal language; however, what you are going to do with the data you collect should be put in ways that you would engage with yourself. Provide people a way of opting out of your data collection that is easy and available at any time.

Having high-quality data allows personalised and customised communication with your personas (or even individuals), and this ability directly supports the promotion of your value proposition. With additional ethically collected data, you can also build better personas with details about the types of content that are preferred and what time of the day they are active, as well as other technical details.

Improved understanding of your personas (or even creating new personas as you learn more) enables more targeted and valuable content to be delivered through your digital presence. The Amazon recommendation system is a large-scale example of increasing the value you deliver to your personas. Your efforts may be more modest. You may learn that a daily short video is overwhelming your persona, and a longer-form weekly video is more appropriate. You may learn that a wordy blog post is not right for your persona, and a short, more "listicle" style is better. You may discover that a podcast is preferable to text because your personas engage better on the move and with audio. Learning from data is an iterative process. You can make mistakes, but digital gives you the capability to learn rapidly, apologise if necessary and take a different direction.

The GDPR provides a framework to create high-quality and ethical connections with your personas. If you can demonstrate to your audience how the aggregation of their data can engage them more personally, give them greater insight, improve a service or even fulfill a wider social need, your audience will be more willing to share their personal information.

TL;DR

Be ethical in your digital presence. Consider what you are asking from the people who will be engaging with your presence in terms of sharing data. If you would not be comfortable with sharing this information, then do not ask your visitors. Strongly ethical personal behaviour will build trust and reputation for your digital presence.

Callout 5.1: Your action – being ethical

At this early stage in the development of your digital presence, achieving your goals being ethical may appear largely conceptual. But being ethical should permeate all your actions from the very beginning. Many organisations (and particularly public organisations) have made it policy to conduct Equality Inclusion Assessments (EIA) for key decisions and actions. The process does not guarantee ethical behaviour across the organisation, but it does set out an intention that the organisation is attempting to consistently consider its actions through an ethical lens. The viewpoint is usually orientated around consideration for those with protected characteristics, and this can be a starting point for your own thinking (Table 5.1). You can consider the actions and outcomes that you have already defined in this light. A positive assessment encourages inclusion of all people regardless of this characteristic. A negative assessment means that the action will exclude and discourage engagement by some people based on this characteristic. Your task is to reframe your actions in ways that move the assessment away from negative and towards the positive.

Give the same consideration to new actions as they become defined. Acting legally (in the UK) would push the actions to neutral, but acting ethically is about attempting to make each action positive (a significant challenge for any organisation or individual).

Table 5.1 A Equality Inclusion Assessment template

Action	Characteristics	Positive	Neutral	Negative
	Age			
	Disability			
	Gender reassignment			
	Marriage or civil partnership			
	Pregnancy and maternity			
	Race			
	Religion or belief			
	Sex			
	Sexual orientation			

Callout 5.2: Case Study – James Hobson (aka The Hacksmith)

From personal presence to an organisation

James Hobson is Canadian and was born in 1990. James and the wider work of Hacksmith Industries could be categorised as backyard engineers – James does have a degree in this field – that have found an audience on YouTube that almost defines a genre in its own right. Since starting the YouTube channel in 2006, James's work has attracted attention because the projects have focused on creating items that were originally props in major Hollywood films. Through the application of engineering skills, these props are turned into functioning objects, including Iron Man's exo-skeleton and Captain America's shield. These projects have attracted sponsors and increased the audience for Hacksmith videos. As a result, James's profile has turned a personal presence into a growing business. The LinkedIn channel for Hacksmith Industries now lists 13 employees, and the website is currently looking for more people to join the company. The LinkedIn channel also reveals a transparency in terms of the source of their income and the persona that they are specifically addressing: "We are social influencers and we make money by selling advertising to companies who want to reach our demographic of young males". James Hobson's Facebook page also boldly reveals a personal progression from engineering graduate to "video creator".

The Hacksmith website uses the Wix content management system.

Channel	Link	Followers	Views	Content
YouTube	www.youtube.com/channel/ UCjgpFI5dU-D1-kh9H1muoxQ	11.1m	983.9m views	660 videos
Facebook	www.facebook.com/thehacksmith/			
Instagram	www.instagram.com/thehacksmith/	558k		2.9k posts
LinkedIn	www.linkedin.com/company/ hacksmith-entertainment-ltd/	1.4k		
Twitter	https://twitter.com/thehacksmith	31.4k		4.1k tweets
Website	www.hacksmith.tech/		Ranked 418,000th website globally	

Callout 5.3: "In Debora's Kitchen" – being ethical

Debora plans a presence that matches their own personal values. The website will be the hub for the presence and will contain a privacy policy as well as a statement of values that will apply to all the connected surrounding channels.

1   Indeboraskitchen will be accessible for people with disabilities.
2   No personal data of visitors will be shared or sold; it will be used only for its intended stated purpose.
3   All data will be backed up securely in accordance with a defined security policy.

4   A privacy policy and full compliance with GDPR will be maintained in letter and spirit.

5   Gender-neutral language will be used for all communication.

6   Any monetisation of the presence will be made transparent.

7   The origins of recipes will be fully disclosed, and any synthesis of ideas from other food bloggers will also be disclosed.

8   Debora's own life story and persona will be presented truthfully with no dramatisation.

Debora intends to build relationships with the key personas and recognises that all relationships (online and offline) are based on trust cultivated over a long period of time.

References cited

Ford, R. and Richardson, W. (1994) "Ethical decision making: A review of the empirical literature", *Journal of Business Ethics*, 13, pp. 205–221, https://doi.org/10.1007/BF02074820

Goddard, M. (2017) "The EU General Data Protection Regulation (GDPR): European regulation that has a global impact", *International Journal of Market Research*, 59(6), https://doi.org/10.2501/IJMR-2017-050

Kansas University (2006) "Steps of the ethical decision making process", https://research.ku.edu/sites/research.ku.edu/files/docs/EESE_EthicalDecisionmakingFramework.pdf

Lazarus, D. (2018) "Facebook says you 'own' all the data you post. Not even close, say privacy experts", *Los Angeles Times*, 19th Mar., www.latimes.com/business/lazarus/la-fi-lazarus-facebook-cambridge-analytica-privacy-20180320-story.html

Mettler, K. (2019) "Female reporter whose butt was smacked on live TV is now seeking criminal charges", *National Post*, 12th Dec., https://nationalpost.com/news/world/female-reporter-whose-butt-was-smacked-on-live-tv-is-now-seeking-criminal-charges

Noyes, D. (2020) "The top 20 valuable Facebook statistics", *Zephoria*, https://zephoria.com/top-15-valuable-facebook-statistics

Pence, E.H. (2015) "Will big data mean the end of privacy?", *Journal of Educational Technology Systems*, 44(2), pp. 253–267, https://doi.org/10.1177/0047239515617146

Reczek, R., Summers, C. and Smith, R. (2016) "Targeted Ads don't just make you more likely to buy – They can change how you think about yourself", *Forbes*, 4th Apr., https://hbr.org/2016/04/targeted-ads-dont-just-make-you-more-likely-to-buy-they-can-change-how-you-think-about-yourself

Singer, N. (2012) "Mapping and sharing, the consumer genome", *New York Times*, 17th June, www.nytimes.com/2012/06/17/technology/acxiom-the-quiet-giant-of-consumer-database-marketing.html

Stetler, B. (2011) "Upending anonymity, these days the web unmasks everyone", *New York Times*, 21st June, www.nytimes.com/2011/06/21/us/21anonymity.html

Vallejo, J. (2020) "Nurse suspended after TikTok video mocking Covid-19 mask rules goes viral", *The Independent*, 30th Nov., www.independent.co.uk/news/world/americas/oregon-nurse-suspended-tiktok-covid-mask-b1764155.html

Wong, J. (2019) "The Cambridge Analytica scandal changed the world – But it didn't change Facebook", *The Guardian*, 18th Mar., www.theguardian.com/technology/2019/mar/17/the-cambridge-analytica-scandal-changed-the-world-but-it-didnt-change-facebook

Further reading

Fosl, P. and Baggini, J. (2007) *The Ethics Toolkit: A Compendium of Ethical Concepts and Methods*, Hoboken, NJ: Wiley.

Part II
Planning

6 What is a Theory of Change?

What you will learn

- The underlying ideas, terminology and purpose of a Theory of Change
- Creating a Theory of Change for yourself
- Defining the process by which change will happen

6.1 A Theory of Change

Through Part I of this book, the focus of attention has been on broad concepts that are the building blocks for your own digital presence. We have heavily and consciously used terms such as "strategic thinking" and "value proposition", as well as introducing some models to link all these concepts together. The underlying narrative is that you need to take the long-term view for creating a successful digital presence in order to achieve your goals. Strategy by itself does not deliver results – it makes your approach consistent and coherent. Strategic thinking also makes your presence ethical, trustworthy and always of high quality. What is now needed is a way to plan the specific actions that will take you from your current situation to achieving your overall goal. To do this we utilise the Theory of Change to link your activities and the planning of your overall project (other project management methods are also available).

TheoryOfChange(.org) is an organisation devoted to promoting the use of Theories of Change and teaching people how to use one. The organisation defines a Theory of Change as

> a comprehensive description and illustration of how and why a desired change is expected to happen in a particular context . . . by first identifying the desired long-term goals and then working back from these to identify all the conditions (outcomes) that must be in place (and how these related to one another causally) for the goals to occur.

Theory of Change is a suitable planning framework for your digital presence because it explicitly articulates how a project is intended to achieve its outcomes with a defined set of actions while taking into account your own assumptions as well as situational and environmental contexts.

The Theory of Change aims to address the linkages between goals, objectives, strategies, outcomes and assumptions. Each Theory of Change is uniquely crafted around an individual or organisation in the way that connects goals with specific actions, and as a result, it is often referred to as a "road map" or "blueprint" for explaining how to get "there" from "here" (Stachowiak 2013). Theory of Change is used in a variety of

DOI: 10.4324/9781003026587-6

organisations, including charities, governments and companies for many purposes, but it is particularly popular in situations in which it is a form of social change that is being sought as the outcome of the project. It is less commonly applied by individuals for their own needs; however, the principles and purpose also readily work at the personal level. The focus of this chapter is to understand the Theory of Change and how this can then be applied to your goal and to developing your digital presence.

Many of the building blocks for your own Theory of Change have already been forming through the actions you have undertaken in the first part of this book. You know that your digital presence will be founded on high-quality visibility and reputation delivered through the right channels. You also know that the right channels are, in part, determined by identification of personas – the personified representations of your audience. These building blocks are all framed around a transparent and consciously ethical approach to building and maintaining relationships. All this work sits on top of the definition of your core value proposition: The value that you offer your audience through personas that you have defined.

Your audience may need even more than that. The power of the audience produces a need for ever more transparency in all our interactions. The value that you create that benefits your audience is reciprocated by different forms of value they return back to you. But audiences are also increasingly interested in understanding the benefits that your actions bring to society at large – by challenging traditional thinking, delivering education, employing others or offering entertainment. This perspective has visibly manifested negatively as calls for boycotts of prominent digital channels such as Amazon (Cook 2020) in the wake of its documented rise in profits during the COVID-19 pandemic. This type of action is not confined to end-consumer movements either. Many large corporations boycotted advertising on Facebook after what was seen as a weak response to hate speech on the channel and in the wake of the reinvigorated Black Lives Matter campaign (Hsu and Lutz 2020; Wong 2020). Your sentiments will align with your audiences and are described in your personas. Like you, they are driven, idealistic and often frustrated with the ways that current forms of capitalism benefit individuals unequally. While you may express many of these sentiments more boldly, many companies also share this thinking and express it through actions such as being a living-wage employer (livingwage.org.uk) or becoming a greener employer (greenmark.co.uk).

Social change is increasingly embedded in all our collective thinking, which further reinforces the benefits of applying a Theory of Change to your own project. This is a key differentiator for the Theory of Change as its purpose does not end with the delivery of specific outputs but extends further to recognise the impact that this change makes as a result. The multiple interrelated actions needed to create visibility and build a reputation for a digital presence require a framework that can take into account the dynamic complexity of the situation and the environment while still being able to bring about the desired change and deliver impact – your end goal (Figure 6.1).

Traditional methods of managing projects that are based solely on delivering a final output do not acknowledge the causal chains of action that bring about this final result or the potential wider impact that is (really) being ultimately sought. Causal chains can be complex and may require multiple iterations of one action before a second one can commence. Similarly, a sequence of actions may have to occur multiple times before a defined output will be realised. Ignoring the mechanisms and interrelationships of actions is described as "black box" thinking. For example, an educationalist may test the hypothesis that classroom attendance results in higher attainment and lower dropout rates.

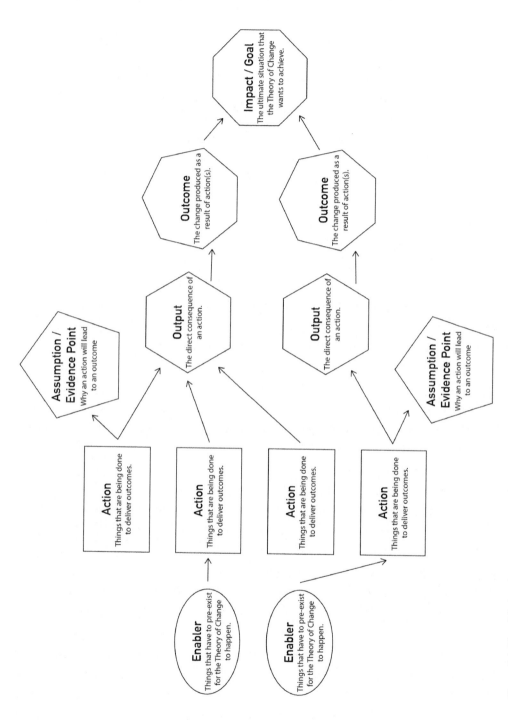

Figure 6.1 Simplified and generalised Theory of Change flow diagram (Why will this happen?)

A trial could be devised to test this hypothesis and a statistical relationship identified. What would not be examined in the project is the underlying causal mechanisms that may or may not also be at work (including the Hawthorne Effect of students altering their behaviour because of the observation itself). A Theory of Change is a recognition that the processes and actions required to change people are generally complex and messy.

Developing a Theory of Change identifies all the stakeholders who will feel the impact of the change that is being planned. A stakeholder is anyone who has something to gain or lose from the project you are initiating. There is definite benefit in analysing the needs and concerns of multiple stakeholders in any project to encourage and recognise multiple perspectives. A process not dissimilar to the development of personas (Chapter 4) and a way of ensuring that the actions undertaken will be ethically sound (Chapter 5). A Theory of Change also shifts thinking away from what you are currently doing to focus on what you want to achieve. This perspective parallels the idea of using strategic thinking and the advantages of taking a long-term perspective (Chapter 3). The value of SMART objectives (§3.2) also directly translates into the outcomes of a Theory of Change. Through the first five chapters of this book, you have developed your understanding of the key concepts. Now with a Theory of Change, you have the mechanism to consciously link them together.

For your own Theory of Change, the outcomes will concentrate on the elements of the presence that are about building reputation and visibility. Your overall goal (your impact in the Theory of Change) may not be evident for a number of months or years and will depend on the specifics of the goal itself. If your goal is to gain employment in a company that suits your own attitudes and sentiments, you may realise success very quickly. If your goal is to found a startup and sell 10,000 units of your product, the progress may take longer. If your goal is to establish yourself as an internationally recognised influencer, then the goal may take longer still. Many of the case studies in this book will also give you an indication of the time frames for achieving these different goals. An advantage of having a Theory of Change is that it demonstrates at least one possible pathway to achieving your intended goals irrespective of how long the change itself may take to occur. By breaking down the black box of setting goals without a route to success, a Theory of Change also considers the real-world setting in which the project is being implemented. These acknowledgements shape the actions that will be undertaken and the order in which they are completed. The most directly relevant example is that of a university student planning their future career. Their time scale is relatively fixed as they must first graduate before moving into a professional role. However, opportunities for undertaking an internship during a holiday period introduces a new action that produces a new output – in the form of work experience – and outcomes that may shorten the pathway to their final goal. In contrast, a risk to the Theory of Change may be the prospect of achieving a lower degree classification. If this risk becomes a reality, the timeline for achieving a goal may need to be extended. This risk will require additional actions that introduce new outputs that reach your intended outcomes through a different route.

6.2 Applying a Theory of Change

A Theory of Change can be used from the beginning to the end of an initiative. It can be a way of planning an idea and developing the strategy that is required to make it a reality. A Theory of Change can also be used as a way of monitoring and evaluating change

(Arensman et al. 2018). Using a Theory of Change when a project is already underway can reveal why the initiative is or is not working.

The idea of a Theory of Change is that it represents reality. When plans for change are made and implemented, there is an implicit understanding that those plans are driven by strategic thinking and purpose. A Theory of Change theorises about strategy by stating that *if* you use this logic, *then* you will realise the stated goal.

A Theory of Change maps out your initiative in stages (and in reverse) (Taplin and Clark 2012):

- Identify your long-term **goal** (or the impact you want to see)
- Recognise any **assumptions** that lie behind this goal
- Mapping back from your **goal**, identify the preconditions or requirements necessary to achieve that goal – these are your **outcomes** (or SMART objectives – §3.2)
- Document why these preconditions or requirements are needed
- Explain the rationale for **outcomes** that are necessary preconditions to other **outcomes**
- Where possible, develop **evidence points** to measure ongoing progress towards desired **outcomes** – these are measures of value that has been produced
- Define the who and what aspects of the **outcomes** – these are your desired **outputs**
- Choose the most likely **action(s)** to produce a desired **output**
- Define the **enablers** found in existing parts of the system that your theory needs to work
- Consider that some **outcomes** may need to exist before some **actions** even commence and subsequent **outcomes** are realised
- Review your theory. Is it plausible, "doable" and testable?
- Write a narrative (and a flow chart) to explain the overall logic of your project

A further distinction found in a Theory of Change is the presence in the system of shorter-term and longer-term outcomes. The shorter-term outcomes are generally achieved earlier in a project and are sometimes also described as quick wins. However, the most vital step in a Theory of Change is getting the long-term outcomes right. An outcome is a situation that does not currently exist but must be in place for your project to work and to achieve the overall goal. Outcomes are the building blocks of your Theory of Change too. All the outcomes in your Theory of Change are preconditions for achieving the goal. This reinforces the need for a clear, compelling goal to help you to remain focused and motivated over time.

To get to your goal in your Theory of Change, you define the pathways that lead to each outcome. You may have multiple pathways, and each pathway may pass through a sequence of outcomes, or it may have only a single outcome. A pathway is the sequence in which outcomes must occur to reach your long-term goal. Pathways also represent the intersecting causal logic of your Theory of Change. It is a reflection of the importance that a Theory of Change places on causal logic that a visual flow chart is so often associated with the work.

A visual approach is also justified for other reasons. The process of "backwards mapping" used in the Theory of Change can be challenging if you are more used to planning activities that start at the beginning and progress forward. "Standard" processes that are generally recognised as effective tend to be applied in this way without critique or deviation. It is exactly this approach that does not produce any form of desired change.

Turning this perspective around, the Theory of Change instead comes back to defining the required enablers at the other end of the planning process. Enablers are the conditions or resources that must already exist as starting points to ensure the success of your initiative. But unlike short-term outcomes that must be crafted as part of the project, the enablers are believed to already exist. In a similar way, a Theory of Change must make assumptions. These are the plausible bridges that link actions through defined outputs to outcomes. The assumptions are the often unvoiced preconditions that must exist for the outcome to be realised. Stating an assumption is a way of connecting the outputs from an action into the wider logic of a Theory of Change. Providing these rationales explicitly explains the logic behind each causal link on the pathway to the final goal.

Evidence points also appear along the pathways in a Theory of Change. These are the mechanisms for testing and checking the progress of the logic with measurable evidence of progress along the pathway. This is usually done by demonstrating how an outcome has been fulfilled. The evidence points reinforce that the overall logic of the theory is sound and that there are no other alternative explanations.

Mapping your project from end to beginning is systematic and more consciously sensitive to the steps that must be undertaken for a project to be successful. Understanding and mapping out the logic for change will also take time and require research. A Theory of Change should be a dynamic plan that can respond to the changing external environment. Shifts in the expected outcomes within the theory may also prompt necessary changes by either providing a more direct route to the goal or requiring the addition of further outcomes (to overcome what has now revealed a gap in the logic).

6.3 Defining your Theory of Change

Creating a successful digital presence is a process involving many elements, is sensitive to external situational change and will evolve as you change yourself (internal change). In other words, the Theory of Change is well suited to supporting a project of this type because it emphasises the linkage between goals, objectives and actions (Vogel 2012b). It is also a flexible tool that can be bent to suit your purposes rather than becoming a straitjacket for your current activities. This is why the Theory of Change is described variously as a road map, a theory for action and a blueprint for strategic planning and learning (Reisman et al. 2007). But there are also critiques of the Theory of Change that argue there is a lack of attention to detail (DuBow and Litzler 2018) and particularly the specific resources required for any particular action. This is a gap that requires attention, and subsequent chapters of this book focus on precisely the filling in of these details for your own Theory of Change.

We have presented strategy as an integrated set of choices that are externally facing (Chapter 3). This means that all your interactions are moving towards predefined outcomes that shape and guide your efforts, but these must also be reconciled and responsive to a constantly changing world.

At this point, it is doubly useful to highlight some possible elements that you could introduce for your own Theory of Change. Developing specific elements for a Theory of Change will reinforce its value and at the same time will assist in the practical need to develop your own thinking for creating your digital presence.

Goals

Your goal is the big change that you want to achieve (Callout 1.2). In some ways, this is outside the scope of this book as the change will not simply be to create a digital presence. But equally, your interest in this book either reflects a desire to do something with an existing digital presence (beyond it being just a bit of fun) or is an intuitive recognition that your goal is going to incorporate a digital presence in some way. There are a range of goals that you can define from the most personal and pragmatic through to the large scale and much longer term. True to the Theory of Change, and irrespective of their actual scale, the goals you define should be sustainable while also reflecting personal ambition.

Some personal and pragmatic goals for a graduate might include

- Gain employment with an organisation that reflects my own beliefs and ethical viewpoint
- Become an influencer with a focus on innovation in my favourite subject area
- Become a recognised innovator in my subject area
- Find a life partner
- Become a prominent member of an international professional community
- Found my own startup specialising in my favourite subject area
- Develop an advocacy programme for under-represented communities in my profession

Thinking about these goals in terms of a Theory of Change, it may be that one or more of the goals are prerequisite outcomes that must be completed before your final goal can be achieved. This causal logic will only be revealed when you work back from your own specific and ultimate goal. The final two examples also hint at a wider set of goals that are more organisational and social in their impact. These latter options and other more organisationally focused goals may be how your Theory of Change evolves as your own goals develop and are achieved. Organisational goals that could be considered for a Theory of Change may look more familiar in that they will echo other strategic-planning processes and particularly the biggest of the externally facing SMART objectives. For example:

- Be the leading source of local knowledge in a specific subject area
- Be the leading retailer of a specific group of products in a region
- Become the national industry benchmark for how a specific service is delivered
- Be recognised as a leading source of innovation for a particular service or product
- Define an entirely new product niche for a sector

These are very large goals that probably challenge other existing businesses and will take time and concerted effort. These goals certainly require a number of prerequisite outcomes to be successfully achieved. These outcomes will already potentially be partially defined – without the assumptions and evaluation points being acknowledged – as inwardly focused SMART objectives including, for example, productivity improvements, changes in the organisational structure or creating new supply chains.

Not-for-profit organisations have a bigger challenge in shaping their goals. Their goals will generally extend beyond the realm of organisational goals and seek to bring sustainable social change. The UK government's Department for International Development (DFID) offers examples of how big these social impacts can become while still sharing many of the qualities of being SMART (Vogel 2012a):

- Improved learning outcomes and staying-on rates for boys and girls
- Poor and vulnerable people, especially women, benefit from economic growth in the poorest states in India
- Reduced poverty and improved security in North and South Kivu
- Women and girls are free from all forms of gender-based violence

These examples are large-scale projects that are based on complex causal pathways that also require significant investment from bodies such as the DFID.

The key to establishing your own goal irrespective of whether it is personal, a startup, organisational or a project for social good is to be ambitious while retaining the qualities of being SMART.

Outcomes and outputs

It is on the outcomes and outputs of your Theory of Change that we will specifically focus here on your digital presence. However, the value of using the Theory of Change is that within your own logic model, there may be outputs and outcomes that you can recognise that are not specifically related to your digital presence. While those cannot be specifically dealt with here in this book, you will be able to recognise yourself the interrelationships among these outcomes. All your outcomes and outputs will also have SMART qualities and will often include specific measures as a way of assessing when the outcome has been achieved.

For a digital presence, your outcomes and outputs will share similarities regardless of the scale or form of your goal. Your outcomes will be specific, in that many of them will relate to outputs that are associated with a specific digital channel. The outcomes will also be measurable by mentioning a specific number of people who will have changed in relation to their engagement with you. This may be a count of your deeper and ongoing interactions rather than simply the number of people subscribing to a YouTube channel or an email newsletter, which themselves would be outputs from those specific actions. Your outcomes need to be achievable in order to ensure that the causal pathway remains viable. It does not make any sense to describe an output of 1,000,000 monthly visitors to your own website if your outcome is to have your CV downloaded by just five people. Your outcomes must also be relevant. If you are an engineer with a goal of contributing to a wider social project through the application of your skills, then you would focus attention on engaging with the right community of practice (for example, engineering-forchange.org) in preference to more generic channels such as LinkedIn. All these considerations also come within a time-bound frame that does not leave the final realisation of the outcome open ended. Subsequent outcomes can never be realised if they are dependent on shorter-term outcomes which do not have any expected date for completion.

Actions

As you work backwards, the actions you must undertake to deliver the outputs and outcomes required will become increasingly obvious. By already knowing the elements of a successful digital presence – the right channels, visibility and reputation, with an emphasis on high quality (Figure 1.7) – your actions will manifest around this combination. There is a tendency to shape each action in relation to specific individual channels. There is a common sense aspect to this approach, and with the guiding logic of your Theory of Change, it will ensure that your actions all remain connected to the goal. In working back from your outcomes, it is worth considering the full scope of channels that can be used. At the core of your thinking should be your own website (Chapter 9), as well as how email could work for you as a channel. Email may not be your preferred channel, but consider your personas. With over 300 billion emails sent each day worldwide (Campaign Monitor 2019), it remains the single largest digital channel and is still a preferred channel for the majority of professional engagements.

Social media channels also figure in your actions and require some consideration. While Instagram, YouTube, Facebook, Twitter and TikTok are at the top of any list of the most popular (Robinson 2020), other channels are more focused on specific locations (e.g. KiwiBox, Taringa, RenRen), social action (e.g. Care2), professionals (e.g. UpStream) or lifestyles (e.g. Wayn) ("Jamie" 2020). Your selection of a channel for your action should not be solely based on its popularity – the sudden rise of TikTok as a channel should be read as a cautionary tale against basing the selection of a channel solely on its total number of users (Mohson 2020).

Actions that address visibility should be framed more directly around how you can become more visible to your personas (rather than just everyone). Considering the format of your content will guide you in specific directions as there is a need to balance the format that best showcases you with the preferences of your persona(s). A long-form video format – and the use of YouTube – may present the best showcase, but your personas are busy people who prefer short-form content. Your compromise might be to use TikTok if your personas fit that channel or, if not, an embedded video in a tweet.

Actions around reputation will be tied to the quality of your content but may be expressed in different channels as earned media. Reputation is the most difficult element to control as its construction lies with your audience. However, some insight from the concepts of big data can help guide your actions for building your reputation. The four *V*s of big data (and distinct from the five *V*s of strategy) are an appropriate lens for improving your reputation. The four *V*s are veracity, variety, volume and velocity. If you view all the content available through digital channels as a complete set of big data, your own content represents only a very tiny fraction of this entire collection.

Building a reputation requires veracity. The significance of veracity will vary if you are building your reputation as a stand-up comedian rather than a medical technician. To consider these two examples, your content needs to sit on a continuum between correctly consistent to consistently correct. This also ties closely to all your actions needing to be ethically consistent and sound. Variety then considers the mixture of content. This may involve multiple channels or a single channel – especially a website – where multiple formats offer different ways of saying the same messages. This type of reinforcement helps represent your own consistency around your core messages and your ability to communicate these messages in different ways. The volume and velocity of your content are interrelated. Rapidly delivering large amounts of detailed content is not sustainable and, as a result, will not build a long-term reputation. Your velocity – your pace of delivery – must be sustainable for your own capabilities and provide enough time for your personas to consume, appreciate and, importantly, share, review and comment upon. The format of the content that you are using also requires consideration of its volume – the size of the content being presented. Videos beyond a few minutes long will be abandoned, email newsletters that require endless scrolling will reduce the size of your audience and intricate information graphics will only attract the attention of the most dedicated. Applying the adage that you should only include one idea in each message will help define actions that build your reputation.

TL;DR

You need a plan to create your digital presence. A good plan flexes as external circumstances change and internal capabilities improve. A good plan also recognises where the assumptions lie and has a clear logic that leads you step by step from your current situation to your ultimate goal.

Callout 6.1: Your action – developing your Theory of Change

With some enablers, actions, outcomes and a goal already drafted, you have the building blocks to create your own Theory of Change flow diagram.

Work backwards from your goal. Do not assume you will have all the outcomes you will need. Document your additional assumptions and ensure that your logic does not make a significant leap from one outcome to the next. If you are not clear what is missing now but you know that something will be required, then place an empty action, output or outcome box in the logic model. You will need to fill out these blanks to create your complete Theory of Change.

Your actions should produce outputs – what will specifically come out of an action and who will be the beneficiaries – that either singly or in combination with other outputs (and outcomes) contribute to an outcome. If the outcomes that you have already defined do not match up with the outcomes that you can define from your outputs, you will also know that there is a gap that requires a linkage either with intervening actions or a sequence of outcomes.

Freely available mind-mapping software or specialist Theory of Change software such as dylomo(.com) can assist you in visualising your flow of logic. If you use Microsoft tools, then PowerPoint can also be used as a quick and dirty visualisation tool.

Callout 6.2: Case Study – Mohd Shahril Fawzy (aka Pojie)

Living what you have learned

Pojie is a journalism and photography graduate from Malaysia. Their digital presence began as a log of personal travel to Thailand. Pojie's posts take a variety of perspectives on travel with different content focusing on food, a location, the journey or the quality of a particular hotel. Pojie also offers travelling tips for different countries as extended "listicles". The advice and travelogue are presented variously in English and Bahasa, clearly defining a persona for the audience. Although initially working for a company as travel writer, Pojie is now freelance and travels full time, with their website featuring travels to a range of countries including China, Indonesia, Norway and Wales. Pojie's digital presence now has sponsorship from a range of Malaysian companies that reflect and support their presence, including Air Asia, Cabin Zero (a luggage retailer), Starwood Hotels, CIMB Bank and Celcom (a Malaysian telecoms company).

The Pojie website uses the Blogger content management system.

Channel	Link	Followers	Likes	Content
Facebook	www.facebook.com/pojiegraphy/	18.3k	18.1k likes	
YouTube	www.youtube.com/pojiegraphy	3.26k	277k views	85 videos
Instagram	www.instagram.com/pojiegraphy/	19.1k	505 average likes	2k posts
Twitter	https://twitter.com/pojiegraphy/	9.1k		98k tweets
Website	www.pojiegraphy.com/		Ranked 2,460,00th website globally	

Callout 6.3: "In Debora's Kitchen" – a personal Theory of Change

Debora's Theory of Change is emerging with many of the key decisions that have already been made.

The original goal describes a desire to "create a 'go to' online presence for busy people to learn how to make simple and healthy Latin cuisine". In a Theory of Change, this now appears to reflect the impact that Debora wants to see and represents a vision for a further business. As a consequence of the long-term outcome that "within the next three to five years, 'InDeborasKitchen' should be in a position to draw in revenue that is sufficiently strong and consistent to become Debora's day job" now better represents the goal in a Theory of Change.

Debora's proposed outcomes can now be identified as a string of causal logic with an action: "To create a website that supports the existing YouTube channel". This implies an unstated assumption about actions relating to the creation of content and leading to an output: "To consistently create and publish content that is fun to watch and easy for beginners to understand". An evidence point can be introduced here that endeavours to quantify "fun" and "easy" that will involve surveys or interviewing to the website at regular intervals. Maintaining a consistently "fun" and "easy" approach will be important as the output links to a short-term outcome – "To grow in subscribers and organic viewers over the next three to five years" – and implies a longer term outcome: "To build a community (using multiple channels including WhatsApp Business) where it is possible to leave feedback and request recipes".

Debora's plans around other social media channels are also prompts for actions (Figure 6.2).

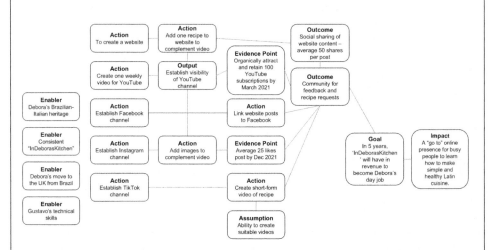

Figure 6.2 First draft of Debora's Theory of Change

Some further metrics that could be added to gauge early success: subscribers, views, Facebook likes, followers, social shares.

References cited

Arensman, B., Waegeningh, C. and Wessel, M. (2018) "Twinning 'practices of change' with 'theory of change': Room for emergence in advocacy evaluation", *American Journal of Evaluation*, 39(2), pp. 221–236, https://doi.org/10.1177/1098214017727364

Campaign Monitor (2019) "The shocking truth about how many emails are sent", 21st May, www.campaignmonitor.com/blog/email-marketing/2019/05/shocking-truth-about-how-many-emails-sent/

Cook, B. (2020) "Why you, too, should boycott Amazon", *The Focus*, 21st Aug., www.thefocus.news/opinion/why-you-too-should-boycott-amazon/

DuBow, W. and Litzler, E. (2018) "The development and use of a theory of change to align programs and evaluation in a complex, national initiative", *American Journal of Evaluation*, 40(2), pp. 231–248, https://doi.org/10.1177/1098214018778132

Hsu, T. and Lutz, E. (2020) "More than 1,000 companies boycotted Facebook. Did it work?", *New York Times*, 1st Aug., www.nytimes.com/2020/08/01/business/media/facebook-boycott.html

"Jamie" (2020) "95+ social networking sites you need to know about", *Make a Website Hub*, 30th Oct., https://makeawebsitehub.com/social-media-sites/

Mohson, M. (2020) "10 TikTok statistics that you need to know in 2021", *Oberlo*, 3rd Sept., www.oberlo.co.uk/blog/tiktok-statistics

Reisman, J., Gienapp, A., and Stachowiak, S. (2007) *A Guide to Measuring Advocacy and Policy*, Baltimore: Organisational Research Services.

Robinson, R. (2020) "The 7 top social media sites you need to care about in 2020", *Adobe Spark*, https://spark.adobe.com/make/learn/top-social-media-sites/

Stachowiak, S. (2013) "Pathways for change: 10 theories to inform advocacy and policy change efforts", *Center for Evaluation Innovation*. Seattle: ORS Impact.

Taplin, D. and Clark, H. (2012) "Theory of change basics: A primer on theory of change", *ActKnowledge*, www.actknowledge.org/akresources/actknowledge-publications/

Vogel, I. (2012a) *Examples of Theories of Change*, London: Department for International Development, https://assets.publishing.service.gov.uk/media/57a08a66ed915d622c000703/Appendix_3_ToC_Examples.pdf

Vogel, I. (2012b) *Review of the Use of 'Theory of Change' in International Development*, London: Department for International Development.

Wong, J. (2020) "'Too big to fail': Why even a historic ad boycott won't change Facebook", *The Guardian*, 11th July, www.theguardian.com/technology/2020/jul/10/facebook-ad-boycott-mark-zuckerberg-activism-change

Further reading

Allen, A. and Roberts, J. (2017) "Evaluating implementation of the early college model through a theory of change", *International Journal of Educational Reform*, 26(3), Summer, pp. 250–257, https://doi.org/10.1177/105678791702600306

McLellan, T. (2020) "Impact, theory of change, and the horizons of scientific practice", *Social Studies of Science*, 25th Aug., https://doi.org/10.1177/0306312720950830

Sullivan, H. and Stewart, M. (2006) "Who owns the theory of change?", *Evaluation*, 12(2), pp. 179–199, https://doi.org/10.1177/1356389006066971

Watkins, K., Lysø, I. and deMarrais, K. (2011) "Evaluating executive leadership programs: A theory of change approach", *Advances in Developing Human Resources*, 13(2), pp. 208–239, https://doi.org/10.1177/1523422311415643

7   Tactics for building your presence

What you will learn

- Key actions for creating your presence
- Key actions for creating your visibility
- Key actions for creating your reputation

7.1 Key actions for building your channel

A successful digital presence is a strategic presence. Having defined the outcomes that are prerequisites for achieving your goal, you can now work back to the specific actions. These actions then coalesce as outputs in your logic model to deliver those outcomes (Chapter 6). This chapter focuses on the specific tactics that build your digital presence – but this acknowledges that there will be other actions in your Theory of Change that are beyond this scope. The tactics you use to build your presence will always be based around creating visibility and encouraging a positive reputation.

The first tactical question is where to start establishing your own presence. You may already have some personal presence on social media channels.

New channels are continuously appearing, and existing channels are in a constant cycle of change. Combined with the fact that all these channels rise and fall in popularity over relatively short periods of time, it can be an overwhelming environment to engage with. There is a sense that it is difficult to get your presence right and that it is all too easy to get it wrong. This is what encourages the "fail fast" mindset (Stark 2019) that tries new approaches to solving a problem. "Fail fast", however, is only a useful perspective when it is linked with the invocation to "learn fast" (Winnie 2020). Failing to learn fast condemns you to repeat failures without success. Your actions need to be rapid, focused and specific. Your tactics should be shaped by available evidence and not solely rely on a "gut feeling".

The first steps with these channels will be to align them all with a consistent name (handle or ID or other label). Some social media channels allow a change after they have been created and some require a fresh start (McGillvray 2014). Just to make things more complex, what is or is not possible can also change over time. The key issue is to construct a consistent identity – in the same way that all your identification lines up offline. Even if you tactically do nothing more with your existing social media channels right now, at the very least you have laid down a clear intention. If you have no social media presence (a statement that will seem unlikely to many), then do not feel any pressure to jump onto every conceivable channel. A strategic approach – and your Theory of Change – should guide your choice of channels rather than any sense of immediate pressure to "dive in" for

DOI: 10.4324/9781003026587-7

fear of missing out. Organisations starting out on the journey to create a digital presence are less likely to have existing social media channels. But even well-established companies may use a change of name to reflect changing purpose and goal. The rebadging of Weight Watchers to the simpler but more enigmatic "WW" signalled a shift from dieting to wellness and new partnerships, such as the one with the Headspace app (Ferris and LaVito 2018). WW is also a more internet-friendly name in its briefness, and its letter repetition makes it easier to type in a quick WhatsApp or text message.

After the immediate (and remedial) action to line up your social media channels with your own identity, you need to establish the hub for your entire digital presence – your website. This is the core owned media of your digital presence. Many of the case studies presented in this book use their websites for a single purpose: as the placeholder that points to all their social media channels. Some also include an email or a direct contact form. Some go further and use their websites to offer more personal details, a blog, links out to podcasts or a full ecommerce setup. Very few (but some) of the people in the case studies have no form of personal website.

Your initial website actions will be driven by your Theory of Change. If your goal is to seek a new role, it may be primarily a summary CV and a link to your LinkedIn profile. If you are founding a startup, you may have a single-page teaser for your new product or service. If you are a small retailer, it will be a page emphasising your street address, contact details, opening hours, how long you have been operating and some quotes from happy customers. The technical aspects of these individual actions are picked up later (Chapter 9). However, the advantage of your Theory of Change is that the initial description of your actions can be expanded out with more and more description that starts to capture this level of detail. A few words in your Theory of Change can be expanded to become a full document (in your favourite word processor or text editor) that can then be turned into the website itself. If you frame your document with a clear logic and use headers, sub-headers and phrases that you believe your personas themselves would use, then you are already on the right path to a high-quality presence. (This point comes back again in a couple of paragraphs.) If your format is more ambitious and involves images, audio or video, then your fuller descriptions could become the brief for a sketch, a script or a descriptive treatment.

Creating your initial presence sets down a marker. Your website will be one of an estimated 1.8 billion that exist worldwide, with around 25% of them considered active (Armstrong 2019). Depending on your existing social media channels, you are also one among 330 million active Twitter users (Lin 2020) and over 1 billion Instagram users (Clement 2020b). Just having a website and social media channels does not correlate to having an instant audience. What you are creating is the opportunity for your personas to access your presence. Achieving your goal will require further actions. In your Theory of Change, a high-quality website (and building the right channels) are outputs that support the delivery of an outcome that then leads in your causal logic to further actions and outcomes.

7.2 Key actions for building your visibility

Gaining visibility is about gaining an audience for your presence. The quality of your website and social media channels is a pivotal consideration for your actions (Part III). Quality does have multiple meanings and is too often reduced to solely the subjective assessment of its visual appeal. However, your human audience will not generally stumble upon your presence by accident (unless they use Mix.com), and your first visitors will be the robots of search engines. Delivering a high-quality presence to a search engine produces better search engine rankings (closer to the top of the first page of results), which, in turn, attracts a human audience because they are more likely to find you in the first place. Achieving this type of quality for search engines is less visual (or audio or video) and more about being logical and textual. Despite their apparent sophistication, search engines, including Google, primarily base their results on the text that they find on a website. If the document the search engine robot finds is logical and well-structured and uses the same phrases that your personas use for their searches, then you are in a good situation.

Having high-quality text for your website also applies to your social media presence. There is a significant difference between posting an image of your portrait with a piece of text embedded in the image (Figure 7.1) and an image accompanied by separate text such as "Shobna Anand: Veterinary surgeon" and some descriptive hashtags such as #vet #yourlocation #yourexpertise. While search engines such as Google do not generally prioritise social media channels in the results (with the exception of YouTube in the case of Google), social media channels rely almost entirely on the textual descriptions that are included with an image or video to make this content findable through their own search functions. If you apply the mantra "text is visible but images are visual", you will consistently deliver a high-quality visible presence that will continue to engage your audience visually once they have found you.

Your visibility is based on the content that will appear on your channels. A content plan will be pivotal to maintaining your visibility over time (Chapter 8), but to begin with, you need to define what designers and developers describe as a minimum viable

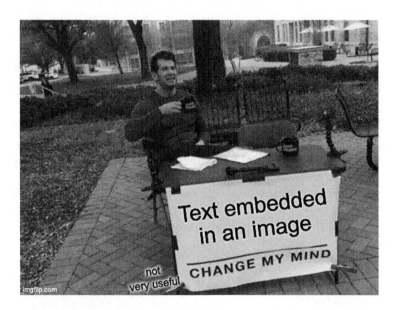

Figure 7.1 Text embedded in an image

Source: imgflip.com/memegenerator

product (MVP). In the case of your digital presence, this is the least amount of content delivered over a defined period on the smallest number of channels that would be of sufficient interest for at least one of your defined personas to warrant a return to your presence in the same defined period. At an optimum, this could resolve to as few as two pieces of content. However, the chances that this would satisfy an MVP for any substantial number of individuals that sit behind a persona is low.

Building visibility could also include actions that introduce the use of paid media. For a personal digital presence, this will not be an option to consider at the beginning of your Theory of Change, if for no other reason than the fact that it costs money. The vast majority of the personal case studies presented throughout this book have not used any paid media to increase their visibility. Instead they have relied on the quality and relevance of their content to engage their personas. However, there will be circumstances when you need to explore the use of paid media for an organisational presence. Paid media gives you a specific form of visibility, although it does not usually contribute positively to your reputation directly. Paid media can even have a negative consequence for your reputation if your personas see the placement of the paid media in the wrong place or the wrong channels or it detracts from their digital experience. Paid media in its many forms is effectively advertising. The use of paid media may still be attractive to kickstart the visibility of many commercial projects. The use of Google Adwords is a relatively low-cost entry point that makes a new business more prominent in relevant search results than would otherwise be possible naturally (or, in the words of the search engine optimisation industry, organic visibility).

7.3 Key actions for building your reputation

Visually appealing websites and social media channels coupled with different forms of interactivity and further relevant content can all engage your human visitors in ways that will encourage favourable earned media – including precious word-of-mouth comments. These are the actions that build beyond visibility to support the creation of a positive reputation. If you were to put this mundanely, your biography is what makes you visible to search engines and to your personas; a portrait picture accompanying the biography is what helps retain your audience and build your reputation.

Retaining and positively influencing your personas in ways that encourage them to create earned media are the primary aims that will shape your actions for building reputation. With an increasingly positive reputation, additional audience members who are represented by your personas will engage directly with your presence. They will arrive directly at your presence without using the intermediary of a search engine. Website analytics are covered later (Chapter 14), but the rudimentary metric is that the percentage of visitors coming from search engine results (what is called organic search traffic) reflects your visibility while the percentage of visitors coming from other websites (aka direct referrals) is evidence of your reputation.

What you do to improve your reputation will follow on in the chain of causal logic from your visibility actions. Without delving directly into the technical mechanisms of creating interactivity, you can define actions that will specifically keep your audience engaged directly with your presence. This can include different forms of live chat, moderated forums or greater levels of sophistication such as an embedded form (a site search function is one straightforward example). The starting point for identifying potential reputation-raising forms of interactivity is to scan your own favourite websites and channels for similar examples of interactivity. The question to ask with the examples that you identify is not "How does it work?" but "How can it add value to my own presence and maximise the value proposition for my personas?" From the technical point of view, if you can identify a form of interactivity on another website, then you can eventually find a way of including it in your own website.

It is also worth considering that the interactive nature of viewing video content – it can be fast forwarded, rewound, paused – is also a route towards greater interactivity on a website that can also improve visibility when it is accessed directly through YouTube. This helps explain why over 500 hours of video content is uploaded to YouTube every minute (Clement 2020a). With mobile phones able to capture (and edit) high-quality video material, it is one of the most straightforward and valuable ways to simultaneously build visibility and reputation. This combination of advantages makes vlogging (video blogging) a relatively easy technical task that bundles together many of the building blocks of a successful digital presence.

Building reputation is also a moderating influence on your actions. You cannot build a high-quality reputation and simultaneously deliver content to every social media channel (or even just the most popular ones). A focus on reputation means that some channels need to be ignored. For example, you probably do not need a presence on more than one long-form video hosting platform. Some channels may need to be retired as circumstances change. A new channel with a more focused reach into your persona or a rising-star channel that is a better host for a specific format might justify this change. A decision such as this would be strategic and need to be reflected in your Theory of Change.

Actions related to the building of your reputation necessarily sit on top of actions that raise visibility. These elements themselves require the starting actions of a presence in the right combination of channels (Figure 7.2).

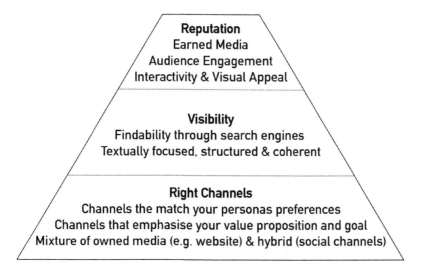

Figure 7.2 Balancing the right channels, visibility and reputation

TL;DR

You need to identify the right combination of channels for your presence. One of these channels will be a website because it is owned media and completely under your control. You need to be visible by using well-written and well-structured text that will be found by search engines. You need to consider visual and interactive content to help retain the people who find your presence through search engines in order to develop your reputation.

Callout 7.1: Your action – your immediate tactics

Identify the channels that you will use in your presence. Identify the actions for creating your presence on these channels within your Theory of Change.

Define the types of content you will develop for these channels that will create visibility. These actions will involve creating text-based content. Add these as actions that link to the outputs of your channel-creation actions.

Identify actions that will then continue on from the creation of text-based content to enhance your reputation. These will be actions that retain people or encourage them to return to your presence. These might involve interactivity, video, audio or static visual content.

Place these actions within your Theory of Change. Consider the causal logic (visibility actions occur before reputation action) and any assumptions that may have been built into your actions. Identify any evidence points that may be needed. For example, you may need a certain number of visitors to your website before you start including video elements.

Callout 7.2: Case Study – Naina Redhu

Diverse channels that reflect personality

Naina is a blogger and podcaster born in India in 1988. Naina has been actively blogging since 2004 and created a website in 2010. Naina's website is now primarily a personal ecommerce portal where personally created original art objects are available to purchase. Reflecting the spirit of the COVID-19 pandemic, Naina's brand was named in *Mans World India* as one of the six face masks to buy (Singh 2020). Reflecting a focus on luxury and a handcrafted approach, the masks are the most expensive choice of the six recommended at ₹2,000 (approx. 27 USD). Naina was also interviewed for the *Times of India* about the benefits of reflecting on past failures and your goal. "A CV of failures would start with deciding on your end goal and then figuring out the success and failure bracket" (Amarnath 2019).

Naina's podcasts are distributed through a range of different platforms and cover a range of topics including blogging itself – this wide range of interests reflects a previous career in management as well as their personal life, art and current issues interests.

The Naina website uses the WordPress content management system, including a WooCommerce plugin.

Channel	Link	Followers	Views	Content
Spotify	https://open.spotify.com/show/5HwVipVYnxARyEjp4onfvp			
Pinterest	www.pinterest.co.uk/nainaco/	10k	426k monthly views	
Instagram	www.instagram.com/naina/	53.1k		3.2k posts
Twitter	https://twitter.com/naina	22.6k		175.4k
LinkedIn	www.linkedin.com/in/naina/			
YouTube	www.youtube.com/channel/UCK5KT0htwvRDIcTft1v03Xg	671 subscribers	80k views	185 videos
Website	www.naina.co/		Ranked 457,500th website globally	

Callout 7.3: "In Debora's Kitchen" – channels, visibility and reputation

Reflecting further on their presence, Debora now adds more details to the Theory of Change to help identify gaps in the logics and assumptions. This involves adding further actions and outputs.

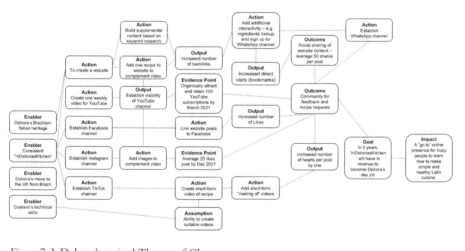

Figure 7.3 Debora's revised Theory of Change

References cited

Amarnath, N. (2019) "Do you need a failure CV?", *Times of India*, 31st Mar., https://timesofindia.indiatimes.com/life-style/relationships/work/do-you-need-a-failure-cv/articleshow/68629228.cms

Armstrong, M. (2019) "How many websites are there?", *Statista*, 28th Oct., www.statista.com/chart/19058/how-many-websites-are-there/

Clement, J. (2020a) "Hours of video uploaded to YouTube every minute as of May 2019", *Statista*, 25th Aug., www.statista.com/statistics/259477/hours-of-video-uploaded-to-youtube-every-minute/

Clement, J. (2020b) "Number of monthly active Instagram users from January 2013 to June 2018", *Statista*, 24th Nov., www.statista.com/statistics/253577/number-of-monthly-active-instagram-users

Ferris, R. and LaVito, A. (2018) "Weight Watchers renames itself to 'WW' as consumers want to be well, not to diet", *CNBC*, www.cnbc.com/2018/09/24/weight-watchers-to-rename-itself-ww-shifts-focus-to-overall-health.html

Lin, Y. (2020) "10 Twitter statistics every marketer should know in 2021", *Oberlo*, 30th May, www.oberlo.co.uk/blog/twitter-statistics

McGillvray, E. (2014) "How to rebrand your social media accounts", *Moz*, 3rd Apr., https://moz.com/blog/how-to-rebrand-your-social-media-accounts

Singh, M. (2020) "Six face mask brands you need to check out", *Mans World India*, www.mansworldindia.com/currentedition/six-face-mask-brands-you-need-to-check-out/

Stark, F. (2019) "Why a fail fast mentality is key to tech innovation in business travel", *Phocus Wire*, 23rd May, www.phocuswire.com/Business-travel-fail-fast-mentality

Winnie, V. (2020) "Why learn fast is better than fail fast", *UX Collective*, 12th Oct., https://uxdesign.cc/why-learn-fast-is-better-than-fail-fast-b7c1fe34c380

Further reading

Holloman, C. (2012) *The Social Media MBA*, Oxford: John Wiley.

8　Content is king

What you will learn

- The importance of content for your digital presence
- Identifying relevant content to build your reputation
- Measuring your content

8.1　Content is king

References to content have already appeared in the discussions across many of the previous chapters. These references have been introduced casually (with the assumption that you already recognise the content that is all around you). In this chapter, content finally gets the attention that it deserves. After all, your visibility and reputation depend on your content. What you "do" with any channel is ultimately about content. This is irrespective of the forms of content that you choose to use or their relative quality.

Depending on your source, there are somewhere between 5 (Guru 2020), 101 (Rattan 2018) and 113 (Ellering n.d.) forms of content. This variability appears to reflect some uncertainty among those claiming to be experts, but the difference can be explained. There are four basic underlying forms that make up any content; text, image, audio and video. For the moment, these are the building blocks for all content, although there is always the potential for a new technology that will unlock a new form that accesses different senses (e.g. through brain implants) (Chapter 18). Each of these forms can also be combined in multiple ways, such as text and image (Figure 7.1); that at least notionally offers 24 potential types of content. These potential combinations can be recognised in content such as a recorded presentation in which the sequence of images from a slide-show (primarily composed of text) are combined with the spoken word of a narrator and offered in a video format. Any one of the content components that are brought together to create the final presentation could be presented in its separate form and still be meaningful to an audience.

A further dimension can then be added to each of the underlying four forms that is defined by length as either short form or long form. This can become the basis for the creation of an entire channel. Twitter's success is based on the value of short-form text. Medium's positioning – and its name – plays with the concept of length in the content that it encourages. TikTok is designed for short-form video, whereas Vimeo and You-Tube are better for handling longer-form material.

The dimension of interactivity defines additional forms of content. Interactive short-form text can be recognised as the basis of messaging services such as Telegram and

DOI: 10.4324/9781003026587-8

WhatsApp. Interactive text-based content is also the basis for the content on channels such as Reddit. Taking this form even further and framing the interactivity around questions and answers provide the basis for channels such as Quora. Interactive image-based content can be seen on sites such as Imgflip, where a visitor can create a meme with the available tools.

The different social media channels mentioned here are only indicative examples – and overly simplify the content. Needless to say, there is a social media channel that specialises in any conceivable combination of these dimensions (Figure 8.1). Most social media channels also bring together combinations of these forms of content to maximise impact. For example, the content focus of YouTube is static long-form video, but the commenting feature incorporates interactive short-form text while Twitter now allows images and video to be embedded with the short-form text.

Your own abilities in relation to the four basic forms of content will guide your decisions about where to focus your initial efforts as well as where to focus your own personal development. There are many online tools – including free options – that can support the development of your content. But for all the high-quality tools, your own comfort with the underlying form is the primary determinant in terms of selecting and prioritising a form of content (or a combination of forms).

Despite the ready availability of quality video recording devices on phones, there are still many people who will become immobilised when they know that a recording is being intended for public sharing. Recording directly facing the camera or speaking into a microphone is a uncommon and intimidating activity for many. In a similar vein, not everyone is a confident artist or a polished wordsmith. Building on your strengths in terms of confidence with a particular basic form of content will necessarily inform your choice of different social media channels. However, the actions in your Theory of Change related to channels will focus on selecting those that are most used by, and suitable for, your personas. This tension reflects the strategic relationship between the venues of your selected channels and the vehicles in the form of the content you produce.

The interplay between vehicles and venues is a balance between what your personas want and where they want it. As with so many aspects of creating a personal digital presence, there is a need for some self-reflection in relation to the content that best suits your skills and your own personality. If the form of your content genuinely reflects you, then you will bring the quality of authenticity to your content. Personal authenticity underpins the development of your reputation. The role of authenticity can work even when you are basing your reputation around making people laugh (Case Study 9.1). The need for authenticity also highlights that high-quality content is not just a synonym for professional production. If your content is capturing "real life" as it happens, then the desire for

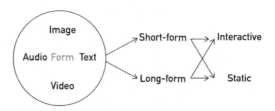

Figure 8.1 Types of content

authenticity will override the need for highly polished and edited content. Being "too perfect" may even detract from the sense of authenticity that is seen by your personas.

Tied to the importance of authenticity, originality is a further consideration for any personal presence and should be a priority. A key premise of social media is the ability to share. The "ShareThis" icon is a familiar symbol across the internet (Figure 8.2) and is a key mechanism for creating earned media and the reputation that you want to build. From this point of view, you want to be creating original content that is shared, rather than sharing content that you find. You want to be at the beginning of the chain of sharing, not somewhere in the middle. Sharing content becomes an action only when it supports your own content and contributes to your Theory of Change. Shared media should not become the dominant vehicles that are being delivered through your venues. Taking this situation to a logical extreme, if your presence is populated with content that is not regarded as your own (or your own opinion), you may face accusations of being a "sock puppet". This is internet parlance for an inauthentic account that is seen as a mule that brings content or even disinformation that promotes other accounts. Becoming a sock puppet is not the outcome that you are seeking.

Following on from the need for authenticity, you should resist becoming involved in the creation of disinformation or "fake news". The late 2010s and early 2020s will be remembered as a low point in the mass propagation of "fake news", disinformation and conspiracy theories through social media channels. The largest of these are now taking action to combat this class of content. The severity of the actions range from labelling questionable content and removal of the content through to blocking an account or completely banning an individual (Slawson and Waterman 2020). Recognising fake news and disinformation can sometimes be challenging because the stories are often engaging and will partially resonate with your own thinking. Social media channels want to retain you and will promote content that you will be most likely to read next – if you read content that is fake news, the effect will be to then amplify even more fake news. The problem of fake news emphasises the importance of content and its importance in the economies of digital channels to retain visitors by offering similar content.

In creating your own content, irrespective of its form, length or interactivity, you need to be cautious that you do not repeat the disinformation and further contribute to its legitimacy. The best approach is to be critical, double check the claimed sources and ensure that the news is being reported independently by multiple outlets. Do not take video or images as evidence without applying the same critical scrutiny. Photo and video editing tools are sophisticated enough to create convincing visual fakes. The same

Figure 8.2 Share this icon

technology that enables any imaginable fantasy film to be created is not just in the hands of Hollywood and Bollywood production companies. The final checkpoint mirrors the final check for considering if something is ethical (Chapter 5). If your "gut feeling" is that the content could not be correct, then deeper scrutiny is required (Mindtools n.d.; Ireton and Posetti 2018).

A potential personal goal that has not been considered in any depth is the case of finding a life partner. The many channels that directly focus on supporting this goal reinforce the need for authenticity and originality in all forms of presence. The way that content is created on sites such as PlentyofFish and Badoo is generally very constrained − filling in answers to a series of fixed questions − and uses a mixture of forms − text and images at least (Light et al. 2008). The expectations on these channels distill down many of the key considerations for creating any digital presence. The result is that advice such as "Do not say general things that mean nothing"; "Don't tell us your sob story", instead present a positive perspective; "Don't be a douche" or, in other words, do not tell your audience what they should be or be doing; and "Don't ignore spelling and grammar" work as rules for all forms of digital presence and possibly life more generally (MenAskEm n.d.).

Content is king. From a strategic point of view, the content you create is the vehicle for achieving your goal. The actions that create content are the bridge from actions related to choosing your channel to outcomes that relate directly to your visibility and reputation. The final compelling evidence that content is king can be found by searching for "worst websites ever" (Kenwright 2014); "worst social media posts" (Calus 2017), which includes the unexpected creation of the word "covfefe"; "worst dating profiles" (Femail 2017); or visiting theworldsworstwebsiteever(.com). For video content on YouTube with very low visibility, use astronaut.io. After experiencing these low points in digital content, the key advice for developing relevant content is "do not do this; do the opposite".

8.2 Developing relevant content

With a focus on yourself (or your organisation), creating the content for your digital presence is, on one level, straightforward. Developing your content is a case of "saying what you see". Your subject is immediately available, and the tools for creating any of the four basic forms of content can be found on a mobile phone − through the built-in camera and microphone coupled with apps. Text editor apps such as EverNote and Jotterpad let you create text on your mobile. Image editors such as Snapseed, Prisma and Adobe's offerings all give you relatively powerful tools to edit photographs while PaperDraw, Adobe Illustrator and other tools enable those who are more creative to create drawings entirely from scratch. More specialised web-based apps such as infogr.am also enable you to create information graphics on your mobile. In all these cases, the advantage of using a mobile device is that sharing with social media channels (and other digital channels) is directly built into the app and accessible with a tap of the ShareThis icon (Figure 8.2) or similar. There is a still wider set of content-editing applications available as web-based tools for free or nearly free. Beyond this attractive price point, there is a further advantage. The design of apps and web-based applications make them intuitively easy to use. This is in contrast to more traditional applications that require downloading onto a laptop or desktop computer. In combination, easy access to the right editing tools that are easy to use makes the ability and capacity to create relevant content for your digital presence an assumption within your Theory of Change.

But with so many tools available, the choices appear daunting. Using a systematic approach to selecting your tools is how to tackle this challenge in a way that avoids repeating mistakes and gets you the best suite of software that suits your own needs.

1   *Identify and list your own needs.* This could include what form of content you are creating, consideration of price, ease of use, the ability to easily share with a particular social media channel, the stability of the app and any special features that you might require. A special feature list may limit your options dramatically but nonetheless is necessary if you can see the need. For example, you may need an image editor that can turn your photos into cartoons or a sound editor that is in a specific format suitable for a particular podcast system.
2   *Rank each criteria* from most to least important.
3   *Weight these criteria* with the most important being 1 and the least important being 0.1.
4   *Identify and research* potential apps that appear to suit your needs.
5   Create a grid with each of your criteria in a column and the potential apps on the rows.
6   Based on available information, *score each app* for each criteria from worst (1) to best (10). For the stability of the app, you should assess this criteria on how long the software has been available, how many times it has been downloaded or how many positive reviews it has received. The higher score for each of these indicate the better (or best) option.
7   *Total the scores* for each app. Multiply the score (from 6) with the weighting (from 3).
8   *Test* the highest scoring app.

This approach to software selection is systematic but not entirely objective as it considers your subjective needs and purpose in preference to the description offered by the developer. This approach is also iterative. As you evolve and develop your needs, you will consider new software with evolving criteria. Identifying software in this way also helps you discover new candidate software. If one app scores high on your criteria, then other tools by the same developer may be attractive to other needs you may have.

With the tools in place and your overall purpose defined – your goal – you already have what you need to start creating relevant and quality content. Using some social media channels is even easier as the tools to create content are embedded in the channel itself. Twitter, Facebook, TikTok and Instagram are all popular because the barrier to entry as a content creator is incredibly low. In fact, you were probably already using these channels before you read the previous seven chapters. However, without developing a Theory of Change, using a strategic mindset and undertaking some self-reflection, the presence you are creating will lack focus, direction and purpose. In combination, all these negatives reduce the likelihood of achieving your goal.

A further opportunity for content creation activities is through collaborations with others. This can take a range of approaches. Having a question and answer (Q&A) session with an expert or someone relevant to you and your personas with a higher reputation is one way of building your own reputation through original content. A Q&A can be in text, audio or video form and is a useful marker for your longer-term outcomes. Deeper collaborations are also possible, including joint authorship of a longer piece of content, an information graphic or a more creative piece of work. Creative collaborations that take longer to complete also lend themselves to another type of content in the form of a time lapse, or the "making of" narrative, the behind-the-scenes viewpoint on the final content. If your development methods are particularly interesting in their own right – for example, a LEGO session, a trip to the seaside or group sketching – this may lead to further content in a "how to" format that explains what you did in the "making of" content. Other forms of collaboration can also be mutually beneficial. If your own skills are best concentrated around text-based activities, then a collaboration with an illustrator can build related content in other forms that make more compelling content in combination. Comic-style content is a good example of the coming together of different collaborators with different complementary skills. Collaborations should always be treated as a reciprocated relationship where mutual value is being realised. There are a number of examples in which self-styled influencers have asked for free services where there is little or no clear reciprocal benefit for the other party. If the basis of the collaboration does not have a clear balance, it is not reciprocal.

A commercial relationship in content development is a further example of collaboration that may offer some benefit to you and avoids imbalance. Freelance sites such as Fiverr(.com) offer a marketplace for services from specialists in different forms of content. The original concept that services would be offered for a "fiver" has long since evolved into a full-fledged business services provider. As you build an ethical presence, do not base your selection of commercial services solely on price. Freelance services give access to an international directory of providers, but you should ensure that you are paying what is considered a fair price for the specified service in your own location.

If "saying what you see" is not sufficient inspiration to craft your own content-making actions, there are some further influences that may help to shape what you "say". Content is primarily found through search. Search engines provide answers to questions as well as matching the implied user intent with the results that it shows. Understanding the search intention of your personas and developing content to match their intent can deliver a "free" audience. Understanding what your personas' search intention will be can take trial and error. Examples drawn from politics can show how this matching might work in practice (Burcher 2012).

> In the midst of the health care debate, the Obama White House started monitoring what questions people were asking online about the health care bill. And they determined that the #1 most searched question was simply, 'What's in the health care bill?' So they actually drafted a blog post for the White house website and titled it, exactly, 'What's in the health care bill?' It worked! During the heat of the debate, if you searched for that phrase, the #1 link that came up was to that blog post on WhiteHouse.gov, which specifically laid out the President's plans around health care. What I love about that story is that you have a team who understood how the web works, how people use the web to seek information, and they used their website to their own advantage. And the best part is that it cost nothing. It cost nothing other than the time it took to actually have that person type up that blog post.
>
> (Lecinski 2011)

In the UK a similar example of matching content with search intent was arguably employed by Prime Minister Boris Johnson in 2019 (Stokel-Walker 2019). Before and after becoming prime minister, Johnson faced significant public criticism about his claims that after the UK left the European Union (so-called "Brexit"), the National Health Service (NHS) could benefit from an additional weekly £350 million windfall. Although subsequently proven to be an inflated claim, the statement had been painted on a bright red bus that travelled around the UK. The claim continued to be damaging for Johnson as a prime minister fresh from a contentious general election. In June 2019 the prime minister did an interview in which he "admitted" that his hobbies included painting model buses made out of old wine boxes. The unusual nature of the hobby raised eyebrows, but the impact on search results suggested an entirely different purpose for his specificity. Content about the unusual hobby came to replace the reference to the big red bus and the claims about funding the NHS (Melia 2019). However, a search for "Boris Johnson Bus" on Google indicates that the claimed strategy has only been partially successful over time. The video and text result show political statements from Johnson and references to his hobby. In contrast, the image results solely show different angles of the big red bus and its claim.

Both of these current affairs examples offer insight for your own content development. Content should offer answers (or at least a response) to the questions that your personas ask. Questions and the intent of the person behind them are an indication of a need or a point of pain for them. There are even tools, such as the Chrome extension "TextOptimiser", that make suggestions for your text-based content based on search internet research. Responding with content that supports this need and reduces pain is successfully delivering your value proposition to your personas in a vehicle they can use and through venues that they choose to use. Content development is not about selling yourself or your services and products. Rather than selling, you are giving your personas the opportunity to find and choose you because of the value that you clearly offer them.

Sometimes current affairs and trends can be an opportunity to develop your digital presence and ride on a crest of interest. This can be done by targeting topics of conversations rather than search intent.

In 2010, a 22-year-old American, Ashley Kerekes, was receiving high levels of attention on Twitter. Ashley's Twitter handle was based on a lifelong nickname, @theashes. The rising interest in Ashley coincided with the England cricket team starting their 2010–2011 Ashes series against Australia. Cricket lovers began following @theashes on Twitter, posting messages and asking Ashley questions. Ashley made it clear that neither they nor their Twitter account had anything to do with cricket – "I am not a freaking cricket match". The confusion and the mystery only amplified the attention that Ashley was receiving (McGuiness 2013).

Brands soon took notice of the combination of events that was happening around Ashley's Twitter account. Vodafone event set up a #teachtheashestheashes campaign so that people with knowledge of cricket could explain the rules of the game to Ashley through Twitter. This rising stardom sparked another Twitter hashtag movement – #gettheashestotheashes.

The Australian airline carrier Qantas picked up on this conversation and tweeted out that they would be providing Ashley and Ashley's boyfriend an all-expenses-paid trip from the USA to Sydney for the final Ashes test match. Vodafone offered to sponsor the couple's tickets as well as a phone to let them tweet about the experience. The couple were given a tour of the cricket stadium with Australian cricket legend Steve Waugh. They were even interviewed by the Australian prime minister and appeared on a BBC interview. Qantas gained immense publicity after the news broke out on leading media outlets across the country, leading to an increase in followers on Qantas's newly launched Twitter account. Ashley also found a way to capitalise on the moment by selling t-shirts that read I AM NOT A FREAKING CRICKET MATCH!!! (Jones 2010; Crane 2010).

Ashley Kerekes's Twitter account is still @theashes. After some gaps in activity that can be measured in years, they have recently started tweeting again, making references to the events of 2010 and the connection with Australia. In 2015 a similar error provoked @ theashes to send the message "Not a wedding venue either . . ." Kerekes's choice of online identity has continued to be a defining moment in their life.

When someone else starts a conversation, if you understand the trend, you can capitalise on it and extend the narrative. It is a case of maintaining relevance with the original message and building on it in different ways, with new information or a fresh perspective. The @theashes experience was undertaken in good spirit and with humour. In other cases your offering may be to offer content that helps explain the conversation to the uninitiated, critically unpicks the debate or offers an alternative perspective. There are always trends of this sort happening within your areas of interest that will relate to your own goal. The challenge is to be able to identify the trend when it is on the rise. Joining the conversation supports an increase in your visibility, and if your content resonates well with the trend itself, it will also contribute to your reputation.

8.3 Measuring content

For your short-term outcomes, you will want to focus on actions that create content. However, over time, you need to measure and understand how your content is being received. The metrics that are available for different channels will vary slightly, but your long-term outcomes around visibility and reputation will guide what you choose to measure. Consider your Theory of Change as a filtering process. While progressing towards your goal, the situation around you will change. The closer to your goal that you measure, the smaller the quantities that you will identify. Actions that establish your presence will tend to have outputs measured in the thousands; the outcomes from these outputs might be measured in tens or hundreds. Longer-term outcomes may only have (or need) a single digit. If your goal is, for example, to find a life partner or secure a professional role, the final quantitative measure will be one. If your goal is to become an influencer, your optimal number will be larger (the case studies throughout the book provide some indicative comparative measures) but will still filter down to deeper, longer-term outcomes. In a similar vein, measures related to reputation will be smaller than any metrics relating to your visibility.

As you start to build the content for your digital presence, it will be measures of visibility that will initially interest you the most. The most straightforward measurement of visibility is the number of visitors. This data can be accessed for a website. Some channels do not make this available, but in most cases, it is just difficult to find. Twitter offers a separate page (analytics.twitter.com/) for your key measurements, including profile visits and tweet impressions (the number of times your tweet has been seen). TikTok lets you access views through the "Overview" and Facebook has an "Insights" link. Because Google is such a dominant force in search, its analytics system can provide wide-ranging insight for a website (analytics.google.com/analytics/web/). This is a sophisticated system, and it can distinguish between the coarser count of total visits to a web page and the more useful count of total users (§14.2). There is a quantifiable difference in your visibility between one visit from 500 users and 500 visits from one user.

Before you begin the development of your content and start measuring its visibility, it is worth doing some comparative research on the presence of others. This will help you get a sense of the scale of activity relevant to your own focus and goal. For websites there are many tools (e.g. moz.com/domain-analysis, majestic.com, suite.searchmetrics.com/en/research/domains/organic) that offer limited free services and will reveal some indication of the popularity of a website as well as popular terms used to find the site through search engines. There are also a number of extensions (chrome.google.com/webstore/category/extensions) that will assist your research if you make use of the Chrome browser. Tools and the latest information relating to measuring content will generally be found with search terms that include the acronym SEO (search engine optimisation). Terms such as "SEO metrics" and "SEO research tools" provide a rich and deep seam of materials to explore.

The depth of website metrics that can be obtained is another reason to consider the benefits of using this specific channel within your own presence. Even if you restrict your measurement activity to Google Analytics, there is still significant insight to be found. Google offers a demonstration account that you explore even before you have created a website (tinyurl.com/google-demo-account). This account will help you familiarise yourself with the terminology and form of reporting used by the system.

Outside directly owned media, there are also options for measuring and comparing your performance against that of others. For social media channels, there are other similar tools available for undertaking comparative research, but their value is determined by the openness of the channel itself. A tool such as Popsters(.com) can analyse multiple channels at the same time and provide comparative insight. For specific channels such as Twitter, there are third-party tools such as twitonomy(.com) that can analyse all your content (or that of another user) on a single platform.

These many tools take the measurement of channels beyond a simple quantification of visibility and push your attention towards the question of reputation. Many of the metrics reported by these tools provide proxy evidence for reputation. For example, website analysis will tell you about the average time on site, the number of sessions, the number of pages visited and the bounce rate.

The bounce rate is a percentage. It is the proportion of visitors to your site who immediately returned to where they came from – usually a search engine result page. The bounce rate tells you if your content is matching search intent. The fact that you are receiving visits is a positive signal, but a bounce means that the full content did not satisfy the searcher's intent. This is a reputation issue as much as it is a visibility issue because some users who have this experience repeatedly will consciously avoid your website when it appears in future results. New actions will be required to better match content with search intent.

A more positive set of measurements for the reputation being built by your website is to have users spending an increasing amount of time on your site, more session per users and more pages per session. All these measures are signals that your intended persona aligns with the actual people visiting your sites and that you are engaging them with a growing volume of content. More time spent on your website will increase the likelihood that a visitor will share your content across their own network, give you earned media on social media channels and, more fundamentally, remember you (or at least bookmark you).

Over time, reputation-building activities will introduce the value of a further metric. If your visitors are all being acquired through the results of search engines, it suggests that your reputation is low. Visits solely from search results means that there are no bookmarks of your website, no links for your website on other websites or in social media channels (a referral) and no one sharing your website through word of mouth.

Tools such as the Ahref website authority check (ahrefs.com/website-authority-checker) provide another way to measure an indicator of reputation. The principle is that when people link to one of your website's pages from their own website (a backlink), it is a confirmation of the authority of your content. It is a type of popularity voting mechanism for websites.

Reputation is expressed in more varied ways across social media channels, although the underlying principles are very similar to those used for websites. Many social media channels provide a way of "liking", "upvoting" or starring content as a first level of affirming reputation. Sharing, favoriting and similar actions are an even stronger confirmation of your persona alignment and reputation.

The different metrics for content highlight what might be seen as a key distinction between visibility and reputation. Visibility is about convincing a machine that your content is good. A search engine robot finds something you have created and will offer users a link to it when their intention appears to match. Reputation is about a person confirming that your content is good. People want to share, recognise and talk about your content when it matches their intent and provides them with value. In this way, a high number of backlinks to your content, as one example, is an indicator of the quality of your reputation.

The many ways of measuring content could appear intimidating. Measuring content, search engine optimisation (SEO) and encouraging reputation growth is a specialist profession in its own right. However, you do not need to become immersed in the full scope of SEO activities. Your goal is specific, and your purpose for creating content for your digital presence is shaped by that goal. Your goal and your Theory of Change will determine what evidence points you may need to confirm progress towards your goal.

TL;DR

You need to create content that your personas will be able to find. You need to create content that your personas will like. Measure your channels to ensure that you are making progress towards your planned outcomes and goal.

Callout 8.1: Case Study – Melyssa Griffin

Turning a hobby into a multimillion-dollar blog

Born in the United Stated in 1989, Melyssa is a former Japanese high school English teacher turned entrepreneur. Melyssa began blogging in 2013 as a hobby with the goal of building an online community. However, this hobby rapidly evolved. Within a few months after starting the blog, Melyssa was offering web design services primarily through a new website. Three months later, Melyssa quit the teaching job, returned to California and pursued creating a design business full time.

In 2015, after building a successful design business (with a six-figure turnover), Melyssa was starting to feel burnt out. Melyssa was done with clients forever at this point and needed to shift focus. The desire was to create something that was sustainable over a long period of time and that delivered value to many people. This is when Melyssa noticed that a lot of website traffic was coming from Pinterest. It was also the time when the availability of online courses and e-learning was starting to gain momentum.

Recognising that these two factors represented a market shift towards online learning, Melyssa decided to leverage this knowledge and created a new online course on Pinterest marketing called "Pinfinite Growth". The course has now produced over $USD 3 million in sales. Since then Melyssa has created multiple courses to help aspiring entrepreneurs grow profitable business.

Melyssa uses high-quality content to build up a loyal group of subscribers who receive regular email newsletters. Melyssa frequently sends out powerful emails that directly speak to these subscribers' interests.

In 2018, Melyssa pivoted again by moving from coaching entrepreneurs about business strategy to coaching people on mindset and personality development. More recently a new podcast called "Limitless Life" encourages people to stop procrastinating.

Melyssa Griffin's success is based around delivering content of high value to subscribers with a focus on supporting and helping subscribers rather than selling products. Melyssa's content is fun, witty and relatable while remaining constantly educational. Combining entertainment and education has been an important cornerstone to creating valuable content.

The Melyssa Griffin website uses WordPress as the content management system and uses a range of plugins including Yoast and ShowIt.

Channel	Link	Followers	Views	Content
YouTube	www.youtube.com/c/ Thenectarcollective	7.6k	217k views	28 videos
Pinterest	https://in.pinterest.com/ melyssa_griffin	88k	392.9k monthly views	
Instagram	www.instagram.com/ melyssa_griffin/	64.7k		1468 posts
Twitter:	https://twitter.com/ melyssa_griffin	17.1k		6.5k tweets
Website	melyssagriffin.com		Ranked 67,150th website globally	

Callout 8.2: Your action – planning your initial content

At this stage you need to bring together what you believe your personas need with what you can provide. This is the continuous fine line that you need to navigate. You need to build on the strength of your current skills while also recognising the channels and content that your personas want.

Create a list of ten topics that will be interesting for your personas. These will be specific to your interests and relevant to your personas. If you are fitness orientated, this might include nutritional supplements or new exercise routines. If you are focused on travel, you might review a new website for booking travel or a location you want to visit. Effectively your ten topics are ten relevant "things" to talk about. Each of these could be at least one piece of content in its own right.

Consider your ten topics. Are there any current affairs that will affect your topic in the near future? Is the situation different in different countries? Every difference, each nuance is a potential new piece of content.

With each of these ten topics, what are the specific questions that people might be asking about them? You might need to talk to people and listen to the discussions online. Each of these questions is a new piece of content. Each question also potentially reflects the search intent of your personas (so title your content with the question).

Now consider the topics more widely. Will any pre-explanations be required for a less-knowledgeable visitor? Are there any pre-existing skills that are required around these topics? Any explanation or contextualising of your original topic, including "how to" and "advanced" discussions, are potential additional pieces of content.

Browse some of the suggested blog ideas (Omnikick n.d.; Engel 2020; Start Blogging Online 2020) for how you might present your topics and the additional content that this prompts. Even if you plan to use images, video or audio, consider how these ideas will translate into your preferred form of content. At this point the ideas for items of content should have expanded exponentially.

Prioritise your long list of content ideas. Calculate (guesstimate) how long each piece of content will take to create and plan a timeline for developing your content. Realistically acknowledge your other life commitments and the time frame for your Theory of Change in this plan. For example, you may plan a total of one piece of content per day. You need to be able to fully produce your content within the space of a day. This is plausible for text but is unlikely for quality video content.

At this point, do a sense check. If this material can already be found online through search, consider what distinctive personal angle you can put to the content. Also consider how the content you are proposing relates to the outcomes in your Theory of Change. If the contribution is not clear, then de-prioritise the content idea or remove it completely.

With a planned schedule for your defined content, we can now move on to delivering your digital presence.

Callout 8.3: "In Debora's Kitchen" – content plan

Topics that will be interesting for Debora's personas

- Easy recipes
- Quick recipes
- Extending the recipes (longer weekend options)
- Sourcing ingredients outside Brazil (South America)
- Substitutes for hard-to-find ingredients
- Other accompaniments for recipes to create meals
- Origins of the recipes (regions/celebrations/influences)
- Recommendation for the best utensils to use
- Pronunciation guide for recipes and ingredients

Ways of presenting these topics

- "How to" video and descriptions
- "Making of" images and video

- Long-form text content
- Searchable function – recipe lookup, ingredient finder
- Lists of suppliers
- Audio descriptions (for commuters; for origins stories)

Content Type: Video, short and long text content, images
Content Frequency: Start out with once a week and then increase the frequency
Timeline to create and publish new content: up to four days

References cited

Burcher, N. (2012) *Paid Owned Earned: Maximizing Marketing Returns in a Socially Connected World*, London: Kogan Page.

Calus, V. (2017) "Social media year in review 2017 – Part II: Worst social media posts", *Planable*, 21st Dec., https://planable.io/blog/worst-social-media-posts-2017/

Crane, E. (2010) "They call me @theashes, so take me out to the ball game", *The Sydney Morning Herald*, 31st Dec., www.smh.com.au/technology/they-call-me-theashes-so-take-me-out-to-the-ball-game-20101230-19b7k.html

Ellering, N. (n.d.) "113 content types to organize with your marketing calendar", *CoSchedule*, https://coschedule.com/blog/types-of-content/

Engel, K. (2020) "103 blog post ideas that your readers will love", *Optin Monster*, 3rd Jan., https://optinmonster.com/50-blog-post-ideas-that-you-can-write-about-today/

Femail (2017) "Are these the WORST dating profiles ever? From fancy dress to thinly-veiled innuendos, it's no wonder these singletons are still looking for love", *The Daily Mail*, 29th June, www.dailymail.co.uk/femail/article-4650878/Are-WORST-online-dating-profiles-ever.html

Guru, D. (2020) "5 different types of digital content proven to boost your revenue [2020]", *UpGrad*, 15th May, www.upgrad.com/blog/types-of-digital-content-to-boost-your-revenue/

Ireton, C. and Posetti, J. (2018) *Journalism, Fake News & Disinformation: Handbook for Journalism Education and Training*, Paris: UNESCO, https://unesdoc.unesco.org/ark:/48223/pf0000265552

Jones, S. (2010) "American babysitter hit for six by Ashes mania on Twitter", *The Guardian*, 29th Nov., www.theguardian.com/technology/2010/nov/29/babysitter-twitter-freak-ashes

Kenwright, S. (2014) "Top 10 worst websites you'll wish you hadn't seen", *Edit*, 30th July, https://edit.co.uk/blog/top-10-worst-websites/

Lecinski, J. (2011) "Winning the zero moment of truth", June, www.thinkwithgoogle.com/future-of-marketing/emerging-technology/2011-winning-zmot-ebook/

Light, B., Fletcher, G. and Adam, A. (2008) "Gay men, Gaydar and the commodification of difference", *Information Technology and People*, 21(3), pp. 300–314, https://dblp.org/rec/journals/itp/LightFA08

McGuiness, R. (2013) "Ashley Kerekes aka @TheAshes: The Twitter user who isn't a cricket match talks to Metro", *Metro*, 12th July, https://metro.co.uk/2013/07/12/mistaken-identity-on-twitter-ashley-kerekes-theashes-the-ashes-3878435/

Melia, J. (2019) "Boris Johnson: The unlikely SEO strategist", *Parallax*, 26th June, https://parall.ax/blog/view/3301/boris-johnson-the-unlikely-seo-strategist

MenAskEm (n.d.) "Are you making these 4 huge mistakes in your online dating profile?", www.menaskem.com/four-online-dating-profile-mistakes

Mindtools (n.d.) "How to spot real and fake news", www.mindtools.com/pages/article/fake-news.htm

Omnikick (n.d.) "Blog topic ideas: 75 Types of blog posts that get traffic", www.omnikick.com/blog-topics/

Rattan, J. (2018) "101 different types of digital content", *Zazzle Media*, www.zazzlemedia.co.uk/blog/digital-content-types/

Slawson, N. and Waterman, J. (2020) "Katie Hopkins permanently removed from Twitter", *The Guardian*, 19th June, www.theguardian.com/media/2020/jun/19/katie-hopkins-permanently-removed-from-twitter

Start Blogging Online (2020) "134 blog ideas: Post topics & unique things to write about", 1st Nov., https://startbloggingonline.com/blog-post-ideas/

Stokel-Walker, C. (2019) "Is Boris Johnson really trying to game Google search results?", *Wired*, 1st Oct., www.wired.co.uk/article/boris-johnson-model-google-news

Further reading

Pulizzi, J. and Barrett, N. (2012) *Get Content: Get Customers*, London: Kogan Page.

Part III
Delivery

9 Build the parts – the components of your digital presence

What you will learn

- Choosing a domain name
- Securing a web-hosting service
- Using a content management system (CMS)
- Setting up your social media channels

9.1 Making choices

With a Theory of Change in place, the relationship between your goal, your content and the different channels that make up the digital presence become clearer. Although some of these choices are technical, this chapter highlights how to make decisions in the same way as for any consumer purchase. In other words, we present the creation of a digital presence as primarily about making decisions rather than being a technical project.

There are four choices that now need to be made in terms of your digital presence. You already started this process of decision-making (Callout 3.1) when you selected a consistent username for social media channels. To develop your website presence, you must now choose a domain name, select a content management system (CMS) and find a web-hosting service. This will be similar to the approach you used to select content authoring and editing software (§8.2). These choices will include some technical criteria, but the priority will remain fixed on building your visibility and reputation. The final key decision will be to identify the mix of social media channels that will best connect you with your personas. This mix of decisions needs to be of a manageable scale that is based on the content plan you have already shaped (Callout 8.2).

A website is the central owned asset in your digital presence. It is created on top of a web-hosting account and is found and identified by a domain name (e.g. yahoo.com, google.com.au or astronaut.io). A content management system makes developing a website increasingly simple and, more or less, automatically incorporates capabilities such as letting users share your content and adding interactive features. There are at least 200 separate content management systems available, but our focus will be on one of the most popular, stable and secure – WordPress.

A domain name is the unique name your audience types into their browser to view your website, which is the hub of your digital presence. Your domain name is one of the largest signposts to your digital presence. The domain name is the part of a website address that often comes after the "www." part but includes the final (suffix) part of the address after the dot (e.g. ".com", ".in" or "co.nz"). You can only use words, numbers

DOI: 10.4324/9781003026587-9

and hyphens in your domain name (and the hyphen cannot be at the beginning or end of the name. If your chosen username is also available as a domain name with one of the original recognised top-levels domains' (TLDs) suffixes, particularly .com or .net, then your decision has already been made (Figure 9.1). If this is not available, then your username followed by the two-letter country code top-level domain (CCTLD) suffix for your own country, such as .ph for the Philippines or .mx for Mexico, is a close second choice. Some CCTLD suffixes are promoted as being category domains. The domain suffix for the Federated States of Micronesia (.fm) is used to promote radio stations, Columbia's domain suffix (.co) is used as an alternative commercial domain and the domain suffix for Tuvalu (.tv) is used in a similar way. The fee that Tuvalu receives for this usage represents about 8% of the country's gross national product and helps to support the tiny Pacific nation of about 11,000 citizens. There are also CCTLD suffixes that relate to territories of countries where there is little or no population – South Georgia (.gs), Cococ (Keeling) Islands (.cc) and CCTLDs for countries that no longer exist, such as the Soviet Union (.su), as well as codes that were abandoned many years ago for alternative CCTLD suffixes, including .oz for Australia and .gb for the UK. Just to make domain naming even more complex (and interesting), it is also possible to get domain names that are not based on the English alphabet or script but instead use Arabic, Chinese or Hindi characters.

There is a further range of newer global top-level domain (GTLD) suffixes that provide a descriptive ending to your domain name. These include ".online", ".website" and ".expert". The list of options is extensive (wikipedia.org/wiki/List_of_Internet_top-level_domains). The domain names of the biggest brands are synonymous with the brands themselves, such as apple.com and Apple Computer (and Apple now also owns the GTLD ".apple" suffix). Your domain name is the biggest gateway into your digital presence (Coyle and Gould 2002) and helps build trust with your personas (Ha 2002) that consequently assists in developing your reputation. One indicator of a successful digital presence is when your audience can type the name of your presence followed by a global top-level domain or country code suffix and discover you (Chen 2001).

Global businesses and brands register their names with multiple global and country domains. But the focus of their visibility and reputation activities is generally coordinated around just one of these domains, with the other domains also pointing to this same content. The organisational preference tends to be to use the ".com" TLD as a result of its being seen as a global domain. Search engines including Google also tend to give higher preference in their results to content located on ".com" domains. The key takeaway from this organisational learning for your own personal presence is that the first domain name you buy will probably not be the last.

The best starting point to buying your first domain name is to use a domain search tool (such as those at name.com, godaddy.com or namecheap.com) where you can identify the availability of different domains and their annual fees. Different top-level domains will have different costs. Avoid free offers or suspiciously low fees for domain names. These types of offers may initially appear attractive but in the long run may become problematic because you do not have clear ownership of the domain name or are technically blocked from transferring the name. For these reasons, it is also valuable to treat the purchase of your domain name as a separate action from the purchase of website hosting. Bundled packages may present a financially better offer, but you should ensure that you have ownership of the domain name and the ability to transfer it away from the web-hosting company in the future.

Figure 9.1 Checking a domain name as well as suggested alternatives and the option to purchase

If you are struggling to think of a name and check its availability, then a service like domainsBot.com will help. You can go to the site and search for your preferred name. The results will show you what is available and will make further suggestions (Figure 9.1). You can click on the link to buy the name, and the website gets a commission from the sale.

You can also add keywords or a location to your name to help you get closer to a suitable domain name.

9.2 Web hosting

Unlike the choice of domain name where your viewpoint is global, your web-hosting choices are better considered at the local level. Buying a web-hosting service is effectively about purchasing some storage space for files that is permanently turned on and connected to the web. If you are consciously considering your budget, you might consider that you could use your own computer and internet connection. However, while self-hosting is entirely possible, you would be taking on a range of technical responsibilities that are more simply covered by a single, generally low monthly or annual fee. Many service providers who provide home internet access also explicitly ban web hosting in their terms of service. Self-hosting not only can bring technical headaches but could also get your access cut off entirely. If you regard web hosting as a service that you buy in the same way as electricity, you are in control as an informed consumer.

Because the intention is to use a content management system on top of your web-hosting service, you should prioritise your search for a service around this combination of needs. A preliminary search for "web hosting" + your location + your preferred CMS will show you the local options you have for your preferred system. For example, a search for "'web hosting' manchester wordpress" produces a number of possible options in the organic results.

Other technical considerations will help shape your decision beyond just the monthly or annual fee. The advantage of a local company is that the technical support team will be available when you are most likely to need them. Sometimes the web-hosting offer includes a 24/7 help desk – although this type of service can come at more of a premium.

Look for the technical specifications (or "tech spec") of the hosting package. The storage and memory offered in most packages is generally sufficient for your needs. If the values are measured in gigabytes, it will be more than enough for your needs. (You host the files with the largest size – videos – on a service such as YouTube and then embed the content in your own webpages.)

Most hosting companies will state that they have an uptime greater than 99%. This is standard and is the key aspect of web hosting that you would most struggle to achieve if you tried to do this at home. Many hosts also refer to unlimited bandwidth or a high number of gigabytes. Bandwidth will not be an issue for your digital presence initially. However, every time a visitor accesses your website, this counts against your bandwidth limit. If you have two 1Mb images on a web page that is visited 1,000 times in a month, that would use 2Gb of your bandwidth allocation. If your presence becomes highly visible and is visually rich, anything other than an unlimited account may bring unexpected costs – or your website may become inaccessible for a period of time – if you exceed the bandwidth limit.

There will also be a statement about a backup routine – usually daily, preinstalled software (including the CMS of your preference) and a visual control panel. Most hosts provide you with a control panel (Figure 9.2). In a manner similar to social media channels, you can log in, and there is a visual and user-friendly set of tools that lets you control all aspects of your web-hosting package.

You should also look for web hosting that offers a free domain transfer. Having bought the right domain name, you need to connect it with your web hosting. Many web-hosting services will do this transfer as an integral part of setting up your account. The offer of integrated email services is also important (Figure 9.3). This means that your email will also contain your domain name (e.g. you@domainname.com) instead of a generic gmail.com or yahoo.com address. Using your own domain for email will also provide a wider range of opportunities to expand your visibility and reputation. At the very least, using your domain name in your email address shows that you are bothered enough about your digital presence to pay for the service (even if this is only a small amount and is included as part of your web-hosting fee).

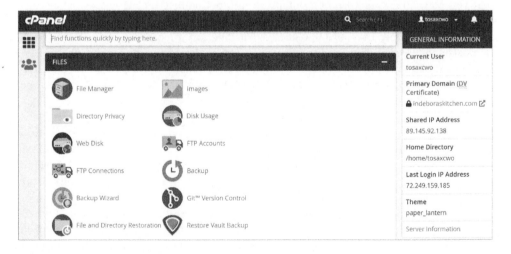

Figure 9.2 Example of a web-hosting control panel

Figure 9.3 Email services within a web-hosting setup

The majority of web-hosting packages now include "free SSL". This means that when you access your website, you can use an address that starts with https:// rather than "http://". This indicates that the connection between your website and the users who visit your site is secured (§16.1). The information that flows between your website and a user's browser is encrypted and cannot be easily intercepted by a third party. Even if your website is not an ecommerce site, this security reassures users, encourages trust and is preferred and encouraged by search engines. The offer of "free SSL" is not a sales gimmick and should be taken as a good indication that the web-hosting company understands the business environment that they are working within.

Fortunately, comparisons of web hosting are regularly produced for individual countries. A search for "web hosting comparison" + your country will offer up-to-date comparisons and recommendations from technical magazines. In many countries, there are also dedicated comparison sites for web hosting, such as hostreviews.co.uk for the UK, hostingcharges.in in India and webhostingweb.co.za in South Africa.

9.3 Choosing and using a content management system

A content management system (CMS) is software that sits on top of your web hosting. Think of a CMS as a container to collect and store your content (text, audio and images). All content management systems share the capability of letting you put content on a website without needing to know anything about the technical infrastructure that builds the web or a website.

A CMS gives you a visual interface that enables you to create, edit and manage website content (Figure 9.4). You use a CMS to create your website, which can then become the hub for your completely owned media. If you choose web hosting with a preinstalled CMS (Figure 9.5), you can effectively focus on the content of your digital presence and your Theory of Change rather having to learn the specifics of the underlying web technology. Think of the situation with this analogy: a CMS is to the web what a modern

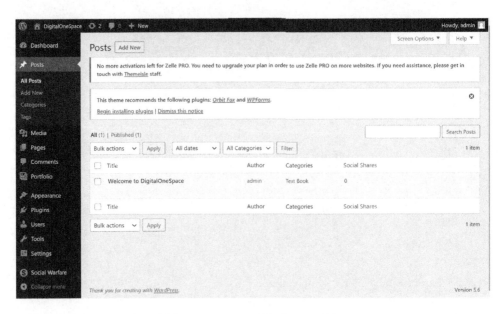

Figure 9.4 The interface for publishing content on a WordPress website

car is to driving. With any recent model car, if you lift up the hood to try and fix the engine, you are confronted by a series of sealed boxes. You could possibly fix them if you knew enough about mechanics. Fortunately, newer cars rarely break down, and the rest of the time, you can drive the car perfectly well from the comfort of the driver's seat with its many easy-to-use gadgets. In other words, you can be a driver without having to be a mechanic. A CMS gives you this same sort of control over your website. As you get more comfortable with the CMS, there are even more advanced settings that let you take a greater degree of control – a type of sports mode for your CMS.

Content management systems are behind some of the most popular and well-known websites. In many cases, it is the same CMS – WordPress – that is behind different websites that are visually unique but have the power and flexibility of the same system. You can visit sweden.se, thewaltdisneycompany.com, snoopdogg.com, mercedes-benz.com and hawaii.edu, all without moving away from WordPress technology.

With so many different content management systems freely available, making a sensible choice appears to be difficult (notwithstanding the fact that we are already encouraging the use of WordPress). The main alternatives to the broad-based applicability of Word-Press focus on a specific set of features. For example, there is even greater ease of use with Weebly, more visual templates with Wix, Joomla is more technically orientated, and Webflow is more orientated towards designers and the creation of more heavily visual websites.

Although your specific goal may draw you to these other options (and it may be worth exploring the options first), there is a clear argument for using WordPress for your digital presence. It has a large user base, an intuitive visual interface and a large developer base that supports ongoing development as well as securing the site against hackers. There are a large number of existing plugins that enable you to add engaging interactivity to your

Figure 9.5 A web-hosting control panel – and accessing WordPress

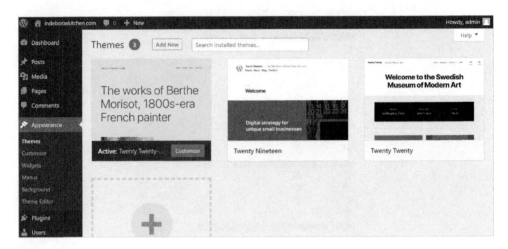

Figure 9.6 Changing the theme on a WordPress website

website without coding (but with the downside of increased security risks), the use of themes lets you customise the visual appearance of your website easily, and it is incredibly flexible if you want to experiment.

Because of the popularity of WordPress, it also has an active open-source community of developers who have created a wide range of features that can be added into the system without technical knowledge. The 58,000 plugins (wordpress.org/plugins/) and 8,000 themes (wordpress.org/themes/) are enough to cover the majority of specialist needs. Freelance websites such as Fiverr also have a vast number of developers willing – for a fee – to create even more themes and plugins.

The major advantage of the CMS approach – and one of the fundamental reasons content management systems were invented – is the separation of form from content (Figure 9.6). This enables you to choose a theme that suits the sensibilities of your presence, and it will be consistently applied across all your content.

9.4 Setting up your social media channels

There is a daunting array of social media channels. Your Theory of Change and the personas that you have defined will guide your choice of channels. Your plan is to use the venues that your personas also use. There is no added value in maintaining a multiple series of channels beyond what you have identified as the essential channels. Working with extra channels places a strain on you and your time as well as drawing the focus of attention for your content creation away from the venues where it can have the most impact.

Do not forget about email. Email is an important channel for many personas and is a form of your owned media that offers you unlimited control and options. Email is also the most pervasive form of online communication. Email is needed for signing up to social media channels and using many websites, particularly ecommerce sites and messaging systems, as well as other casual uses. If your personas regularly use email in their professional roles, a regular email newsletter for your most engaged audience is an appropriate destination for some of the content that you have planned.

An additional bonus in creating a WordPress-based website is that there are many newsletter (or list-building) plugins available that manage and automate the newsletter signup and distribution process. These plugins include features such as ensuring that the subscriber is giving consent to receive email and that there is a clear and easy mechanism for unsubscribing if (or when) the subscriber is no longer interested (Figure 9.7). This approach confirms the philosophy of a CMS by letting you focus on content rather than the technical details.

Choosing the content for an email newsletter does require some consideration. Each email message that arrives in a user's inbox demands attention and action. One of the fundamental characteristics of email is that anyone who has a person's email address can send email messages to that person. Consequently, email messages reduce the boundaries between yourself and your personas. The systematic use of email with a newsletter encourages deeper ongoing conversations on a one-on-one basis. The flow of actions for a visitor from visiting a website to signing up for a newsletter, receiving an email and then personally contacting you may mirror the causal linkages also defined in your Theory of Change. A personal exchange of email may even represent an output that leads to the achievement of one or more of your long-term outcomes.

The selection of content should consider the flow of actions that eventually brings a visitor to your newsletter content. The newsletter will be extension material that develops the ideas in the content of your website. Or, to put this in strategic terms, greater value for your subscribers can be found in the newsletter because your newsletter subscribers are more valuable than your website visitors.

Other social media channels assume different roles in your Theory of Change. This is determined by content forms that they encourage or prioritise. Four of what are generally regarded as the five most popular "global" social media channels (other than email) encourage short-form content; Instagram, Facebook, TikTok and Twitter are signposts to your longer-form content and owned media channels. The purpose of using one or more of these channels is to increase your visibility and stretch beyond the mechanics of search engine results. The content for these channels will be short, timely and to the point. The content you place on these venues is a gateway to richer content on your owned media. For many of these social media channels, it is a case of ensuring that your profile is fully populated – including a link to your own website and your new email address that uses your domain name. If you have content on owned media that directly relates to a conversation or thread on a social media channel, offer a link along with some short explanatory text. The opportunities to add a "flying signpost" into a live conversation should be taken cautiously and with clear relevance to the point in order to avoid any accusations of spamming. Spamming (or just the suggestion that this is what you are doing) is reputation damaging, so the opportunities to add links that point to your own content elsewhere should always be balanced against this ethical consideration.

With the short-form format, the other purpose for their use and the reason for monitoring them are their interactivity. Because you are dealing with people through these channels, being responsive is an opportunity to directly build reputation. Engaging with

Unsubscribe Manage preferences

Figure 9.7 Well-designed WordPress newsletter plugins include clear options in the footer of each email sent to subscribers

the conversations that are happening in each channel is a further reason you cannot maintain a large network of social media accounts.

The long-form exception in the social media channel "top five" is YouTube, which is owned by Google, making a compelling case for using this channel. The internal search engine in YouTube is often claimed – by Google, among others – to be the second-largest search engine (Funk 2020), and while this is disputed, it is still an important channel for raising visibility. Creating video content is not a task to be taken lightly (unless you are an experienced videographer – in which case, YouTube is already on the top of your list of preferred channels). In a self-referential twist, searching for "how to make videos for youtube" on YouTube's internal search engine freely provides hours of tuition. There are ways of starting a YouTube channel with minimal investment in equipment. You could consider a software solution that makes your work "quirky" while at the same time hiding the lower production quality produced by your equipment. There are filters such as cartoonisers that convert video into a cartoon experience. Software such as screencast-o-matic(.com) simplifies the process of creating videos by just using your existing laptop or computer. The other advantage of considering YouTube as one of your channels is the ability to embed a video that is on YouTube into your own website. This lets YouTube deal with all the complexities of hosting video content and serving it up to visitors – all without affecting your monthly web-hosting bandwidth limits.

Your location should also influence your choice of social media channels. The most regularly cited social media channels are biased towards the English-speaking world and particularly to the USA, Canada, the UK, Australia and New Zealand. But the list of channels by active users (Clement 2020) lists five Chinese sites amongst the top 15 channels globally. Vkontakte and Odnoklassniki are the second and fifth most popular channels respectively in Russia (Melkadze 2019). Some sensitivity to these regional variations should influence your choices around social media.

Interest-based social media channels will never hit the top ten lists of global users. That is not their purpose. Identifying channels based on your goal may require research if you are not already part of the community. LinkedIn is a high priority if your goal is identified in any way as gaining a professional career. But other networks also exist with more focused criteria, such as valence(.community) for black professionals and academia(.com) for academics.

Other, more lifestyle-orientated channels may also need to be included on your list of actions. There are channels for knitting (Ravelry), book reading (Good Reads), gaming (Twitch), beer drinking (Untapped) and just automatically networking with everyone (ncludr.com), as well as local community-level channels such as Nextdoor – in some locations, at least.

Following your personas' own preferences will often lead to a network of channels that support a community by using the best features found in each channel. The communities that emerge around a specific game provide useful indicative examples. The Pokémon GO community is a diverse global community focused on Niantic's mixed-reality game. The game is sometimes considered a social channel in its own right. However, out of concerns for safety, the opportunities are limited within the game itself, although there is a mechanism for linking your Pokémon Go and Facebook accounts. The community itself is self-organising at multiple levels that reflect the direct relationship that the game has with physical location. At a local level, players coordinate themselves around Facebook and WhatsApp groups to maximise personal opportunity for progressing in the game. There has also been global coordination within the community. For example, a publicly shared Google document continues to actively collect teaching resources for a "Pokémon GO syllabus" (tinyurl.com/pokemon-go-syllabus). A similar network of channels has built up around the Nintendo game Animal Crossing and includes animalcrossingcommunity(.com) and nookipedia.com – which is a wiki (or collaborative encyclopedia) based entirely on the game.

Finally, you should maintain a watchlist of the new channels that are regularly emerging. For example, Triller(.co) has the prospect of challenging TikTok in the short-form video space, and Bubbly(.net) may finally introduce a social media channel based around the spoken word audio form. These are not necessarily channels for engaging with right now. But if they fit your goal, they should be monitored and rapidly engaged with if the intentions of your personas match the channel.

Once you have email set up and your chosen key social media channels are all signed up, you can add social media icons to your website. There are even plugins available that make this process simply a case of adding your username for the appropriate social media channels ("Simple Social Icons"). You can also investigate the use of social sharing plugins such as "Sassy Social Share". This allows visitors to your website to share with their own network on different channels. Using a plugin that monitors usage of social sharing will also help prioritise the channels that are important to your personas and move beyond solely selecting channels based on global popularity.

TL;DR

Select a domain name that uses your own name or handle. Buy "local" when identifying a company that will host your website. Choose based on the features that are included such as "SSL certificate" and unlimited bandwidth rather than solely by price. Consider the value of an email newsletter as a channel for reputation building. Use a small number of social media channels that best reach out to your personas.

Callout 9.1: Case Study – Mehdi Sadaghdar (aka Electroboom)

A humorous and homebrew view of electronics

Mehdi Sadaghdar is an electrical engineer born in 1977 in Iran but now based in Canada. Despite Mehdi's technical training, the Electroboom content seemingly involves a significant number of electrocutions, explosions and shorted power sockets, all achieved with the deadpan style of an unsuspecting victim. Mehdi's content – particularly through YouTube videos – is a constant warning for caution around electricity that is done with a humour reminiscent of 1930s slapstick movie actors.

Mehdi has been creating educational videos for YouTube since 2012. In 2013, they produced "How not to make an electric guitar", which by itself has now had 14 million views. The video effectively sees Mehdi create a guitar with strings that have electricity running through them. Consequently, Mehdi's attempt to play a chord results, somewhat inevitably, in a massive shock.

Despite the relatively light production values of many of the videos, there are a number of indications that each video is carefully edited. Any swearing is carefully bleeped out, and on occasion, overlaid multiple copies of Mehdi are introduced into the video.

The Electroboom website uses WordPress as its content management system with the Twenty Eleven theme.

Channel	Link	Followers	Views	Content
YouTube	www.youtube.com/channel/UCJ0-OtVpF0wOKEqT2Z1HEtA	4m	354m views	150 videos
Facebook	www.facebook.com/ElectroBOOM	573k	547k likes	
Website	www.electroboom.com/		Ranked 696,200th website globally	

Callout 9.2: Your action – assembling your digital presence

Register a domain name that captures your name (or your consistent online handle). Even if your current Theory of Change does not include a website, you should reserve the space proactively.

Identify your preferred web-hosting service and purchase their most modest offering that satisfies your needs (and considering the basic technical needs described in this chapter).

Enable your CMS if it is not automatically enabled on your web hosting. Many web-hosting services will set up WordPress automatically when it is selected as the preferred CMS during the account setup. However, if a manual installation is required, the easiest method is to use the one-click install available through the web-hosting control panel (usually CPanel or Plesk). Under "Software" in the control panel, you will see "WordPress Manager by Softaculous" next to the WordPress icon – the ornate capital *W* (see Figure 9.5). Clicking on this option will reveal a button labelled "Install". Clicking this button will then reveal another screen (Figure 9.8). An automatic installation by the host or a manual installation by you should be done under the top level of your domain. In other words, typing just your domain name into a browser should show your WordPress front page (Figure 9.9).

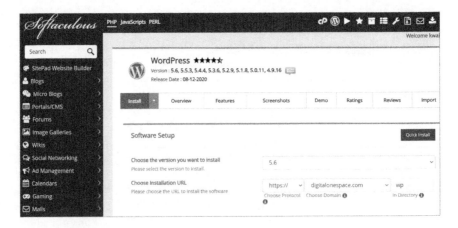

Figure 9.8 Enabling the CMS on a web-hosting account

Figure 9.9 The front page of your new WordPress system

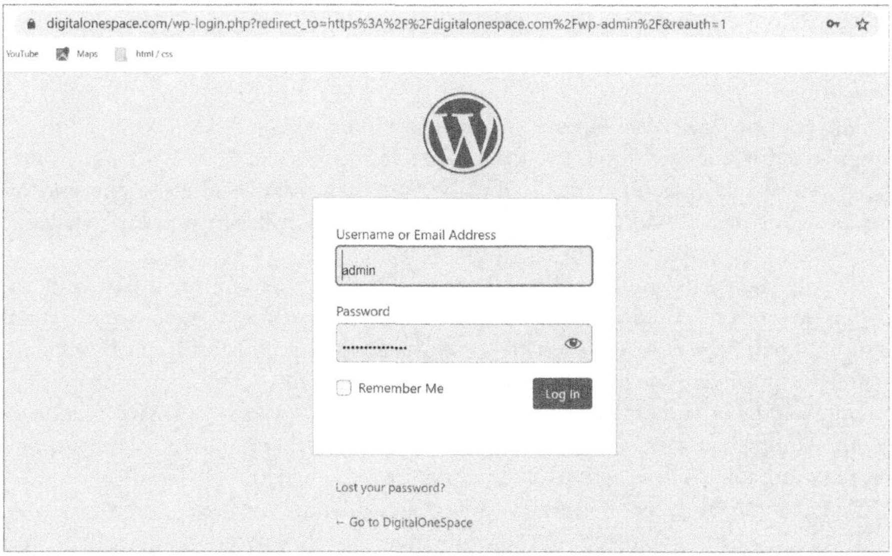

Figure 9.10 The WordPress login screen (e.g. example.com/wp-login/)

Once the installation is complete, you will receive an email to the address that you provided during the setup. The email will contain the credentials to the control panel for WordPress itself, from which you can publish your first piece of content after you log in. If your installation is at the top level of your domain, then typing yourdomain/wp-admin/ will take you to the login screen for your WordPress setup (e.g. http://example.com/wp-admin/) (Figure 9.10).

Set up what will be your primary email address for your domain name (e.g. yourname@yourdomain) (Figure 9.11) and test it by sending emails to and from this address. In your web-hosting control panel (not the WordPress control panel), click on Email Accounts under Email (see Figure 9.3). Follow the prompts, and you will be able to set up your first email account.

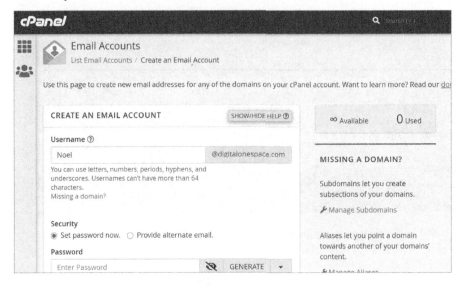

Figure 9.11 Setting up your first email address

Add your first piece of content to the CMS (Figure 9.11). It does not need to be lengthy, but it does set down the marker for your presence. Start with something biographical that has some depth. Include your new email address at the end of the post. Include a mention of concepts or ideas that will be interesting to your personas.

Identify the small number of social media channels that will form part of your digital presence. If you do not already have active accounts on these channels, then sign up. Spend the time on each of these channels to populate the profile details as fully as possible – including your new domain name (which is now also your website's address) and email address. Channels such as LinkedIn provide feedback on the completeness of your account and provide tips that help you complete the profile more fully. These actions will help improve your visibility significantly.

Add at least one piece of content to your new channels. Make it appropriate in style for the channel and relevant for your personas. In short-form channels, this could be presented as a rhetorical question: for example, "What's the big thing in the world of free-climbing right now?"

Return to your website and add links that point to your social media channels (Figure 9.12) by installing a plugin (such as Sassy Social Share or Simple Social Icons). At the same time, add a social sharing plugin that will allow visitors to share your content across their own networks (such as the AddtoAny plugin).

In the example on digitalonespace.com, the installed plugin is Menu Icons by ThemeIsle (wordpress.org/plugins/menu-icons/), which creates icon links to Facebook and YouTube on the top-right menu bar (Figure 9.12). The installed WordPress Social Sharing Plugin – Social Warfare plugin (wordpress.org/plugins/social-warfare/) enables the first post, "Welcome to DigitalOneSpace", to be shared by visitors to their own social media communities. There are icons for Twitter, Facebook, LinkedIn and Pinterest between the title and the body of the content that simplify the sharing process for visitors.

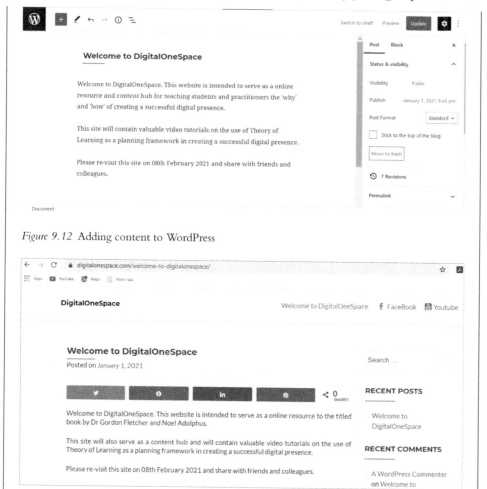

Figure 9.12 Adding content to WordPress

Figure 9.13 Social media plugins interacting with website content

Individually email close friends and family announcing your new website – using your new address.

Your presence is live and in its infancy. There will be little traffic, but you can share your website's address (your domain name) whenever it is appropriate. Monitor your new email address as well as your social media channels. Engage and be responsive.

Once you are ready, you should start producing and delivering the content that you have planned (Callout 8.2)

References cited

Chen, S. (2001) "Assessing the impact of the internet on brands", *Journal of Brand Management*, 8(4/5), pp. 288–302, https://doi.org/10.1057/palgrave.bm.2540029

Clement, J. (2020) "Most popular social networks worldwide as of October 2020, ranked by number of active users", *Statista*, 24th Nov., www.statista.com/statistics/272014/global-social-networks-ranked-by-number-of-users/

Coyle, J. and Gould, S. (2002) "How consumers generate clickstreams through web sites: An empirical investigation of hypertext, schema, and mapping theoretical explanations", *Journal of Interactive Advertising*, 2(2), pp. 42–56, https://doi.org/10.1080/15252019.2002.10722061

Funk, M. (2020) "YouTube 2nd biggest search engine – The myth that just won't die", *Tubics*, 7th Feb., www.tubics.com/blog/youtube-2nd-biggest-search-engine/

Ha, H.-Y. (2002) "The effects of consumer risk perception on pre-purchase information in online auctions: Brand, word-of-mouth, and customized information", *Journal of Computer-Mediated Communication*, 8(1), https://doi.org/10.1111/j.1083-6101.2002.tb00160.x

Melkadze, A. (2020) "Ranking of social media platforms in Russia Q3 2019, by users share", *Statista*, 14th Dec., www.statista.com/statistics/867549/top-active-social-media-platforms-in-russia/

10 Look and feel – make your presence reflect you

What you will learn

- The persuasive importance of the visual
- The importance of consistency over "art"
- Telling more with visual communication

10.1 The importance of the visual

"Look and feel" is a phrase that found favour with programmers in the early 1980s. This period marked a key transformation in the history of computing. People started interacting with computers by clicking a mouse and interacting with graphical elements that appeared on the screen. Prior to the development of graphical interfaces, using a computer involved typing commands after a text prompt appeared. There were no images, sounds or videos. Everything was text. The only variation that was possible was the choice of changing the colour of the text – and in some cases, this involved twisting a physical knob on the side of the screen.

With graphical user interfaces (GUIs), computing became popular, and people became users. Attention to design was an integral aspect of the earliest GUIs – including the Apple Lisa and then Microsoft's Windows. It is worth noting that while Apple brought the GUI into the hands of household users, it was the Microsoft product that popularised its usage. Apple sued Microsoft for copying the "look and feel" of their system but lost on the basis that despite the visual similarities, the underlying technology was different (Power 1997). Despite the legal nuances, it is the visual aspects of the way a computer operates and what is presented by individual software that are noticed first and are the impressions that last. If you ask ten people to comment about what they think of a website, nine of them will talk about the colours, the size of the text, the images and the styling of the navigation components. In other words, the look and feel.

Despite the attention to design that informed the earliest graphical user interfaces, there was a period when this sentiment was briefly lost. The consciously designed GUIs of the 1980s gave way to the "wild west" of the World Wide Web. The web's original intention was to enable scientists (and particularly physicists) to use the internet to share technical information (Berners-Lee n.d.). The focus of this development was on the simplicity with which a document could be placed "on the web". The tradeoff for this ease of use was the lack of any clear separation between form and content. The result was a blending of the logic of a document, such as its headings, paragraphs and footnotes, with its visualisation.

Evidence of the confusion and poor experience that this can create is found through the Wayback Machine (web.archive.org), which has been capturing snapshots of websites

DOI: 10.4324/9781003026587-10

since the 1990s. Browsing to currently familiar websites through this site reveals their history. The evolution of a site as it develops over time reveals the improved experience that comes from genuinely separating form and content. The more recent enthusiasm for "dark mode" settings on phones, in apps and on websites and its claimed benefits are easy to achieve because of the same conceptual separation of form and content (Kostadinov 2019)

A key advantage of using a content management system for your website in combination with selected social media channels in your digital presence is that the logical separation is managed for you and is largely invisible. This means changing the look and feel – what is called the theme – with a CMS such as WordPress is achieved with a few clicks (Figure 10.1). The theme can just as easily be reversed without having to individually change each piece of content that you have on your website. The hallmark of good design is that you do not notice it. Contrariwise, poor design is intuitively obvious because it creates jarring effects.

However, the implication is not that look and feel do not matter because they can be changed. Look and feel do matter, and you should be endeavouring to get them right from the start. As a result, you should not have to change the theme after your first choice.

The look and feel of your digital presence is also much wider than a WordPress theme or changing a single setting within your social media channels. Think of the look and feel of your digital presence in the same way as the clothes you put on each day. Although the clothes you wear change from day to day, there is a general consistency around the style, the colours and the items themselves. Even though you wear different forms of clothing for different activities, such as going to work, going to the gym or going to a film, there still remains a consistency that others who know you will recognise. Your digital presence across multiple channels should give the same sort of consistent impression that reflects your identity. Humans are largely visual in their responsiveness and generally recognise this type of consistency in a subconscious way. The challenge in preparing your own look and feel for your digital presence is to lift this awareness to a conscious level that critically unpicks its elements.

Because of this visual focus of attention, perhaps the most recognisable design element for your own presence are your own images. The most common approach is to use a

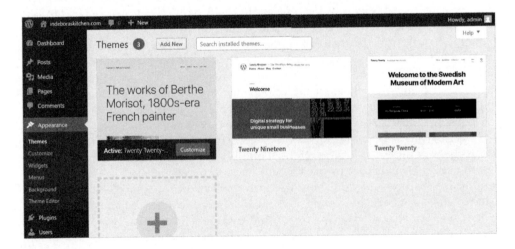

Figure 10.1 Changing a theme in WordPress

consistent image of yourself across all your channels. However, if you make the investment of using a professional photographer, there may be an opportunity to get a small set of images with a variety of poses to create a more dynamic impression. Your passport photo is not the solution as a profile picture anywhere, ever.

Your portrait should attempt to capture your personality. You might choose a traditional head and shoulders portrait as the most personal and direct image of yourself. This standard format can be played with and become more playful or casual with different angles of lighting, a tilted camera or tightly cropping the final image (so not all of the top of your head is showing). Your hands could also become a prop in this format of portrait. Variants on the *Thinker* pose could be considered cliched, but in combination with other props or playful variants, lighting may open up creative opportunities. Hands may also be used to shade or hide part of your face. Madonna's 1990 "Vogue" video is an object lesson in all forms of portrait photography that may inspire your own images (youtube. com/watch?v=GuJQSAiODqI).

Moving the camera back to a three-quarter portrait provides an image that reaches from your head to your knees. Moving back again, a full-length portrait will almost certainly require a professional photographer to get all the elements working together in a harmonious way. Both three-quarter and full-length portraits require some consideration of your surroundings and what is appearing in the background. Portraits of this type can fail dramatically when they incorporate a rubbish bin or scenes of industrial blight. For most people, their domestic setting does not produce good backgrounds for full-length portraits. However, there is also opportunity in full-length portraits as the setting can be used to convey extra meaning about you. A forest footpath for an outdoorsy and active person, the urban backdrop of an iconic city from a high vantage point for the adventurer, a laboratory setting for the chemical engineer. Your portrait can say a lot about you, and Pinterest can provide numerous visual idea starters if you search for "portrait photography".

Colour also reflects personality, and your colour combinations are another visual element that sends a message. The psychology of colour tells us that blues are cool, reds are warm and grey is neutral. More importantly, colours have meanings that can vary dramatically from culture to culture (McCandeless 2009). One of the most dramatic variations is the colour of death, which varies between black, white, grey and green, depending on your location in the world. Your own favourite colour may have different meanings for your personas too. This is why some persona templates include a favourite colour as an integrated aspect of the portrayal.

The meanings become more complex when used in combination, but more importantly, you are looking for a colour scheme that works in a complementary way and that you can apply in whole or partially across all your channels. Colour combinations are infinite, but some work better than others. Fortunately, Pinterest again provides some insight with a search for "color schemes". WordPress itself also offers practical assistance for your website (and insight for your other channels, depending on how much they can be configured) with a browsable directory of its themes (wordpress.org/themes/), including many free options.

The themes offered through the WordPress(.org) site also highlight a further element of the visual impact of your presence: its typography. While text is generally black, there are many thousands of typefaces – the ways that the characters are shown – that contain multiple fonts. In effect a font defines the size, weight and style used with a typeface; for example, Times New Roman 8pt, Bold is a font that makes use of the Times New Roman

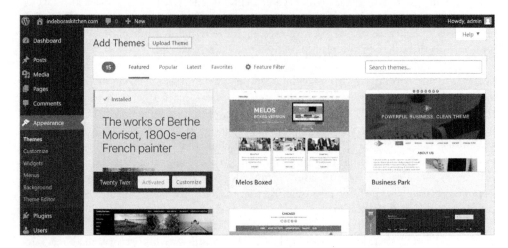

Figure 10.2 Uploading a theme you have found for your website

typeface. But because these definitions get confused in day-to-day usages (and in software such as Microsoft Word) searching for either "font" or "typeface" on Pinterest will provide hundreds of examples. Sites such as dafont(.com) also offer a searchable directory ranging from the simplest and most traditional to the most ornate and unreadable. However, to keep your own presence uncomplicated, it is better to find the closest match to your preferred typeface through the WordPress(.org) themes selection. Downloading a theme from the web and installing it on your WordPress website is done through a single page on your WordPress control panel (Figure 10.2). If you have developed a strong understanding of the typography that best reflects your design sentiments and your preferred theme does not match this perspective, you can apply a further plugin (such as Easy Google Fonts) to let you select the typeface you want to see with your preferred theme.

Once you have started considering these aspects of your own look and feel, you will begin to recognise other elements of your presence that you will want to shape in a reflection of your own personality.

10.2 Being consistent

There are many principles of good design. But any individual author will identify different principles for their own list. The difference is a result of content and purpose. Many lists of design principles also combine the skills (the enablers), actions, outputs and outcomes for creating good design, a combination of logic that you will already be familiar with from your Theory of Change.

For the digital experience and context, the outcome of good visual design is an unambiguous and unobtrusive experience for the observer. As an aspect of communications, good design is about reducing the potential for misinterpretation between the sending and receiver. This has led some designers to speculate on the possibility of creating a universal graphical language that could be shared between languages and cultures such as semantagraphy (Bliss 1965) or, more recently, thenounproject(.com), which has a mission statement of "building a global visual language that unites us". However, there are many challenges to universality. Dreyfuss (1984) cites the example of the South African

Chamber of Mines erecting signs to encourage its illiterate workers to keep the mine tracks clear of rocks (Figure 10.3). The three panel cartoon carefully laid out the steps for removing the rocks. Unfortunately more rocks appeared on the tracks than before. After investigation, the embedded assumption that the illiterate workers would "read" the cartoon from left to right was realised. Workers who saw the sign interpreted the message from right to left and were dutifully moving rocks onto the mine rails. Getting feedback from your personas is clearly important.

As the creator of your message, you will recognise the intention of your symbols, design and content. You need the feedback of others to improve and to focus your message for clarity. It is a process that is valid for any type of content – but especially longer-form static material.

Good design is not the same as good art. For anyone in the creative sector, this statement is overly obvious. Our own experience, however, is that those beginning the journey to developing their own digital presence will explain the poor design values of their first efforts as a result of the fact that they are not an artist. Presumably, their intention is that they will either eventually become an artist (an unlikely transformation) or that their presence will automatically evolve and improve (an impossible transformation).

The key skills for bringing good design to your digital presence have already been described in earlier chapters as self-awareness and critical reflection. If you think your design does not look quite right, it is unlikely that others will disagree. Visual comparisons with similar content on the same type of channel is the rule-of-thumb guide to use. Some channels make it incredibly difficult to break away from the overall "house style". For example, Twitter offers you effectively no options to format text in any way differently from its millions of other users. However, even this does not stop some creative use of characters to create "character pictures" (Kirkbride 2018). But as you move towards using your fully owned media, including websites and email, the opportunities to alter the visual style of your content are completely unrestricted.

This returns to the one key rule for all your design actions. Be consistent. Even if you are attempting to be a rule breaker, you need to understand the rule in order to break it – and have applied it previously in your own content. Consistency is the hallmark of all good digital design. The rule can be applied to all the elements involved in your design. Using the same typeface across the body of your text content and the same (or a contrasting) typeface for the headings is an everyday example of consistency that also applies to any form of printed or digital document.

While a casual glance at any block of text might suggest there are few other opportunities for applying the rule of consistency, a deeper examination highlights how much

Figure 10.3 A visual sign can be misinterpreted (after Dreyfuss 1984)

is taken for granted. The consistent use of text alignment (e.g. left, justified or centred) is only seen when it is not applied. The preference for italicising, bolding or underlining for emphasis in a block of text works in a similar way as alignment. The scourge for many new university and college students is completing a list of references correctly. There appear to be so many rules and exceptions to learn with referencing guides, and most of this advice never states the one underlying rule – consistency. Apply the citation rule once to a book, and this is the same rule you will apply for all books from there on. Many undergraduates look at each citation as a new problem to be solved – "How do I reference this item?" – rather than recognising the rule: "This is a book, so its citation will look the same as the previous book I cited".

Underneath the structural level of consistency is an even more fundamental aspect of the document that is based on your own style and use of language. The way your document (as well as other forms of content) is received is shaped heavily by the language that you use. It should address its intended audience – your personas – in a manner that they are familiar with and that would be generally considered appropriate for both receiver and sender. Many organisations have failed to recognise the need for this type of consistency. The Monterey Bay Aquarium received significant criticism for a Tweet about one of the sea otters in 2018 (twitter.com/montereyaq/status/1075120423744860160) that took the form of a type of rap "Abby is a thicc girl/What an absolute unit/She c h o n k/ Look at the size of this lady/OH LAWD SHE COMIN/Another Internetism !" A subsequent tweet included the hashtag #bodypawsitivity. Although the content received significant attention with 54.4k likes, 17.8k retweets (shares) and more than 999 comments, the aquarium subsequently apologised for its use of vernacular terms that are used specifically in relation to Black women's bodies.

Other, more subtle uses of language appear in individual writing and create a signature style. Preferences for pronoun use can often reflect an individual's schooling and the resistance to using personal pronouns including the first person. "I" in content may make you appear distant and disconnected. Similarly, awkward phrasing in an attempt to be gender neutral, such as "he/she" instead of the preferable "they" and "their", or being unintentionally gendered: "manhole" instead of "accessway" and "manpower" instead of "labour", can also disconnect you from your personas. Word usage, patterns of punctuation and phrasing are difficult to change. Be aware of your own style with text. Time and the creation of more and more text-based content will help you evolve your style in ways that improve your engagement with your personas.

Using a consistent colour scheme for your digital presence follows the same rule. There is always room for creativity in applying the rule of consistency. In fact, the rule of consistency is what enables your creativity. For example, if you employ a consistent theme of black, yellow and white across your website, then breaking the rule with a splash of red with one item of content emphasises the specific message combined with a sense of urgency. Other options might be to use your preferred colour scheme but with a changing emphasis of colours between each of your channels.

Continuous self-awareness and a critical view on your own work will help you improve. Consciously being consistent will help create a design sentiment for your digital presence that is a recognisable aspect of your own identity.

10.3 Communicating visually

Visual communication is at the intersection of considering your look and feel and your plans for content creation. Lists of types of content generally include information graphics, posters and other forms of visual communications that lie between the purely visual images and text forms of content. A real benefit of visual communications such as information graphics is that it can be shared across social media channels as a complete bundle. Your look and feel are maintained irrespective of the channel, your content is engaging because it is visual and, when it is done well, it conveys a longer-lasting message than text forms of content. Edward Tufte, whose work as a statistician is overshadowed by his capability as a visual communicator, lays down the value of information graphics and other forms of visual communication content as a type of challenge. "Graphical excellence is that which gives to the viewer the greatest number of ideas in the shortest time with the least ink in the smallest space" (Tufte 2006b). As a form of critical benchmark for your own visual communications, this is the aspirational standard.

Tufte also coined the term "chartjunk" to describe visual communications that confuse, add unnecessary noise or are more complex than the original data they set out to represent. The concept that "less is more" is particularly true for visual communications. Many software tools that are regularly used to create visual communications by default do the opposite. Microsoft Excel graphing capabilities have a tendency to add "chartjunk" such as duplicated keys and additional lines. A critical design sentiment is required with software that is being pushed to do actions that were not in their original specifications. For example, with Excel charts, it is often a case of selecting and deleting all the unnecessary elements until only the key message is revealed. Tufte is also critical of PowerPoint in poetic terms, "PowerPoint is like being trapped in the style of early Egyptian flatland cartoons rather than using the more effective tools of Renaissance visual representation" (Tufte 2001). This criticism is justified as Tufte elaborates in his extended essay on PowerPoint, in which he identifies the automatic hierarchy in the software as unhelpful and capable of distracting attention from the key points of a message. In this particular essay, he dissects the Power-Point presentation used by NASA engineers that identified the potentially fatal flaw in the space shuttle's design. The presentation was made before the Challenger was affected by the fault with significant loss of life. However, the key points and warning were under a third-level header of a text-heavy slide and consequently were ignored in the decision-making process that led to the fatal launch of Challenger in freezing temperatures (Tufte 2006a).

The starting point for visual communications, however, is not the software to create the content but the message that you want to get across to your personas. If you consider your content creation in relation to your personas' intent, then the starting point will be a key question. Your content then sets out to answer this question through visual communications. Thinking in these terms then enables you to recognise the type of question and the direction in which this may take your content. "How" (and especially "how much") and "when" questions lend themselves to quantitative forms of images such as charts, timelines and logic flow charts. In contrast, "who", "what" and "where" questions point to more qualitative and representative types of images that include portraits and maps. While we have tended to associate mapping with services such as Google Maps, there are also soft maps that take the form of a locational sketch based on what is observed rather than satellite precision. "The Soft Atlas of Amsterdam" (Rothuizen 2014) presents the city in a series of pen sketches by the author that includes small text notes of the author's observations at that location. The soft atlas focuses on the "who" and "where" questions simultaneously by asking "Who is observed in this space?" with locations such as a supermarket, a houseboat, an air traffic control tower and Anne Frank's house.

"Why" questions are more complex to represent and will often incorporate a mixture of data and explanations. "Why" questions make for the most interesting – but most complex – visual communications that will provide a rich explainer for your personas.

The sources of your data for creating visual content will vary depending on the need. There is a wealth of data to explore through sites such as Wikipedia, where the Creative Commons license regime enables you to reuse and repurpose according to your needs. A simple information graphic of milk bottle tops by type, by country and by colour was compiled by one of the authors entirely from Wikipedia data in 2012 (Figure 10.4). A second information graphic compiled from publicly available data shows the local government election results in Salford in the UK in 2012. The representation is by ward and ordered within each ward by the individual party vote (Figure 10.5), showing a win for the Labour party in all but two. Some information graphics can be useful on an ongoing

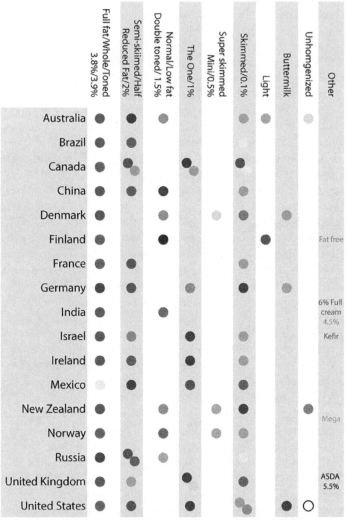

Milk Bottle Lid Colours by Country by Type
source: en.wikipedia.org/wiki/Milk_bottle_top

Figure 10.4 Information graphic of milk bottle tops by country by colour

(Full colour version: 217lemurs.tumblr.com/image/21660163737)

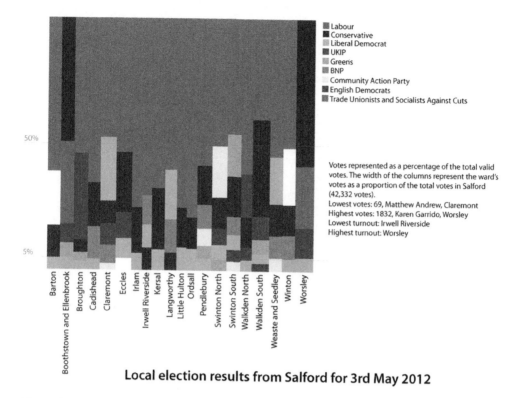

Local election results from Salford for 3rd May 2012

Figure 10.5 Information graphic of local government elections in Salford, UK, 3 May 2012

(Full colour version: 217lemurs.tumblr.com/image/22672908625)

basis. The retronator(.com/clock) visually displays the current time in relation to the most popular times for the current day of the week on a selection of social media channels. A graphic of this type can guide your own decision about when and to which social media channel to add content when it is likely to receive the most attention.

There are a range of tools for creating visual communications. The choice will depend on your own skills with creative tools and the time you have and are prepared to invest in developing your technical competency. Of course, in a sharing economy where people are crafting their own digital presence, you will readily find content specifically designed to support your skills development through YouTube, Pinterest or other channels. Full-scale tools including Adobe's Creative Suite are a significant personal financial investment – although current students at many universities and colleges may have access to this suite through an institutional licensing arrangement. It is worth enquiring if you do have a currently valid student card.

Other tools have been designed specifically for the purpose of creating visual communications content. The licensing and options do vary. There is value in applying the same systematic selection process as choosing your content authoring applications (§8.2). Your selection criteria will depend on the type of visual communications you are planning. Tools to consider include piktochart(.com), visme(.co), infogram(.com), canva(.com) and easel.ly.

TL;DR

Be consistent in your design: colours, typography and style. Break any or all of these design sentiments once you understand them, and you can create additional impact for emphasis. Break these principles consistently and your design sentiments simply break down into an incoherent stream of content.

Callout 10.1: Case Study – Stacey-lee May (aka Queen of Smoke)

Challenging gender stereotypes

Born in 1997 in Johannesburg, South Africa, Stacey-lee May is a former law student and spinner (or drifter). Stacey-lee was taught how to spin by their father as a response to bullying at school at the age of 16. Stacy-lee's skill with cars has attracted significant media attention, and that has led to filming with Charlize Theron in a range of locations such as London and Pakistan. Increasing awareness of Stacey-lee beyond South Africa has also produced sponsorship from Red Bull.

Stacey-lee crafts deeper visual meanings into her spinning activity. A trademark pink livery is a reference to breast cancer awareness and a remembrance of Stacey-lee's grandmother, who died from the condition. Stacey-lee also regularly works in a local soup kitchen and does a sponsored charity drive each year to provide essential supplies to those in need.

Stacey-lee's digital presence is currently underdeveloped, although the potential is clearly evidenced by the number of followers that have been gained through multiple different channels with minimal content. By challenging the stereotypes associated with the sport of drifting, Stacey-lee is an interesting presence to specific personas that are readily defined.

Channel	Link	Followers	Views	Content
YouTube	www.youtube.com/channel/UC4VGLYM9RV6UasN6GoIj1eg	1.2k	13k views	6 videos
Fundrazr	https://fundrazr.com/teamstacey			
Facebook	www.facebook.com/staceylee.may	17k		
Instagram	www.instagram.com/team_stacey/	48.9k		409 posts
Twitter	https://twitter.com/staceym325i	239		26 tweets

Callout 10.2: Your action – defining your own look and feel

Start with a reflective analysis. What design sentiment do you already project personally in real life? Do some research with friends and family about the design sentiment they think you project.

Considering what you discover, assess whether this design sentiment would work with your personas and your goal. What aspects of your current design sentiment require modification (or tweaking) within your digital presence.

Return to the WordPress themes page and browse the available themes to find something that closely matches this design sentiment. Download and install this theme for your website. The theme you choose and use should reflect your design sentiment, but be aware of your personas. The theme also needs to be suitable for them. You can describe this as considering the persona experience (although, in the technical literature, it is called user experience or UX and is a more expansive topic than just the selection of a WordPress theme).

Taking a cue from the WordPress theme you have now chosen, consider what aspects of your social media channels can be configured to reflect a consistent sentiment.

If you are using email, create an email footer that will appear at the base of every email that you send which will also reflect this same sentiment.

Reflect on your planned content (Chapter 8) to see if any of the ideas are suitable for development through information graphics. Select information graphics software to develop suitable content into visual communications for your digital presence.

References cited

Berners-Lee, T. (n.d.) "History of the web", *World Wide Web Foundation*, https://webfoundation.org/about/vision/history-of-the-web/

Bliss, C. (1965) Semantography *(Blissymbolics). 2nd Enlarged Edition. A Simple System* of 100 *Logical Pictorial Symbols, Which Can Be Operated* and *Read Like* 1 + 2 = 3 in all *Languages*, Sydney: Semantography (Blissymbolics) Publications.

Dreyfuss, H. (1984) *Symbol Sourcebook: An Authoritative Guide to International Graphic Symbols*, New York: Van Nostrand Reinhold.

Kirkbride, A. (2018) "Ways to be creative with text-only tweets", *Twirp Communications*, https://twirp.ca/2018/06/ways-to-be-creative-with-text-only-tweets/

Kostadinov, P. (2019) "The pros and cons of Dark Mode: Here's when to use it and why", *PhoneArena*, 19th Dec., www.phonearena.com/news/Dark-Mode-iPhone-Android-interface-feature-pros-cons-versus-light-mode_id116978

McCandless, D. (2009) "Colours in culture", *Information is Beautiful*, Apr., www.informationisbeautiful.net/visualizations/colours-in-cultures/

Power, A. (1997) "Web 101: A history of the GUI", *Wired*, 19th Dec., www.wired.com/1997/12/web-101-a-history-of-the-gui

Rothuizen, J. (2014) *The Soft Atlas of Amsterdam*, Amsterdam: Nieuwamsterdam.

Tufte, E. (2001) *The Visual Display of Quantitative Information*, Cheshire, CT: Graphics Press.

Tufte, E. (2006a) *The Cognitive Style of PowerPoint: Pitching Out Corrupts Within*, Cheshire, CT: Graphics Press.

Tufte, E. (2006b) *Beautiful Evidence*, Cheshire, CT: Graphics Press.

Further reading

Jong, C. (ed) (2017) *Ten Principles for Good Design: Dieter Rams*, Munich: Prestel.

Omniglot (n.d.) "Blissymbolics", https://omniglot.com/writing/blissymbolics.htm

11 Curation – sharing with your audience

What you will learn

- The value of collections
- Using curation to develop your presence

11.1 Collecting content

Collecting content and curating what you find are other ways of encouraging wider engagement with your personas. The desire to collect is a core human drive. This is a desire that ties humanity back to its hunting and gathering origins on the African savannah. In the modern era, that desire is still present, even if the need that lay behind it no longer is. During the colonial period, this desire manifested itself in the controversial gathering of artefacts from occupied countries and their acquisition and display in the museums of the colonisers. Attitudes of this type can still cause ongoing international political controversies such as the original friezes from the Parthenon in Athens or the so-called "Elgin Marbles" that are held by the British Museum in London (Smith 2020).

Personal collecting was actively encouraged through the late twentieth century in parallel with the rise of consumer culture. Mainstream collecting focused on coins, stamps, comics and sports cards. More unusual collections focus on traffic cones, garden gnomes and air sickness bags (Hickman 2020). In effect, any class of item can become the object of a collector's attention. Obsessive collecting also attracts media attention (Larbi 2017) as behaviour that is aberrant because of its excess while still being relatable to most people.

All these examples mean that collecting in the digital context is part of its normality rather than surprising. There are so many ways in which you could already be collecting digital artefacts. If you are studying and writing essays, then every list of references you create is part of a collection that you build over your career as a student. Very few people make any use of this collection after they graduate, and it is a largely untapped opportunity. The bookmarks that you accumulate as you browse the web are another collection that you are continuously building but you may be doing very little with other than using them as a personal *aide-memoire*. The examples continue across other forms of content too. Creating a series of playlists on Spotify or other music streaming websites is an audio collection that can also be shared and accessed by other users of the services.

There are a number of social media channels that focus on building collections for access by others. Pinterest(.com), Mix(.com), Juxtapost(.com) and Dribbble(.com) all provide ways of collecting content from multiple sources. Some channels provide a generic platform for creating collections while others, such as Foodgawker(.com), have a clearly stated focus.

DOI: 10.4324/9781003026587-11

Creating a good collection takes planning and commitment. Some initial guidance for a good collection can be discerned from two of the largest digital collections. The Internet Archive (web.archive.org) began collecting snapshots of websites in 1996 and continues to collect massive numbers of sites on a regular basis. Its collection policy is guided by collaborating with public libraries around the world that suggest significant sites to archive and track their evolution. The technology used to collect the websites for the archive is the same as that used for creating the database that sits behind search engines, including Google.

The difference between the Internet Archive and Google is that the archive can be searched by a website address and then by its snapshot in time. The intention is for the collected content to be viewed in the way a museum might be visited. Google's focus, in contrast, is on monetising its collection by providing the most accurate results to a specific query (combined with the paid results that also appear in response to the query). Google does, however, provide a way to move back through its own snapshots of the web by clicking on the "tools" menu and then selecting a custom date range. Both collections are extensive and obsessive in scale. The Internet Archive has collected 514 billion web pages. Although Google does not publicly share the number of web pages it has stored since the 1990s, the scale of its current operations would indicate that it exceeds the size of the Internet Archive. Both these operations are only possible because the collection and storage of the web pages is entirely automated.

Both Google and the Internet Archive have also undertaken significant digitising of (primarily pre-1990s) printed, audio and video materials. The results are also expressed in slightly different ways. Google's projects present an extension to the iconic single simple search page with books.google.com and scholar.google.com. The focus still remains on responding to the intent of the person doing the search. The Internet Archive, in contrast, uses the analogy of a lending library, with just under two million items for its subscribers. The comparative examples of Google and the Internet Archive highlight some key learning for your own collections.

Using the nine principles of a good collection defined by the United States' National Information Standards Organization (NISO 2007), it is possible to determine whether the Internet Archive's and Google's collections can be assessed as "good". If the objective of your collection is completeness (or an approximation of this state in the vast digital environment), then the consequent qualities of sustainability must be considered. Google sustains its collection by using a commercial approach to accessing items – effectively, it juxtaposes advertising alongside the extracts of its collection. The Internet Archive, in contrast, relies on donations and corporate support to sustain its operations over time as a not-for-profit organisation.

A good collection respects intellectual property rights. It is unethical and unsustainable to simply gather up materials and re-present these as your own. The history of Google is punctuated with a number of legal challenges around intellectual property rights (Heinze 2013). The Internet Archive has also been challenged in a similar way (Romano 2020). The challenges are founded on very different motivations from the plaintiffs, but the challenge to any large-scale collection is that entirely respecting rights holders can be difficult and inevitably will not satisfy all the parties involved.

A significant difference between Google and the Internet Archive is found in the way they share information about the items they hold. "Collections should be described so that a user can discover characteristics of the collection, including scope, format, restrictions on access, ownership, and any information significant for determining the collection's authenticity, integrity, and interpretation" (NISO 2007). Google's material from its search results generally lacks this form of transparency, whereas the Internet Archive attempts to document these aspects of its collection as much as can be determined. This difference in the visible "meta-information" is at the core of what Google offers as a search engine while the Internet Archive is a preservation project, even though the underlying technology for collecting is similar. This variation in perspective is further reflected with the principle that "A good collection has mechanisms to supply usage data and other data that allows standardized measures of usefulness to be recorded" (NISO 2007). For example, consider Google Trends. This service documents the rising and falling popularity of a search term, but the way that it is reported reveals a percentage rather than an absolute number. Comparative searches with two or more terms could be more useful, but with a popular term shown against an obscure one, this charting only reveals this one already-known fact.

These principles make a case for any type of collection that you develop being founded on transparency and ethical behaviour. You should be aware of the permissions related to an individual item and whether you can reuse directly or can only provide a link to the web page. The Creative Commons license (creativecommons.org) is a widely used system for clearly indicating how content can be reused and shared. *Wikipedia* makes significant use of this licensing approach with its own content and the use of the recognisable CC logo.

Equally important is the link between your collecting behaviour and your own strategic perspective.

> Digital collection development has now evolved and matured . . . where simply serving useful digital collections effectively to a known constituency is not sufficient. Issues of cost/value, sustainability, and trust have emerged as critical success criteria for good digital collections.
>
> (NISO 2007)

If you consider building collections as part of your presence and can identify the added value that this will offer to your personas, then you need to consider focus. You will not be recreating Google – your focus will be on specific topics, themes or concepts. You can add further value to your personas by being selective in your collecting practice and assessing the items in your collection for their comparative quality. In other words, your collection must be curated.

11.2 Curation as part of your presence

The curation of collections encourages a positive impression of your knowledge and skills, can be used to make the value of your offering more distinctive and supports the development of a positive reputation. "A good collection is curated, which is to say, its resources are actively managed during their entire lifecycle" (NISO 2007).

Taking a strategic perspective on the collection means that your starting point is a focus on what you will collect and curate – the vehicle – rather than the venue that you will use for your collection. The collection will be relevant and targeted to your personas. This will include consideration of the form of the content as well as its topic.

The original development of Yahoo! is a useful and indicative starting point for determining the theme of your collection. Originally developed in 1994 as "Yet Another Hierarchically Organised Oracle" (or "Officious Oracle, depending on the source), the original Yahoo! had a contrasting approach to discovering content on the web from those of the search engines available at the time. The Oracle presented a top level of topics and then presented a hierarchy of subcategories that could be navigated through down to a small, selected list of websites that were a close match to the narrower topic. Browsing the original Yahoo! pages through the Internet Archives Wayback Machine (web.archive. org/web/19961220154510/www.yahoo.com/) may also be useful for identifying potential topics for your own collection. However, you should explore the specific subtopics in the directory deeply as you are not attempting to curate the entire web or even a significant proportion of its contents.

Yahoo! is also its own cautionary story about collections and the challenge of curation. Yahoo! is now a news portal. The directory that gave Yahoo! its name (Sullivan 2014) was closed in 2014 as the scale of the web made an humanly maintained directory of the entire web impossible, and the power of Google's search engine made it difficult to compete. The structure of Yahoo! also made curation difficult, even with significant resources. The definitions of the topics and the subtopics did not have the consistency or rigour of sound library practice. Systematic classification systems such as Universal Decimal Classification (UDC – udcsummary.info), the Dewey Decimal System (DDS – wikipedia.org/wiki/List_of_Dewey_Decimal_classes) and the Library of Congress Classification (LCC – loc.gov/catdir/cpso/lcco/) all provide ways of grouping the entire scope of human knowledge in a consistent way. One of these systems will be familiar as they are used in your local library or nearest university library. Navigating down the topics in these systems will also help highlight potential areas for building a collection of content. You may also more intuitively recognise the basis for a potential collection with an examination of your Theory of Change.

The principles for curating your content are relatively straightforward and help create a sustainable and valuable collection over a period of time.

- Maintain a focused topic – and avoid topic creep
- Have a clear and critical rationale for what is included in the collection – this includes consideration of the value of the content to your personas
- Attempt to gather all the relevant meta-information about the content, including an attribution of authorship and source (it is the reference list for your collection)
- Remove items from the collection that no longer meet your rationale – you are not building an historical record
- Focus on quality rather than the size of the collection
- If there is clear permission to share – such as use of the Creative Commons license – use the item directly; if not, then link to the content

Select a social media channel that best suits hosting your collection – or consider using your own website if no other service will fit while still maintaining these principles. There are WordPress plugins that can be used for creating and maintaining your own collection. There are some specific tools such as MyCurator and NorDot worth evaluation (§8.2). But there are other options that, at first impression, may seem obvious choices. The many ecommerce plugins such as Odoo and Shopify (WPBeginner 2020) are also options for creating a collection. The underlying principle for an ecommerce system is the same as a curated collection of content. If you consider the concept of a collection broadly, what you are presenting is a list of broadly related options to your personas, and they are able to browse these options. Your collection simply does not include prices against each item or have a checkout option. Highly configurable ecommerce plugins will allow these features to be disabled and provide you an alternative collection system for your website.

In some cases, it may be that you need to be part of a social media channel such as Pinterest because the value is within the community itself, and your personas are present in these type of venues. In this case, the principles for curating your collection are still relevant, but they will be shaped by what is (or is not) possible through the channel of your choice.

TL;DR

Creating a curated collection can help build visibility and reputation for your presence. A collection can be added to your website or created through a specialised social media channel. An actively curated collective with a clear rationale and focus will build your reputation as an authoritative source for resources relevant to your personas as well as your own goal.

Callout 11.1: Case Study – Hikaru Nakamura

Chess is a game that people still play

Born in 1987 in Japan, Hikaru Nakamura moved to the USA at the age of two. At 15 Hikaru became the youngest-ever American Chess grandmaster (although this record has now been broken three times). Hikaru was playing chess at an internationally competitive standard by the age of ten. By the age of 17 Hikaru was competing – and winning – in competitions around the world. Hikaru's chess career is extensive and heavily documented through an extensive Wikipedia page.

Hikaru is sponsored by Chess.com and is a regular commentator on the Chess-Ninja website.

Hikaru's digital presence accelerated during the COVID-19 pandemic through a resurgence of interest in the game and almost daily activity on Twitch. A claimed tenfold increase in audience during 2020 saw an average audience of 14,000 for Hikaru's Twitch stream and significant increases in both YouTube and Twitch followings in the same period.

Hikaru's website is created with WordPress.

Channel	Link	Followers	View	Content
Twitch	www.twitch.tv/gmhikaru	701k	8.2m views (Nov/Dec 2020)	
YouTube	www.youtube.com/ gmhikaru	509k	92.8m views	805 videos
Twitter	https://twitter.com/ GMHikaru	223.5k		2.6k tweets
Website	https://hikarunakamura. com/		Ranked 2,159,500th website globally	

Callout 11.2: Your action – developing a collection

Using one of the classification systems and observation of websites that you see as most relevant to your Theory of Change, identify one or two potential focal points for a curated collection.

Work back through any material you have gathered previously to identify if you have the beginnings of a relevant collection.

Identify a collection-based social media channel that best suits your goal. If there is no suitable fit, consider potential WordPress plugins that could be used for your collection.

Create a document that defines what you are collecting, what the purpose of the collection is and the outputs and outcomes you want to see from maintaining the collection. (This will relate to visibility and reputation.) Define how much time you will set aside on a weekly/monthly basis to maintain your collection. This time will define how large your collection can become.

Start your collection.

Seek out comments from family and friends about your collection. Seek out comments from your personas (in the form of individual visitors and through a feedback form on your website, using a plugin such as Mopinion or WPForms). Be responsive to any comments, suggestions or additions that you receive.

References cited

Heinze, H. (2013) "Intellectual property rights: Google vs. publishers", *DW*, 24th Feb., www.dw.com/en/intellectual-property-rights-google-vs-publishers/a-16625280

Hickman, M. (2020) "10 wonderfully weird collections", *Treehugger*, 16th Jan., www.treehugger.com/wonderfully-weird-collections-4862656

Larbi, M. (2017) "Meet the woman with the world's biggest Barbie collection", *Metro*, 6th Aug., https://metro.co.uk/2017/08/06/meet-the-woman-with-the-worlds-biggest-barbie-collection-in-the-world-6832072/

NISO (2007) "A framework of guidance for building good digital collections", *National Information Standards Organization*, www.niso.org/sites/default/files/2017-08/framework3.pdf

Romano, A. (2020) "A lawsuit is threatening the Internet Archive – But it's not as dire as you may have heard", *Vox*, 23rd June, www.vox.com/2020/6/23/21293875/internet-archive-website-lawsuit-open-library-wayback-machine-controversy-copyright

Smith, H. (2020) "'Product of theft': Greece urges UK to return Parthenon marbles", *The Guardian*, 20th June, www.theguardian.com/world/2020/jun/20/product-of-theft-greece-urges-uk-to-return-parthenon-marbles

Sullivan, D. (2014) "The Yahoo directory – Once the internet's most important search engine – Is to close", *Search Engine Land*, 26th Sept., https://searchengineland.com/yahoo-directory-close-204370

WPBeginner (2020) "5 best WordPress ecommerce plugins compared – 2020", 21st July, www.wpbeginner.com/plugins/best-wordpress-ecommerce-plugins-compared/

Further reading

Slavic, A. (2008) "Use of the universal decimal classification", *Journal of Documentation*, 64(2), pp. 211–228, https://doi.org/10.1108/00220410810858029

12 Connect – find friends and create advocates through social media

What you will learn

- Building visibility and reputation through social media
- Using social media with impact
- Building trust
- Building a community

12.1 Social media visibility and reputation

Achieving the goal in your Theory of Change will require you to engage with a volume and variety of people through social media channels. So far the concentration of your activity has been on creating content (Chapter 8) and setting up the channels that can be the venues for this content (Chapter 9). But direct interaction is also inevitably part of the causal logic that will make you more visible and build your reputation. Your starting point is friends and family. And from there friends of friends. But the goal in your Theory of Change will push you towards gaining an even wider level of visibility.

It is through social media channels that the activities of individuals and organisations become highly transparent and open to scrutiny by others. Getting positive responses through your interactions beyond friends and family takes concerted hard work. Poor behaviour can rapidly demolish a good reputation. As a result of the permanence of most social media channels, any poor behaviour will stay with you for a long time. The mangled cliche that "what happens online stays online" (Jamieson 2016) is worth subconsciously applying to all your interactions. The risk of being taken out of context either immediately or in the future (boyd 2008) is continuous. The risks become even greater when the message is a poorly received attempt at humour or a misapplied meme (Griffith 2018). The value of pausing and reflecting on your message before clicking "send" should always outweigh the pressure for any immediate witty reply.

Poor practices will also be highlighted and amplified through social media channels with similarly negative consequences. The Swedish clothing chain H&M was exposed through social media for the practice found in two of its factories in Myanmar of employing 14-year-old workers (Butler 2016). This online exposure came after a devastating fatal fire in a Pakistani factory that provoked petitions about working conditions on change. org (Prentice and De Neve 2017). The attention did force some change in the practices of H&M and other fast-fashion retailers (Robertson 2020), although the assessment is that the entire sector is still on a journey to reach fully sustainable and ethical practices.

There are many examples of poor personal practice that have had a damaging impact on reputation. Elon Musk's reference to "Pedo Guy" in a tweet about the rescue of stranded

DOI: 10.4324/9781003026587-12

Thai schoolboys led to a well-documented court case. The legal defence involved a debate about the meaning of the phrase used by Musk and the basis of its use in his childhood home of South Africa (Waters 2018). The British actor Laurence Fox eventually quit his social media presence after a series of outspoken and provocative comments online and on television that caused upset and impassioned responses from a range of different people (Bagwell 2020).

These examples help evidence some of the key principles of managing reputation in a personal context while also restating the work of Schreiber (2011):

1   Reputation is intangible – it represents all your past actions and your ability to deliver value to your personas.
2   Reputation emerges out of your actions and behaviours. It is a "collective representation" shared between yourself and your personas – and not owned by you.
3   Reputation is considered in context and in comparison to others; it does not exist in isolation.
4   Your reputation is the way that others who do not know you decide whether to trust you.
5   Reputation is based on the combination of your behaviours, communications and relationships.

Summarising reputation into a single concept, it can be seen as the trust that your personas have in you to deliver value to them on an ongoing basis. This summary rests heavily on the meaning attached to "trust" and "value". Value takes many different forms and can vary with context and circumstances. Value for your personas can be as "simple" as you delivering an emotional connection. Personal stories make a social media connection human, and it is humans who create reputation, not technology.

Considering the top ten most reputable global organisations (RepTrack 2020) also helps reinforce the meaning of "reputation" and how it is constructed. The names of each of these reputable companies will be familiar in any context. This is a key indicator that visibility must precede reputation. Reputation also crosses national boundaries – and sometimes more easily than the products themselves – as not all the more reputable companies are US-based corporations. Although five out of the ten do have US origins, more extraordinary is that four of these corporations were founded in California.

1   LEGO
2   Walt Disney Company
3   Rolex
4   Ferrari
5   Microsoft
6   Levi's
7   Netflix
8   Adidas
9   Bosch
10   Intel

Both LEGO and the Walt Disney Company have continuously been in top ten lists for global reputation over the past decade. This persistence in terms of reputation reflects a consistency in their actions and behaviours as companies combined with ongoing excellence in their products and services leading innovation in their sectors and their ability to grow and evolve with purpose while still remaining true to their underlying vision. The commitment and priority that LEGO displays towards maintaining the quality of its products manifested itself as shortages in the lead-up to Christmas in both 2015 and 2020. In 2015 the shortage was brought about by the unexpected success of *The LEGO Movie*. In 2020, the combined effects of the COVID-19 pandemic on the supply chain and the unexpected success of the Disney+ series *The Mandalorian* created high levels of demand for its kits.

For organisations, including these top ten, a good reputation also activates positive consumer behaviour (RepTrack 2020) that is expressed through:

- A willingness to buy
- A willingness to work for the organisation
- A willingness to give the organisation the benefit of the doubt

This final point also highlights another concept that is closely tied to concepts of trust and reputation: that of goodwill. High levels of trust and positive reputations build goodwill, which means that in times of crisis or in moments of poor decision-making, there is a preparedness by others to forgive. Although reputation is difficult to quantify, a good reputation stores greater reserves when the need to be forgiven arises. For LEGO, having two supply shortfalls in five years can be forgiven when the company has spent the rest of this time engaging with its most passionate community through its ideas website (ideas.lego.com) and encouraging suggestions for new and contemporary kits. LEGO also responded to requests from fans by pausing the marketing of its police-oriented kits in 2020 following the death of George Floyd and the renewed emphasis on the messages of the Black Lives Matter movement (Heater 2020).

12.2 Using social media with impact

It is a significant observation that reputation is an intangible asset that is neither "online" nor "offline". The converging distinction between media systems and media content (Johnston and Sheehan 2020) makes reputation one of your own assets rather than "just" part of your digital presence. You should protect this reputation and secure your asset. However, this does not ask the impossible by locking down something that is intangible. Your reputation is secured through a consistency in approach, being transparent and genuine and regularly engaging with your personas.

The concept of impact, creating impact and being impactful, however, takes the meaning of reputation one step further to make it proactive in purpose and intent. In other words, attempting to create impact is trying to actively influence news opinions and perspectives among your personas. For organisations, being impactful is about generating new sales – changing a consumer's opinion. For individuals, the impact you are seeking relates to your goal. Your individual impact may resolve to convincing an employer to select you, finding a life partner or building a sustainable income as an influencer.

Creating impact also amplifies the approach of previous chapters. Previous chapters talk about the creation of content as a largely passive activity, based around neutral subject materials. Attempting to create impact is about presenting a perspective or position based on your own knowledge and opinions. Attempting to create impact does bring a degree of risk and is not something that you should be attempting until you are comfortable with your channels and understand your personas. Choose the topics to engage with carefully. Engaging with debates in social media channels that are entirely based on speculative opinion can rapidly lead towards the amplification of disinformation.

The COVID-19 pandemic and the range of controversial and unsubstantiated conspiracy theories that emerged in its volatility and uncertainty are case studies in the negative and dark side of social media. The use of the #SaveTheChildren hashtag on social media by the anonymous QAnon conspiracy theory has drawn many urban middle- and working-class women into its orbit (Peterson 2020; Andrews 2020). The problem with any unsubstantiated conspiracy theory is that any rational argument that attempts to counter the opinions will be challenged by the circular logic of the theory itself.

As a useful example of this echo chamber effect, the crop of conspiracy theories during the COVID-19 pandemic claimed that the virus was a hoax, that the media suppressed the truth of the virus and that any vaccine was a mind control experiment by an anonymous global elite. Becoming immersed in conspiracy theories through social media channels also reinforced these theories as the channels are designed to continuously find more relevant matching content to follow on from what was previously viewed. The result is that conspiracy theories that originated in a US context were increasingly picked up and amplified by multiple British celebrities (Barrie 2020; Cockerell 2020). The impact on the personal reputations of these individuals can only be assessed subjectively, but in all cases, it has been detrimental.

A safer and softer step towards proactivity and impact can be achieved by offering relevant or humorous but responsive commentary to current affairs and events. There are a number of examples of personal profiles on short-form text form channels, but especially Twitter, that take this approach. The humourist and writer James Felton regularly provides this type of commentary through his Twitter channel (twitter.com/JimMFelton), weaving in references to his own work. For example, on 21 December 2020, after travel from the UK to France was blocked, the UK transport minister Grant Shapps said, "France's ban on UK transport came as surprise". and James Felton tweeted, "How could we possibly have foreseen other countries banning travel to plague island the day after we stressed the situation is so dire we were making it illegal to leave Kent". Later on the same day, he tweeted, "Congratulations to the government for finally ending freedom of movement". Felton also retweets content with a similar style and sentiment, so on 21s December 2020, Sky News tweeted, "Supermarket Sainsbury's has warned that if the travel bans on the UK continue 'we will start to see gaps over the coming days on lettuce, some salad leaves, cauliflowers, broccoli and citrus fruit', and Sarah Dempster (@Dempster2000) replied "this would not be happening if we'd voted romaine".

In the US, Mark Hamill (@HamillHimself), better known for his *Star Wars* role, has been actively countering Donald Trump's (@realDonaldTrump) most inflammatory social media statements. In one statement Trump said,

> Michael Wolff is a total loser who made up stories in order to sell this really boring and untruthful book. He used Sloppy Steve Bannon, who cried when he got fired and begged for his job. Now Sloppy Steve has been dumped like a dog by almost everyone. Too bad!

To this, Hamill responded, "Congratulations, sir! This dignified, statesman-like tweet is the perfect way to counter the book's narrative that you're an impulsive, childish dimwit". Ivanka Trump (@IvankaTrump) tweeted a picture of her family and a *Star Wars* character with the words "The Force is strong in my family", to which Hamill responded, "You misspelled 'Fraud'.

#GoForceYourself".

Impactful social media content can build visibility and reputation, but doing it well is an art that is best undertaken modestly at first, tested gently in the most forgiving of channels and practiced carefully with balance and wit.

12.3 The role of community

Building an effective online community is potentially the single most impactful thing you can do to grow your presence. By interacting with the right communities, you can move beyond family and friends (and friends of friends) to create a community of advocates. Community is built through a combination of impactful activities and developing trust. The lifestyle activity of wild swimming provides an exemplar of how these parameters intersect to engage and then build community around your own presence. Wild swimming is swimming outdoors in the sea, rivers or lakes. It has gained popularity in colder countries as a reaction to the controlled spaces of swimming pools in gyms, leisure centres, hotels and apartment complexes. Partially in response to the lockdown of facilities that was brought about by the COVID-19 pandemic, wild swimming has enjoyed renewed and increasing popularity as an activity and as a topic of conversation on social media channels. Wild swimming is a useful example of how to work with an existing community because it relates directly to physical locations and, as a result, the knowledge and information being shared is highly contextual. Because wild swimming – particularly in colder climates and in winter – does involve an element of risk for participants, the importance of trust is also accentuated. Disinformation about good spots to swim can bring the real prospect of danger to life.

Before exploring a wider community, some of the details of digitally enabled communities need to be explored. Your organic community is your family and friends. Content added to any social media channels will generally be seen by your organic community. However, the reach and, consequently, the impact of the content that is shared with your organic community will be limited. To extend the reach of any of your content will require additional information that describes the content to a wider community and, as a result, connects it to an ongoing and wider conversation. The technical label for this description is "metadata", but in many social media channels, content is labelled in this way with techniques such as the use of hashtags. The importance of this form of metadata cannot be underestimated – it is a combination of signposting (for people) and categorisation (for technology). The search function on Twitter has the hash symbol (#) as its icon. Any word or phrase that follows a # without spaces can be a hashtag. There is no set list of words to use, no permission or additional resources required to use a hashtag. There are a variety of stories – possibly all apocryphal – of managers telling their social media managers to go and buy a hashtag. Similarly, examples of minimalist content hidden amongst a sea of hashtags should be seen as a warning against this approach. Do not drown your content in hashtags. It is poor visually and does not help your reputation. The challenge is to use a minimum of high-quality hashtags that capture the intent of your content (Whatman 2020). Instagram has a list of banned hashtags that vary from the weird and rude through to disturbing and obscene (Instavast 2019). Nonetheless, a casual examination will immediately highlight what a low-quality and low-value hashtag looks like.

Simply making up a hashtag and adding it to your content is a hit-and-miss affair. If you are lucky with this approach, the hashtag you choose may be a term used by a wider community. If you are unlucky, it may associate your content with a completely unrelated community or even initiate a hashtag hijack (Setup 2016). Some research is required to understand the communities that you are engaging with. The example of the wild swimming community is usefully indicative. While the obvious hashtag of #wildswimming is used by much of the community, there are a number of other popular alternatives, such as #swimwild. But there is a danger of slipping over into another community, as #freeswim is used by council schemes in the UK to offer free swimming in gyms and leisure centres to under-fives. The similar #swimfree is used by some wild swimmers, but it is also associated with the release of captive whales and dolphins back into the wild.

Using this example, the temptation might be to include all the tags you find. However, this then tips your content towards accusations of being spam (Figure 12.1). If you view your hashtags with more of a cataloger's eye, you will recognise "wild swimming" as the overall category of activity, and you may then consider what auxiliary information would help provide better context for the content. For a wild swimmer, knowledge of the location is a vitally important piece of information in order for someone else to be able to swim there. Wild swimming is a lifestyle activity because it does not just involve the activity of swimming itself but the camaraderie, the clothing (especially warm, dry clothes after the swim and a hot drink) and the relationship to nature. The result is that a lot of wild swimming content includes photography as a form of evidence of the event. A locational hashtag ties these wider lifestyle actions together when applied to a combination of photography and narrative. A further auxiliary of affiliation or grouping will help communicate back to an informal or formal group while also adding authority to the overall content. In some cases, this additional tag will be obscure, such as #swooshers, #TOWS or #HOWLS (Outdoor Swimming Society 2020), but this links your content with the local narrative and forms a trust association with the local group (Figure 12.1). In total, three hashtags – #wildswimming, #location and #group – tie your content to context and community.

This systematic approach uses the smallest number of quality hashtags to connect with a community. The approach draws heavily from the classification schemes used by libraries (§11.2). Most useful of these are the auxiliary tables found in the Universal Decimal Classification (UDC) scheme, which recognises that any given topic has nuances and subtleties of meaning that can be more precisely anchored with a range of qualities (Table 12.1). These qualities can be used to focus your content and its description in unambiguous and useful ways.

Building a new community is best done cautiously. Does your goal require the creation of a new community or do you simply need to engage with an already-established

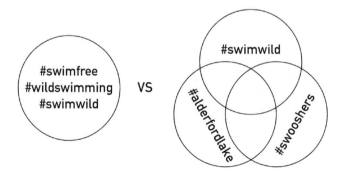

Figure 12.1 Quality hashtags to connect with a community vs spamming hashtags

Table 12.1 Auxiliary descriptors for hashtags

Auxiliary qualifiers	Usage and example
Language	To associate with a language community when the content is not in that language e.g. #deutsch
Form	Defining the intended form of an image e.g. #map
Place	To position content in relation to a specific physical location or area, e.g. #wirral
Grouping, ethnicity, nationality	Association with a human grouping whether large or small (possibly with minimal meaning outside that group), e.g. #MRUFC
Time	Connecting a post with a specific timing of the day, week or year, e.g. #wintersolstice
General characteristics	A catchall category used sparingly unless it has meaning in a specific community that could focus on the material of a thing, e.g. #stainlesssteel; the size of a thing, e.g. #big; the age of a thing, e.g. #millenial, as well as a number of others qualities such as speed, style and shape

Source: Based on UDC auxiliary tables

community? It is important to recognise that a community is not synonymous with a single channel and exists across a networked presence (in the same way that your own digital presence uses multiple channels). Often the community is linked between channels through the use of a consistent hashtag or identifier (again, in a similar manner to your own presence). The community you are engaged with may conduct some of its activity through private channels with services such as Discord(.com). Although often associated with games-based communities, Discord has many other interests represented, with group membership that can number into the millions (top.gg/servers/list/top). There is significant value in exploring the full extent of the channels used by a community before concluding that your needs are not already supported. This research will itself take time as you must build trust with the community in order to gain access to private groups.

The need to build trust with communities is an issue for leaders, organisations, salespeople and researchers, as well as for you. The various models outlining the actions that nurture trust are remarkably consistent, irrespective of the context (Tung et al. 2001; Jaffe 2018; Grenaway 2020). The actions for building trust can be synthesised down to six attitudes:

1 **Be transparent** – do not obscure the purpose of your presence in the community.
2 **Be respectful** – of the existing prevailing hierarchies, practices, quirks and opinions in the community (even if these do need to change).
3 **Be humble** – do not imply that you know everything about the community (or its focus of interest).
4 **Be reliable** – if the community places expectations upon you, be clear about your availability, capacity and capability.
5 **Be giving** – contribute to the community without immediate expectation of reciprocation.
6 **Be genuine** – do not try to create a persona within the community that you cannot maintain.

Only after you have gained trust and full access to a community can you fully assess the value that it provides back to you. If your conclusion still persists that your goal requires a new community, it should be undertaken as an evolutionary development out of an existing wider community and with full transparency. Most importantly, you must consider that attempting to establish a new community will result in a loss of trust and reputation from the members of the existing community.

If you still identify the need for a new community to service your goal, you will need to undertake the development of a digital presence for the new community. In effect, at this point, you would return to Chapter 1 and substitute "you" and "your" through this book with "the community" and "the community's".

TL;DR

Your presence needs to be visible through social media channels. Use a few high-quality hashtags (or similar) in your content. Build reputation by actively engaging in communities that are important for yourself and your personas in ways considered appropriate by that community. Attempting to build your own community should be done cautiously and only as a last resort.

Callout 12.1: Case Study – Oscar Ukonu

Afrorealism on social media

Oscar Ukonu is a Nigerian artist born in Lagos in 1993 who creates hyper-realistic portraits with a conventional blue ballpoint pen. Oscar is self-taught and has been drawing since the age of nine but only switched to the signature pen style at the age of 21 because it felt more natural. Each of the portraits takes over a hundred hour hours of work to get the high levels of detail required to produce the realistic style.

Oscar's work has attracted international media attention with articles in lifestyle and art magazines as well as stories for the rolling news media. The work itself does have a deeper political meaning too. Portrayed as Afrorealism, Oscar's work is a highly observant documentation of African people and their experiences. It is a self-conscious perspective that Oscar is proud to communicate through interviews and in their digital presence.

Oscar's website presence uses the Squarespace system.

Channel	Link	Followers	Views	Content
LinkedIn	www.linkedin.com/in/oscarukonu/			
Facebook	www.facebook.com/oscarukonuarts	71k		
Twitter	https://twitter.com/ukonuoscar	5.1k		200 tweets
Instagram	www.instagram.com/oscarukonu/	74.8k		60 posts
Website	www.oscarukonu.com/		Ranked 5,115,000th website globally	

Callout 12.2: Your action – community building and engaging

Build your organic community by ensuring that you are engaging family and friends through your different channels and that they are aware of your presence.

Identify the existing key communities that you need to engage with in order to achieve your goal.

Ensure that trust-building actions with these communities are now defined within the logic of your Theory of Change. Identify the types of outcomes that will define success in your engagement with these communities.

Observe these communities to understand the hashtags that they use and the many different channels that combined to create the community. Record these hashtags and ensure that you use them consistently in your own content.

References cited

Andrews, T. (2020) "'It feels like she's been swallowed up by a cult': Families are being torn apart by QAnon", *The Independent*, 23rd Oct., www.independent.co.uk/news/media/qanon-4chan-conspiracy-theory-cult-families-b1012147.html

Bagwell, M. (2020) "Laurence Fox quits social media following question Time backlash: 'I Am Fearing For My Future'", *Huffington Post*, 25th Feb., www.huffingtonpost.co.uk/entry/laurence-fox-quits-social-media-question-time-twitter-statement_uk_5e552d22c5b65e0f11c71a54

Barrie, T. (2020) "Why have British celebrities started endorsing American conspiracy theories?", *GQ Magazine*, 9th July, www.gq-magazine.co.uk/politics/article/british-celebrities-conspiracy-theories

boyd, d. (2008) "Taken out of context American teen sociality in networked publics", Unpublished thesis, www.danah.org/papers/TakenOutOfContext.pdf

Butler, S. (2016) "H&M factories in Myanmar employed 14-year-old workers", *The Guardian*, 21st Aug., www.theguardian.com/business/2016/aug/21/hm-factories-myanmar-employed-14-year-old-workers

Cockerell, I. (2020) "More celebrities join the growing conspiracy theory movement", *Codastory*, 29th July, www.codastory.com/disinformation/more-5g-conspiracies/

Grenaway, C. (2020) "Making the invisible visible: 5 ways to build trust with communities", *Chanel Grenaway*, 23rd Jan., www.chanelgrenaway.com/post/making-the-invisible-visible-5-ways-to-build-trust-with-communities

Griffith, E. (2018) "19 massive corporate social media horror stories", *PC Magazine*, 17th Apr., https://uk.pcmag.com/features/45759/19-massive-corporate-social-media-horror-stories

Heater, B. (2020) "Lego pauses marketing of police sets, amid protests", *TechCrunch*, https://techcrunch.com/2020/06/04/lego-pauses-marketing-of-police-sets-amid-protests/

Instavast (2019) "Instagram Banned Hashtags", https://instavast.com/instagram-banned-hashtags/

Jaffe, D. (2018) "The essential importance of trust: How to build it or restore it", *Forbes*, 5th Dec., www.forbes.com/sites/dennisjaffe/2018/12/05/the-essential-importance-of-trust-how-to-build-it-or-restore-it/

Jamieson, D. (2016) "What happens online stays online", *EngageWeb*, 11th Mar., www.engageweb.co.uk/what-happens-online-stays-online-11352.html

Johnston, J. and Sheehan, M. (2020) *Public Relations: Theory and Practice*, London: Routledge.

Outdoor Swimming Society (2020) "Wild swim groups: The UK list", www.outdoorswimmingsociety.com/uk-wild-swimming-groups/

Peterson, A. (2020) "The real housewives of QAnon", *Elle*, 29th Oct., www.elle.com/culture/a34485099/qanon-conspiracy-suburban-women/

Prentice, R. and De Neve, G. (2017) "Five years after deadly factory fire, Bangladesh's garment workers are still vulnerable", *The Conversation*, 23rd Nov., https://theconversation.com/five-years-after-deadly-factory-fire-bangladeshs-garment-workers-are-still-vulnerable-88027

RepTrack (2020) "2020 global RepTrak study – Executive summary", www.reptrak.com/blog/2020-global-reptrak-study-executive-summary/

Robertson, L. (2020) "How ethical is H&M?", *Good on You*, 30th Sept., https://goodonyou.eco/how-ethical-is-hm/

Schreiber, E.S. (2011) "Reputation", *Institute for Public Relations*, https://instituteforpr.org/reputation/

Setup (2016) "Hashtag hijacking: The good, the bad, and the ugly", https://setup.us/blog/hashtag-hijacking

Tung, L., Tan, P., Pei, C., Koh, Y. and Yeo, H. (2001) "An empirical investigation of virtual communities and trust", *Proceedings of ICIS 2001*, https://aisel.aisnet.org/icis2001/35/

Waters, M. (2018) "Elon Musk on the stand: 'Pedo Guy' doesn't mean 'pedophile'", *Wired*, 4th Dec., www.wired.com/story/elon-musk-pedo-guy-doesnt-mean-pedophile/

Whatman, P. (2020) "Social mythbusters: Does using Instagram hashtags mean more engagement?", *Mention*, 25th June, https://mention.com/en/blog/instagram-hashtags-engagement/

Further reading

Strauss, J. and Frost, R. (2014) *E-Marketing*, Harlow: Pearson Education.

13 Search – build visibility and draw an audience to you

What you will learn

- Optimising your visibility
- Using paid media to reach further
- Attracting a wider audience

13.1 Optimising your visibility

A new digital presence will have few visitors. This can be a frustrating point in the project after a lot of planning and energy has been expended for what appears to be a low return. Success will come from continuing to work your Theory of Change and being strategic.

Building reputation begins with someone else linking to your website or your profile on a social media channel. Your personas may arrive through a link embedded in social media content or on a website. However, search engines will be the primary means through which your site will be found and your visibility will be built. About 80% of all the traffic to one or more of the channels in your presence will come from clicking on a link found on a search engine result page.

Understanding the importance of keywords is a strategic advantage. Keyword research is the process of identifying your personas' intent on search engines such as Google, YouTube and Bing. In parallel with hashtags (§12.2), a keyword can be a single word or a phrase – although, unlike hashtags, a phrase can retain the spaces between the words. Keyword research goes beyond identification of a persona's intent to uncover different variations of related words that can also lead to the discovery of new topics and ideas. Understanding keywords also directly contributes to providing a better experience for your persona (or "user experience" in the technical literature).

You can categorise keywords to better recognise a persona's intent and how you could respond in terms of the content that you offer. It is possible to position these categories of keywords in a hierarchy ranging from those that are most specific and focused to the most generic and the most obscure combination of terms (Table 12.1).

The hardest persona intents to reach are the specifically identifiable keywords such as brands or specifically named products. These are searches that include "proper things" or proper nouns – any words that you are inclined to capitalise will be included in this type of keyword. Brands such as "Apple" or "Microsoft" already flag a tightly defined intent, and there may be very few opportunities to break into the intent with your own content (unless you are the thing being named). Even if your own content makes references to these specific things, it will have less weight in search engine results than content

DOI: 10.4324/9781003026587-13

mentioning those things on a domain that is the name of that thing (for example, a search for "Excel" will prioritise results found at microsoft.com and live.com over your own website).

Of course, there is also the contrary opinion, and some companies have specifically built their keyword strategy with paid media around the higher-risk tactic of presenting an alternative option to the existing "thing". The paid media strategy for Shark vacuum cleaners following the search intent for Dyson is one recent UK example of this practice.

Keywords that combine a category of things with an auxiliary qualification (Table 12.1) reveal a broader persona intent. The intent of this type of "qualified things" search is to narrow down options in order to make a final selection or decision (compare §8.2). A search of this type indicates that what is being sought out is partially known, and the purpose is to refine the options down to a personal context. Examples of these searches include "laptop in Cairo", "twilight wild swimming" and "crochet groups for millennials". Because the "thing" is a generic keyword, there are many forms of content that address this intent. Review sites base their business models on results pages for matching a location auxiliary with a particular category. The other form of content that ranks highly for qualified things is "listicles". The listicle is a list of the top five or ten (or any number) of items that match the intent of the search. For example, "Top 5 places to stay in Paxos", "Top 10 Christmas Movies", "Top 6 girl's names". Hidden behind this intent is a question, and your own content could be the answer to this question. The value of the listicle is that you are not committing a response for a single-focused intent but at a broader decision-making level.

When the intent becomes more focused, multiple auxiliaries creates a separate type of search. Because the search contains multiple auxiliaries, the phrase will have three or more keywords, and as a result, a search of this type will, in most cases, produce far fewer results. In the search industry, this category of search is described as the long tail. The term is a statistical reference that describes a situation in which the frequency of occurrences drops away from the main concept as a consequence of adding multiple additional conditions (the auxiliary terms). When this concept is visually graphed, there is a visible tail. Keyword combinations of this type are searched for infrequently and have less relevant content that the search engine can match to the intent. As a result, any content that matches this intent will be high in the result page because it targets a very specific audience. For example, a search for "Best accounting firm in São Paulo for a graduate" produces a relatively small set of useful results that would be a good starting point for anyone with the underlying intent exposed by this search.

The broadest searches are those that only identify a general category of things. The intent of these searches is more difficult to identify, and, as a result, creating content that offers a sensible response can be equally difficult. Although the volume for this type of search is very high, there are also many large organisations competing for attention around these search keywords with paid media and their own content. For example, a search for "Shoes" will produce results with paid advertisements from global brands and (if you are using Google with location awareness) results for the largest local shoe retailers. A search for "Running" will produce listicles from highly visible and reputable sources such as *Runners' World* and *Coach* magazine, as well as a Wikipedia entry and (in the UK) a link from the government's National Health Service (NHS).

Most search engines, including Google, attempt to identify the underlying intent of the combination of search keywords rather than, more simply, mechanistically trying to match terms in the keywords with the words in a piece of content. In this way, search engines are often more sophisticated than the search function offered by individual web-sites. On most individual websites, the search function is often a more traditional database that is simply trying to match words in the search with the words it finds in the content. This is why search engines for a specific site will produce different (and often better) results than the site's own search function. Searching on Google for information about the UK government's Brexit position ("Brexit site:gov.uk") produces noticeably different results from the internal function (on www.gov.uk).

The key lesson is that your content should address your personas and their (assumed) intent. Over time you will learn what content is matching persona intent and what is not. This learning can then be applied to new content – and depending on the channel, you may also set out to retrospectively tweak, edit or even delete older content.

You can experiment with intent yourself. Using the hierarchy of keywords (Table 13.1) and starting with a search for a broad category, examine the results that you receive back. To make it more relevant, use words and searches that relate to your own goal. As you move through the hierarchy, you will notice that the type of content and the source of the content will shift as you become more and more specific with your search keywords. Pay particular attention to sources around keywords that are more decision-making in their intent. The sources for the content in these search results are worth investigating as they will be particularly relevant to your goal. You can also learn more about the style and structure of this content as it can also guide you in constructing content for your own channels.

Table 13.1 A summary hierarchy of keywords

Category	*Intent*	*Potential Content*	*Scale of Results*
Proper Things	Locating	Review, Unboxing, Usage	Tiny
Category of Things with one auxiliary	Decision-making	Reviews, Listicles (of available options), Slideshow	Small
Category of Things with multiple auxiliaries	Decision-making or Locating	Discussion, Contextual description	Tiny
Category of Things	Exploring	Listicle (of decision criteria), Definition	Vast

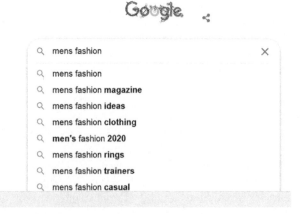

Figure 13.1 Autocomplete searches in Google reveal broad intent

You can explore search intent still further with Google. The autocomplete function in Google's search box tries to help you by adding suggestions based on the intent of previous searches and current trends around the topic.

As you continue typing more words, Google will provide further, more specific recommendations (Figure 13.2). If your focus and content are oriented towards current affairs, typing the beginning of generic phrases such as "when is", "who are" or "what is" into Google produces a list of current affairs topics. If you are able to rapidly produce content with quality commentary and insight (and it is relevant to your goal and overall value proposition), you can gain high-ranking results. However, as a word of caution, this is a tactic already employed by some traditional daily newspapers whose journalists are tasked with undertaking exactly this form of activity.

Understanding intent and keywords is big business. This type of research is the basis for the successful operation of the largest online businesses. As a result, there are a number of commercial keyword research tools available. Some of the most common tools are SEM-Rush, Ubersuggest, KWFinder, Ahrefs Keyword Explorer, KeywordTool(.io), Google Keyword Planner and Moz Keyword Explorer.

These tools all work in a similar (and simple) way: by entering a word or phrase that interests you. The response includes a list of related keywords along with search volume per month and the SEO (search engine optimisation) difficulty (SD) (Figure 13.3). A higher SD is an indication that it will be more difficult for your own content to compete with what is already available. Ubersuggest also highlights the top ten websites in the results page for the keyword (this is the SERP or search engine result page), the estimated number of visits that this keyword generates for the website, the number of links pointing to that website and a DS (domain score). The information about which websites benefit most from the visits based on this search term is a benchmark of reputation for the topic. Both sets of numbers indicate what a quality website channel looks like for this topic, with higher numbers indicating better quality.

Creating content that will attract an audience beyond the organic network of family and friends takes some research and development. By creating for your persona and their (assumed) intent, you are already creating content that is relevant and will support the

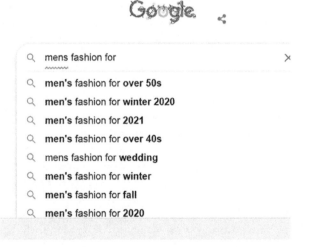

Figure 13.2 Narrowing potential intent for a topic

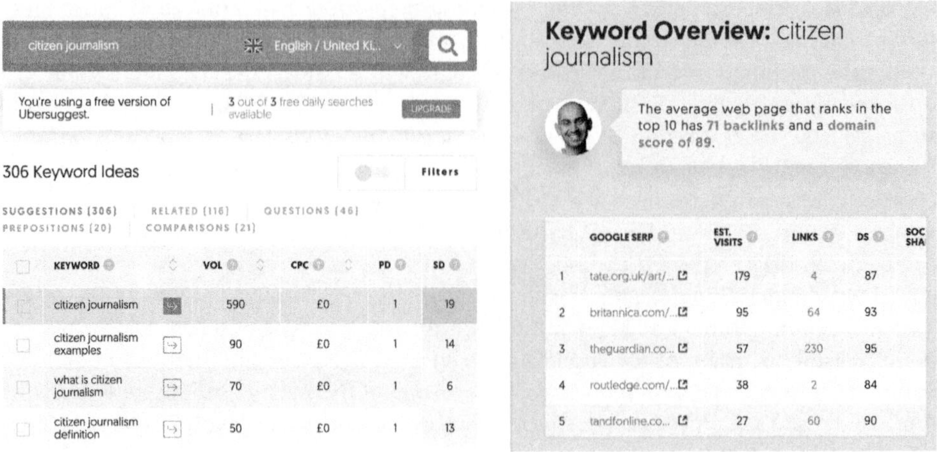

Figure 13.3 Keyword research with a commercial tool

Source: Ubersuggest

development of your visibility. The most effective focus is to create content for searches coming from long tail keywords – these are searches that describe a category of thing combined with multiple auxiliaries: the who, what, where, when, why type of questions. More research (using keyword tools) will find keywords (and combinations) that are relevant to your value proposition and have a high search volume (VOL) and low competition (SD score). Although these combinations are rare, they are worth discovering as you will be responding to an untapped need that supports the development of your reputation.

13.2 Using paid media

If your efforts to become visible in search results that are relevant to your personas are working, then you can safely ignore this section. However, sometimes a presence needs boosting to reach out beyond your organic network and build greater visibility. Paid media covers a variety of options, including print advertising, posters and banner advertising. However, in the context of this chapter and in developing your presence, the most important form of paid media will be paid search engine listings.

Using paid media will have little or no value until you have produced some content and have positioned it on your website. Focus on building the core of your presence with some rich and relevant content before using paid media.

If you have an understanding of the keywords that work best for your personas and their intent (§13.1), then you have done a lot of the development required for this approach. Effectively, paid search engine listings means bidding on your preferred keywords in order to promote your result towards the top of the first page (and have the little "[Ad]" annotation added to the front of the result). The higher the bid, the higher up in the results you will appear. If you consider the hierarchies of keywords (Table 13.1), it is clear that there are choices on which you could waste your money very quickly with minimal benefit. For your personal presence, bidding on the two extremes of the continuum with "proper things" or "category of things" may bring little value, and these are areas of activity to consider only after gaining some experience with the Google Adwords systems (or the systems used on other search engines globally or regionally).

If your research has been successful, you should be able to cover the "category of things with multiple auxiliaries" through your organic search tactics based on content development (§13.1). This leaves the "category of things with a single auxiliary" to focus on. Depending on your specific keywords and the auxiliary focus you are attempting (although it is most likely to be a city or region location), this can be a competitive space. Identify one or two keywords that you will focus on and set yourself clear budget limits. Your tactics should be to improve the quality of the results you can achieve with the budget you have set and not to succumb to a constant cycle of extending the amount being spent on a monthly basis.

The focus of much search engine optimisation (SEO) advice and information is based on the paid media aspect of working with search engines. However, the work of SEO practitioners is also often detached from any strategic perspective, aiming towards a defined goal or, most crucially, towards a personal digital presence. Despite these reservations, a significant amount of value can be gained from SEO practice for your own purposes.

Because SEO work heavily revolves around Google – and paying money to Google for the bids you make on keywords – the tools used for placing advertisements are free. (It is just the act of your link in the actual search results being clicked on that costs money.) Making use of these tools can help both your organic search results and the paid ones. Signing up and navigating the Google Ads interface is the starting point. (There is no demo account to test first.)

The Google Ads system is full of information to learn from. However, when you start, there is no history from your own campaigns as you have not spent any money yet.

In the Google Ads interface, the "Tools & Setting" icon in the top centre of the screen holds the key for some initial research. Clicking on this icon and choosing the "Keyword Planner" option gives you access to a space where you can test keywords and see what the expected outcome will be in a live campaign. Clicking "Discover new keywords", then adding a new keyword and "Get Results", will show the range of prices that will place your ad in the first page of results and the number of monthly searches. Tweaking the terms and using the keyword ideas offered by the system help. There are also options to broaden and refine keywords. There is a lot of information directly available to you, and with some effort, you can roughly estimate the size of the audience for your interests.

With some insight from the keyword ideas tool, you can return to the main screen and click the "+ New Campaign" button. You will be given a number of options at this point asking for your goal. Initially your focus is on "Website Traffic", although, over time, the real purpose of paid media will be to create "Leads". You then select a campaign type. In the early phase, you will focus on "Search", but if paid media proves to be effective for you and you have a bigger budget, then the "Display" and "Discovery" options are also worth exploring. After clicking "Continue", you can configure a number of options. To keep things simple, use only the "Search Network", target your own country, set your daily budget and select "Clicks" as your Bidding focus. From here you can set up the text of your ad and the link that will be where someone who clicks will be taken to visit. The Google Ads interface holds your hand through the process (unsurprising when this is Google's primary source of income), so you are alerted to any errors or missing information in your campaign setup.

The key function of the campaign setup is to add a keyword that will be part of your new campaign. There are three primary choices for the type of match that will be applied to the keywords you add. Broad matches are widely distributed and lack focus. The Ads interface says that "Your ads may show on searches that include misspellings, synonyms, related searches, and other variants of all the following words" (Google Ads). A tighter and more focused approach is to use phrase match, in which "Your ads may show if the phrase ' ' or close variants, appear anywhere in the search, with additional words before or after" (Google Ads). The phrase is completed when you add a keyword. The final option is an exact match where "Your ads may show for searches that are exactly, or close variants of: ' '" (Google Ads). Returning to the example of "Wild Swimming", the difference in the three forms of keywords can be tested before committing to your campaign by searching Google with these three variants; swimming, +wild +swimming, "wild swimming". Although there will be overlaps, you can also see that there is a different response from the search engine.

The use of search modifiers to replicate the matching behaviour of Google Ads is a hint to even greater sophistication with your campaigns. If you are not familiar with search modifiers, there is value in exploring their use more broadly as it can improve the relevance and accuracy of your results by better communicating your intent (Hardwick 2020). Among the most useful modifiers for general use are the "site:" modifier for searching only a specific domain. For example, "accommodation site:faroeislands.fo" produces nearly 500 links about accommodations on the official Faroe Islands website. For your campaign, other modifiers may be more useful. The negative sign narrows your search intent by specifying a keyword that must or must not be present in the results list. Using a negative (e.g. "'sports journalism' -football", instructs the search engine to not include results with that keyword. Some caution needs to be applied in the use of search modifiers as part of your keyword campaign (Google n.d.[b]). The use of modifiers is not common and overengineering your personas' intent may result in hiding your presence through paid media rather than enhancing it. If you are using paid media, it is advisable to start with some simple (but relevant) keywords and to learn from the response and effectiveness of your initial experiments.

Once you have set the bid rate for your keyword and shared your payment details with Google, you are ready to go live with this particular form of paid media.

13.3 Attracting a wider audience

The "Keyword Ideas" tool in Google Ads may very well direct you to new ideas for content and even how you present your content and the form that it takes. Expanding your content plan (§8.2) in this way will invariably extend your audience.

Google recognises the value of and the need for audience expansion by providing a checkbox that extends your ads to a wider audience (Google n.d.[a]). If Facebook is one of your preferred channels, you also have the option to increase your visibility by purchasing advertising (www.facebook.com/business/ads). The same is also true for Twitter (business.twitter.com/en/campaign/welcome-to-twitter-ads.html) and Bing Search (about.ads.microsoft.com). Multiple campaigns on multiple platforms will soon mount up the cost of your presence and may ultimately call into question its sustainability.

Before pursuing an expensive route to building an audience, you want to improve the reach of your organic search results and the integration of your separate channels into a clearly linked coherent presence. Having each channel link to your other channels will support this coherence. Taking the integration even further, you can incorporate tweets directly into your WordPress content (if it is relevant), and with the installation of a plugin (for example, youtube-embed-plus), you can embed your YouTube content into your WordPress website. You can also encourage live conversations about content on your WordPress site by automatically tweeting when you add to your website by (again) using a plugin such as WP to Twitter. As you build your presence, look for WordPress plugins that relate to your other social media channels, including email newsletters. Your website is not just a pivotal hub for your presence but can also be the workhorse to automate and manage a range of tasks that improve your visibility (another advantage of having owned media).

Having a link to your own website on the first search engine result pages is the goal being sought by all active digital presences. The central element to this improvement is about your content, but it is not about creating a greater volume of content as most people – including your personas – are saturated by competing demands on their eyes. The challenge is to create content that is concise, self-contained and ages well, even when it is linked to contemporary issues.

With a steadily expanding body of content on your website, you can also work to improve its visibility to search engines. WordPress (and other CMSes that use plugins) has a number of search engine optimisation (SEO) plugins that will help improve your visibility. You only need one plugin for SEO to be installed. An SEO plugin will integrate with the built-in publishing tools of the CMS. The plugin is useful in many ways as it enforces good practice in terms of search engine optimisation as well as, more fundamentally, good quality writing. The various plugins analyse the content and score the material for readability, sentence length, word complexity, well-structured headings and useful keywords. SEO plugins also encourage you to add meta information about your content – effectively, hashtags for your website's content. Plugins such as Yoast (yoast.com/wordpress/plugins/seo) are well respected and popular. Even if you only follow the recommendations that Yoast makes for your content, you will widen your audience by making your work more visible to search engines. The attention Yoast pays to your content will also ensure that those who visit your content will get a high-quality experience that is more likely to build your positive reputation.

TL;DR

Gain attention for your digital presence by focusing on the intent of your personas. Focusing on the "long tail" of search will help you define your content more precisely around, for example, "topic" + "location" + "another qualifier". Use an SEO plugin with your website to ensure consistency and improve visibility. Only use paid media as a last resort if your "organic" search results need a boost.

Callout 13.1: Case Study – Roi Fabioto (aka Roi Wassabi, aka Guava Juice)

Do what you enjoy – challenges and music

Roi Fabioto was born in the Philippines in 1991 and then moved to the USA at the age of two. Guava Juice is a film studies graduate who mixes a range of comedy, challenges and music into an extensive digital presence. Roi first started putting content on YouTube in 2006 and gained 100 million views with a parody of the Carly

Rae Jepson song "Call Me Maybe". Guava Juice also became the host of the *Sponge Bob Square Pants*–oriented game show "Sponge Bob Smarty Pants". The show was produced by Viacom and distributed through Nickelodeon's social media channels. In some cases, the challenges are better known than Roi and have included filling a bathtub with gummy bears and building an igloo out of plastic cups.

Although Roi is primarily on YouTube, there are also other elements to the digital presence including a website that is set up for selling merchandise. Roi creates custom-made t-shirts and hoodies with prints and stickers on them that are in high demand. Roi also has a monthly Guava Juice subscription box available through Amazon.

Reflecting the primary purpose of the website, it is built with the Shopify eCommerce system.

Channel	Link	Followers	Views	Content
YouTube	www.youtube.com/channel/UCM NmwqCtCSpftrbvR3KkHDA	16.2 m	7.8bn views	1.6k videos
Twitter	https://twitter.com/GuavaJuice	476k	1.3k likes	7.9k tweets
Instagram	www.instagram.com/guava/	1.3m		855 posts
TikTok	www.tiktok.com/@guavajuice	5.3m	64.9m likes	4 posts
Website	https://guavajuice.com/			

Callout 13.2: Your action – being search friendly

Undertake some research and development using Google Ads' keyword discovery tool to identify potential new opportunities for content and ways of focusing your content plan around your personas' intent. Give attention in your content plan to "long tail" keywords that you identify with the discovery tool.

Investigate plugins for your website that will better integrate your social media channels and the website.

Install an SEO plugin such as Yoast into your website. With the SEO plugin installed, go back and check your published content to identify and undertake any improvements that are recommended.

References cited

Google (n.d.[a]) "Using audience expansion", https://support.google.com/google-ads/answer/9496929

Google (n.d.[b]) "About negative keywords", https://support.google.com/google-ads/answer/2453972

Hardwick, J. (2020) "Google search operators: The complete list (42 advanced operators)", *Ahrefs*, 3rd Aug., https://ahrefs.com/blog/google-advanced-search-operators/

Further reading

Aull, J. (2014) *WordPress SEO Success: Search Engine Optimization for Your WordPress Website or Blog*, Indianapolis, IN: QUE.

14 Measure

From SMART to SMARTER

What you will learn

- Using analytics
- How to use Google Analytics
- Getting smarter with predictive analytics

14.1 Analytics and metrics

An important aspect of the Theory of Change is the need to iterate by revisiting your goal and outcomes. You will use metrics to understand your progress, success, challenges and issues. By using metrics in your reflection and assessment of progress, your process will be informed by real data. Measurement of long-term outcomes – including creating a successful presence – will not be possible without suitable data. By using metrics to see where you are and where you want to be against your SMART outcomes, you can assess your situation and change as required in order to stay on track.

A metric is data that can answer questions about your presence and provides the measurability for SMART outcomes. Metrics are generally quantitative – numbers focused – but could be qualitative (using the outcome of surveys, benchmarking or interviews). These are all tangible values but are, by definition, reporting what has happened in the past. As an example, analysis of your website might reveal that 500 people visited your website last month, and this was an improvement of 35 visits over the previous. This reporting should prompt a further "why" question as you endeavour to identify the ways this performance could be repeated or improved upon in the next month.

Taking the step from knowing the numbers found in the data to converting them into actions is the role of analytics. Analytics are the ways in which data provided by metrics is converted into information and knowledge. Analytics should be used to answer questions relating to your own strategy and goal. The real value and power of being strategic lies in focusing on the future (Chapter 3). Analytics focuses on the future.

Web analytics specifically is the collecting, reporting and analysis of data drawn from website activities (Usability n.d.). In contrast, digital analytics is a wider project that includes data from your website as well as other digital channels that comprise your entire presence, including email activity, social media use and organic search results (Hudson 2020). This positions web analytics as a subset of digital analytics, but nonetheless, with tools such as Google Analytics, it is a powerful part of that overall mixture.

DOI: 10.4324/9781003026587-14

14.2 Using Google Analytics

Your website is at the hub of your presence and an increasingly linked-in tool that interacts with your other channels (Chapter 13). Google Analytics is a free web analytics tool that reports on the data that it collects from your website. Google Analytics occupies about 84% of the global analytics market share (W3Techs 2020), a reflection of its powerful capabilities as well as the predominance of Google in terms of enabling your search engine visibility.

You need to sign up to Google Analytics in order to get analytics information about your website. Once you have completed all the details, your account will be created, and you will have a tracking ID. This is the unique number for your Google Analytics account. In your CMS, you can then add an analytics plugin. The majority of the plugins will walk you through the steps required to include Google Analytics on your website. You could consider MonsterInsights or GA Google Analytics, both of which are GDPR compliant for European websites, or Exact Metrics. There are many other plugins available, and applying a systematic selection process (§8.2) would be useful to support your final decision.

There are two methods to collect data about visitors to your website. The older method is through log file analysis. Every time a visitor looks at any page on your website, this data is stored, including a timestamp, an unique identifier of the visitor and the page that was visited. Your own website may already be storing a log file that can be found through your website control panel. With some web-hosting services, you have to actively switch on this collection process. As an older method of gathering data, its purpose has a more technical focus to ensure that the website is stable and performing as expected. Log files are not specifically designed to understand the intent or actions of the visitors to your website. At best, it is possible to partially infer intent from a log file.

As a result of the limitations of log file analysis, a second method called "page tagging" was developed. Google Analytics is a page-tagging tool that works by placing a small piece of code on every page of your website. Fortunately, this process is automated when you use a plugin within a CMS such as WordPress. The code is the way that data is collected and sent to Google Analytics for collation. When someone visits content on your website, the code is triggered and sends some data about that visit to Google. This process is repeated millions of times every day with websites around the world. The type of data that is sent includes

- What content was seen
- When the content was seen
- Which website the visitor came from
- A unique identifier for the visitor
- Some technical details such the browser being used and whether the content was viewed on a mobile device

In order to produce accurate data and to recognise the same visitor when they return to view your content again, your page will give an identifier to your visitor's browser, which it will store. This is a second-party cookie (Chapter 5). A cookie makes it possible for you to see what content an individual has seen when they visited, how long they were on your website and whether they have visited before. All these metrics are useful indications of a growing reputation for your presence and that your content is aligned with the intent of individual visitors. Taken together, an increasing average for these metrics indicates that you have a growing reputation amongst your personas.

Google Analytics collects two types of data. Dimensions are the "characteristics of users, their sessions and actions" and is a description of an individual's visit that can be used to categorise and align that visitor with one of your defined personas. Dimensions have a name and value. For example, "How did the visitor reach my website?" The source and medium reporting answers this specific question, and it can have many different variables.

Metrics are the "quantitative measures of users, sessions and actions". These are the behaviors of your visitors that can be measured and expressed with definite values. For example, "87 visitors arrived at your website through Google organic search which represents 0.63% of your incoming visits" (Figure 14.1).

Different combinations of metrics and dimensions let you answer specific questions. Using Google Analytics lets you measure specific outcomes in your Theory of Change, such as increasing the overall average time spent viewing content on your website. Measuring change at this specific level will provide you with the short-term outcomes that may be currently absent from your Theory of Change and will enable you to bridge any current gaps in your causal logic that may still exist. In general, your outcomes will be to increase the time that visitors spend with your content (pages) and the number of pieces of content that they visit in a single session as measures of increasing reputation. You may also want outcomes that increase the total number of visitors through specific sources/mediums as a measure of increasing visibility. Google Analytics does not improve your digital presence automatically; it provides the insight and focus that enables you to iteratively improve your digital presence.

You cannot expect Google Analytics or any web analytics tool to be completely accurate. What makes these tools valuable is that the data they collect and represent to you as analytics insight is consistently internally accurate. Consistency within a single tool enables you to measure trends over time in the form of a time series that can guide your actions and their progress towards a defined outcome.

Google Analytics includes more than 500 dimensions and metrics (Ritwick 2019). You cannot use every available dimension and metric. The goal and long-term outcomes in your Theory of Change will guide you towards what should be measured.

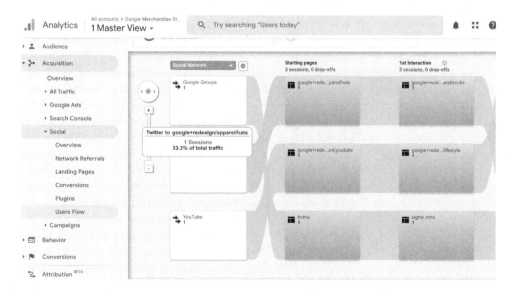

Figure 14.1 Google Analytics screen under Acquisition → All Traffic → Source/Medium tab

14.3 Smarter predictive analytics

Too often plans are made, some SMART outcomes are defined and the actions to achieve those outcomes are clearly laid out. Then all the planning and the drive towards a defined goal fades as the digital presence gets up and running.

Digital analytics can be used reactively or proactively. Using the analytics tool solely as a reporting device for what has happened is reactive. Much of the focus in literature and industry efforts centres on the reactive use of analytics to demonstrate the value that a presence has produced in previous cycles.

A mindset focused on measurement shows ambition, but it must be built on the purpose of shaping actions that support the achievement of outcomes in the future rather than just reporting. A proactive approach sets out actions based on the insight from analytics that consciously improves your digital presence. Once the actions for improvements have been deployed, there is then further measurement undertaken to understand the extent to which change has occurred.

Moving to a smarter use of digital analytics sees the challenge as a statistical one that is focused on continuously improving your understanding and definition of your personas rather than just increasing metrics such as the number of visitors or pageviews. A proactive and statistical understanding turns data into insights that feed future actions. If you listen to the sales pitches of large technology companies, it may appear that the promise of machine learning or artificial intelligence is required to move into the work of predictive analytics. However, turning data into future insights is possible now with well-established techniques.

Because digital analytics data are a time series – that is, data collected over an extended period of time – it is possible to apply predictive trend analysis techniques found in other industries such as the technical analysis of stock prices. A moving average is calculated from a subset of your available time series data – for example, the previous twelve weeks of visits – and then similar averages are calculated for each twelve week of visits, stepping back one week at a time. By charting a rolling average, you can then extrapolate which way your trend will move. Your planned actions should be seeking outcomes that not only match the trendline (as this is the steady-state situation) but exceed its performance. Using moving averages for analysis requires some understanding of your situation and context. For example, changing the rolling average calculation from a twelve-week to twenty-four-week calculation will smooth out the variations in the rolling averages and flatten down the trendline. Shortening the time period has the opposite effect. You can also bring greater sophistication to your predictions by applying exponential smoothing. This is effectively a technique that gives more emphasis in your moving average calculation to the latest numbers and downplays the numbers that happened further back in time. How comfortable you are with maths and making calculations will determine how deeply you choose to explore these types of analytics.

Analytics should understand the factors that may influence your forecast or project. A good example for searches and website traffic is the factor of seasonality. Choice of keyword search terms is affected by the season and the weather. What people do and what websites they visit also change over holiday periods such as Christmas, New Year's and more regional or religious special dates. For an academic, the break period over Christmas and New Year's is often a time for exploration. The activity on social media channels connected with academics (such as academia.com) changes as new authors and writing are discovered when there is less pressure to deliver activities against tight deadlines. Different patterns for similar reasons can be identified with other communities such as the retail sector, professional services or bargain shoppers. Understanding the seasonality on

Table 14.1 Comparison of basic and predictive analytics

	Reactive Digital Analytics	*Predictive Digital Analytics*
Purpose	Understanding audience behaviour	Improvement and differentiation from others
Decision Type	Operational	Strategic
Technology	Reporting	Predictive
ROI/ROO	Low/Medium	Medium/High
Measures	Acquiring an audience	Retaining an audience
Rely on	Information about an audience	Information from an audience
Scope	Focus on digital presence improvement	Focus on persona improvement
Learning	Single loop – repeated attempts at the same outcomes	Double loop – iterative and evolutionary with modification of outcomes if necessary

Source: Adapted from Bose (2009)

your own website will help you better understand and define your personas, and it will shape your content plans around these ebbs and flows of activity.

Fortunately, Google Analytics provides an export option for your data, and Microsoft Excel includes a moving average trendline option in its charting function.

More sophisticated statistical techniques such as regression analysis and attribution modelling can also be applied to your website time series data. Regression analysis enables you to spot any relationship that might exist between the dimensions and metrics that Google Analytics presents. Identifying this relationship shows you something of your personas' intent and how your own website is meeting this intent. The purpose of any analysis should always be to produce actions for your Theory of Change and not solely to prove your mathematical prowess.

Predictive digital analytics is also a knowledge management tool (Table 14.1). Having the opportunity to recognise patterns in your visitor activity and then making improvements should always steer you towards planned long-term outcomes and the goal in your Theory of Change.

TL;DR

Measure your presence. Use Google Analytics to better understand your website. With this insight, evolve your website to better engage with your personas. Predictive analytics can show you the expected performance of a website and the benchmark that you need to improve against.

Callout 14.1: Case Study – Harumichi Shibasaki

The "Japanese Bob Ross"

During the COVID-19 pandemic, Harumichi Shibasaki found unexpected interest in the watercolour paintings they do that are inspired by Eastern Japan and that are shared on YouTube. Born in Japan in 1947, Harumichi is described by the English-speaking media as the "Japanese Bob Ross". Harumichi watched and is inspired by this soft-spoken American who found fame in the 1980s with an effortless and soft-spoken narrative technique. Harumichi also provides instructional videos for watercolour painting. After a lifetime of painting and teaching, this change in approach only happened when, at the age 70, Harumichi taught themself how to create videos for YouTube. Harumichi presents a mixture of Japanese and English with the Japanese commentary being translated off screen by an interpreter. The style is simultaneously instructional, soothing and philosophical.

As the pandemic persisted, Harumichi also expanded their repertoire with videos about digging bamboo shoots and harvesting wild vegetables.

YouTube	www.youtube.com/channel/ UCPiQ_mEXdEbB-3Yhiq7gq5w	740k	31.5m	347 videos
Instagram	www.instagram.com/shiba_watercolor/	35.1k	3k average likes	214 posts
TikTok	www.tiktok.com/@ watercolorbyshibasaki	354.8k	3.3m	

Callout 14.2: Your action – getting analytics

Sign up with Google Analytics. Ensure you complete all the details. Make a note of the tracking ID once the account is confirmed.

Choose and install an analytics plugin for your website. Configure this plugin, including your tracking ID. And wait.

After a couple of weeks, visit the Google Analytics page to start exploring your own data. Identify the number of visitors, how long they stayed on your website and what content they viewed.

With these metrics, return to your Theory of Change and revise or refine the short-term outcomes that you have defined in relation to your website. Consider if these revisions also have an impact on your longer-term outcomes.

Revisit your Google Analytics report regularly (at least once a month) and identify any additional actions required for achieving your outcomes.

References cited

Bose, R. (2009) "Advanced analytics: opportunities and challenges", *Industrial Management & Data Systems*, 109(2), pp.155–172. https://doi.org/10.1108/02635570910930073

Hudson, E. (2020) "How to blend web analytics and digital marketing analytics to grow better", *HubSpot*, 23rd Nov., https://blog.hubspot.com/marketing/digital-marketing-analytics

Ritwick, B. (2019) "500+ dimensions & metrics of Google Analytics (with definition)", *DigiShuffle*, 25th May, www.digishuffle.com/blogs/list-of-dimensions-metrics-google-analytics/

Usability (n.d.) "Web analytics basics", *US Government*, www.usability.gov/what-and-why/web-analytics.html

W3Techs (2020) "Market share trends for traffic analysis tools", https://w3techs.com/technologies/history_overview/traffic_analysis

Further reading

Alhlou, F., Asif, S. and Fettman, E. (2016) *Google Analytics Breakthrough: From Zero to Business Impact*, Hoboken, NJ: John Wiley & Sons.

Dietrich, G. and Livingston, G. (2012) *Marketing in the Round: How to Develop an Integrated Marketing Campaign in the Digital Era*, Indianapolis, IN: QUE.

Part IV

Maintenance

15 Maintaining your digital presence

What you will learn

- The role of maintenance in a successful digital presence
- Keeping pace with change and horizon scanning
- Reflecting and revising

15.1 Maintaining your presence

As the scale of your content grows and the visibility of your presence matures, it is important to create a manageable routine that ensures that the technical systems that deliver your content are all up to date. This routine of updating ensures that any known technical issues or risks are effectively addressed. Using a content management system such as WordPress represents a fine balance between consistent ease of use and the need for regular updates of the underlying system. WordPress recognises the importance of regular updates, and the dashboard provides direct access to the current version information and whether an update is available. Recent versions can also automatically update the system. Keeping the process of updating simple is also an important aspect of maintaining the reputation WordPress has in relation to other content management systems and in relation to the web overall. Checking for WordPress on a monthly basis covers a significant proportion of the technical maintenance that your presence will require. Despite the simplicity of updating a WordPress website, a 2018 estimate suggested that over 90% of websites using WordPress were using older versions, with nearly a third overall on significantly older versions (Rashid 2018).

Maintaining a routine of regularly auditing your existing website content is also good practice. This type of audit should not be an onerous task, but a regular sense check for accuracy, quality, relevance and appropriateness is a wise precaution against undesired attention at a later date. This may be a witty comment that is not witty anymore, spelling errors, awkward phrasing or a factual error. You may have read through your content a number of times and still spot a previously unnoticed spelling error. Content that is titled "The 2019 guide to the best cities to visit in South America" was clearly outdated in 2020 and definitely in need of significant revision by 2021. An article like this needs to be thoroughly updated to include the latest circumstances. By looking at your Google Analytics data, you will be able to determine the performance of individual pages. By looking through your WordPress (or another CMS) content repository, you will be able to identify pages that need to be updated in order to stay relevant.

DOI: 10.4324/9781003026587-15

For minor updates, you regularly see websites where a piece of content will have a note such as "Updated: 21st April 2021". Some sites go even further by describing the changes that have been made – particularly for points of accuracy. Major revisions should be made transparent in this way – a reassuring marker of the attention that you give to your own content. These actions are also another way of building trust and creating reputation with your personas.

Your social media channels should also be revisited with a similar critical eye. Unlike the fully owned media of your website, there is no need to worry about technical issues as these are managed by the channel itself. An audit of your social media channel content will be a lighter touch as the editing options for existing content is different across the channels – and in some cases, it is a single binary option of keeping it as it is or deleting it. Nonetheless, your own ethical considerations (Chapter 5) coupled with shifting social norms may make the option of deleting an older piece of content the very best decision.

A less regular but further consideration for your social media channels is of much greater significance. As your presence evolves, some social media channels may become redundant for your purposes. The decision, then, is whether you should retain your presence on the channel. For example, as Triller gains leverage, should your TikTok account be retired? Reviewing the content that makes up the social media aspect of your presence should become at least an annual activity.

As you are establishing your presence, reviewing and learning from your content (through Google Analytics) should be done more frequently so that you build an intuitive understanding of your presence. An audit of your content should offer insight into many aspects of your personas. This could include:

- The content that brings the most visitors from search engines
- The forms of content that your personas prefer
- Content that needs to be updated because interest has dropped off
- Generating ideas for new content that will be appealing to your personas
- Removing content that no longer reflects your goal
- Identifying pages with misleading or incorrect meta-tags (that were added through your analytics plugin)

A regular backup of your website's content ensures that if there is ever any form of a technical failure, you can retrieve your content and not lose any content that sits at the heart of your digital presence. You should schedule backups of your site, especially before you install a new plugin or update the core WordPress system. How often you backup your website depends on how frequently you update it.

A more sophisticated approach to maintaining your website is to create a second mirror version of your site. This second version of your site can be set up with the same WordPress site (same theme, same plugins, same settings as your main site). Use the mirror site to test any updates before running updates on your live site. This is where you can test out new plugins before setting them up on your main site. You can do this on your webhosting account or you could set up a version of your website on your own computer (with a WAMP setup for a Windows computer – sourceforge.net/projects/wampserver/).

15.2 Keeping up with change

A less regularly considered aspect of maintaining your presence is the need to keep pace with the wider changes that are continuously happening with websites, content management systems and social media channels. There is a continuous evolution going on behind the scenes in all your channels. The updates that occur regularly with content management systems including WordPress reflect some of this evolution, but at the same time, there is an increasing sophistication in what is possible with the web more generally.

You can keep up to date with your existing channels by monitoring their change logs (or similar). For example, Twitter maintains a release notes page that is updated monthly with "new" features as well as "updated" and "fixed" notices (twitter.com/i/release_ notes). In most months, there are only small changes, but on some occasions, there is a significant change. For example, in November 2017, Twitter doubled its character limit for a single tweet. The impact of this one change went to the core tenets of how content is structured for this channel. However, even a number of years later, few individuals or organisations can definitely prove that they have taken real advantage of this change.

Other channels such as TikTok (newsroom.tiktok.com/en-us/product) and Facebook (developers.facebook.com/blog/) maintain similar types of pages; although the intended audiences for the announcements are more technical, there is still some insight that can be gained from monitoring these pages.

WordPress also maintains a detailed change log for each of its versions, as well as release candidates and maintenance releases. The named releases such as "WordPress 5.6 'Simone'" are the most useful for keeping up to date with the meaning and impact of the changes. One of the most significant announcements in "Simone" now makes working with WordPress even easier: "[F]or years, only developers have been able to update WordPress automatically. But now you have that option, right in your dashboard. If this is your first site, you have auto-updates ready to go, right now!" (Josepha 2020).

Beyond keeping pace with the changes being made with your existing channels is the need for horizon scanning beyond your current presence to explore new opportunities. Horizon scanning is an activity that is encouraged in all organisations, although available resources and time mean that strategic monitoring is done irregularly at best and not at all in the worst case. There is value in doing horizon scanning from your own personal point of view too. What you are doing is stepping outside your usual routines, normal patterns of behaviour and regular bookmarks. Your horizon scanning will almost certainly start with some searches. Do a search for "new social media channels". You will find lists and reviews of new services and systems – add the next year to your search to narrow the scope.

There are a number of trendwatching services that can also support your discovery. Trendwatching(.com) and Springwise(.com) are well-established websites that provide regular updates on a wide range of trends in different sectors and around the world. The vast majority of the trends that are reported include at least some aspect of being digital in their description, irrespective of the location or sector where the trend is occurring. The majority of these scanning services provide a free service with their website and as a regularly emailed newsletter. There are also paid subscriptions that offer greater detail and insight. The commercial service is intended as a type of permanently outsourced horizon scanning service for larger companies.

A further tool for continuous horizon scanning is a straightforward news feed or discovery service. Services such as Flipboard(.com) and Mix(.com) provide an app- or browser-based system that can be customised to show your preferred content on a daily basis. Because services such as these are highly customisable, identifying topics that are of interest to you will produce a stream of new content that is relevant. You can customise the feeds you receive still further by flagging the content you see as being more or less relevant. A news feed may also assist in prompting you with more immediate content ideas for one or more of your channels.

All these actions will keep you up to date with topics relevant to your goal as well as key changes that will affect your digital presence in the medium- to long-term.

15.3 The role and value of reflection

The need to regularly maintain your presence and to stay up to date with developments in social media and the web all point to the value of the wider skills of reflection, self-awareness and having a critical mindset. Just as you maintain the technical aspects of your presence by updating and auditing, you should consider applying the same attention to your Theory of Change. As short-term outcomes are achieved and you progress towards reaching your goal, there is a need to review the causal logic of your Theory of Change. As you learn more about creating and maintaining different social media channels as well as becoming more comfortable with WordPress, the timings for your planned actions will shift around. New knowledge will shorten some of your timings towards a successful outcome, but greater awareness may also bring recognition that some outcomes will take much longer and require further intermediate outcomes.

Shifting experience and knowledge may also prompt you to reconsider some of your earlier choices. A good example will be the plugins or themes that you initially chose. A primary criteria – even if it was unspoken – will almost certainly have been to choose low- or no-cost options. Your setup will now reflect this decision-making process. But increasing visibility and reputation may force a change based on what you now recognise as missing functionality for your website that is not present in the free options you are using. Using paid plugins and themes may be a decision that is now needed. Recognising missing functionality should still come through your Theory of Change. A missing outcome or the need for intermediate outcomes that can then support the achievement of already-defined outcomes will be the rationale for changing a theme or adding a plugin and not, more mundanely, because a new functionality looks "really interesting".

Greater personal digital maturity and more regular experience with the communities that you are participating in may also make you reconsider the purpose of your presence in a specific channel. This realisation will not be solely shaped by technical decisions but by your wider social and cultural experience of the channel.

The COVID-19 pandemic highlighted the fact that many corporate risk registers and disaster recovery plans were primarily paper exercises for compliance purposes. Considering what you will do in the worst possible circumstances is something for your own presence as it is for any organisational situation. A backup is one aspect of the answer in this equation. But what do you do if you have a laptop or phone stolen? What if your laptop unexpectedly and irretrievably crashes? Storing your key files in the "cloud" may be one part of the solution. You can, for example, synchronise your laptop files with a Google Drive account that produces an automatic copy in two separate locations. A further reflection is the risk to your digital presence and your Theory of Change if your own circumstances change. If you were to change your course of study or your job, get a life partner or move countries, what would happen to your digital presence? Would you continue along the pathway of the same Theory of Change, or would your goal and the longer-term outcomes shift substantially? These are all reflections on a much larger scale than solely your digital presence, but as we recognised earlier (Chapter 3), your Theory of Change itself may be much wider. Your website and social media channels are only a specific part of this much bigger picture.

TL;DR

Be reflective. Be self-aware. Be critical. Maintain a mindset that lets you explore new opportunities and then incorporate the most relevant of these into your digital presence. Consider technical improvements if they support achieving your goal. Reflect on your digital presence as part of a wider project of change.

Callout 15.1: Case Study – Meagan Kerr

Fat fashion and self-love

Born in 1985 in Gisborne, New Zealand, Meagan is of Maori heritage and has a degree in Design and Visual Arts. Meagan started their digital presence in 2012 with a blog while they were still studying. Meagan has a professional role in social media but is known because of a digital presence that combines a strong body positivity message with a keen interest in fashion. The focus of these messages is on making runway fashion more accessible in terms of price and size as well as to a New Zealand audience. Through this presence, Meagan has also become a commercial advocate for Loxy's Hair Boutique and a writer for FashioNZ.

On Meagan's social media channels, Meagan self-models the fashion items described in the content.

Channel	Link	Followers	Views	Content
YouTube	www.youtube.com/c/ thisismeagankerrblog	3.3k	604k views	85 videos
LinkedIn	www.linkedin.com/in/ meagan-kerr-19571667			
Pinterest	www.pinterest.co.uk/ thisismeagank/_created/	3k	164.5k monthly views	
Instagram	www.instagram.com/ thisismeagankerr	28.6k		1.4k posts
Bloglovin	www.bloglovin.com/ blogs/this-is-meagan- kerr-4072472	495		
Facebook	www.facebook.com/ thisismeagankerr	28.5k	28k likes	
Website	www.thisismeagankerr.com/		Ranked 3,855,400th website globally	

Callout 15.2: Your action – reflecting

Identify the sources that will assist you in maintaining a wider awareness of developments about your own interests.

Set up a routine for spending time with this material and learning from it. Jeff Bezos from Amazon describes a daily routine that includes some "puttering": time that lets him think, explore and learn (Scipioni 2020). It is a regular issue for people in all types of roles to become consumed by a daily routine of management time.

Their working days are divided up into 30-minute and one-hour blocks that are then consumed by meetings. Setting aside "maker time", unstructured blocks of two or three hours, enables more time to focus, to be creative and to horizon scan.

Take some time to consider your current plugins (wordpress.org/support/article/managing-plugins/) in relation to your Theory of Change. Over time, you may want to reconsider the use of free plugins and either get the enhanced paid version or replace a plugin entirely with a better, more appropriate paid option.

References cited

Josepha (2020) 'WordPress 5.6 "Simone"', *WordPress*, 8th Dec., https://wordpress.org/news/2020/12/simone/

Rashid, F. (2018) "How WordPress is eliminating old versions from the internet", *Decipher*, 24th Oct., https://duo.com/decipher/how-wordpress-eliminating-old-versions-from-the-internet

Scipioni, J. (2020) "Why Jeff Bezos sets aside time to 'putter' every day", *CNBC*, 25th Dec., www.cnbc.com/2020/12/25/why-jeff-bezos-makes-a-pointto-putter-every-day.html

Further reading

Hill, A. (2018) "Your digital self – Why you should keep every byte you create", *Medium*, 11th June, https://medium.com/textileio/your-digital-self-why-you-should-keep-every-byte-you-create-3a73bf0b3eb1

Sensum (2016) "The digital self: Why do we express ourselves on Social Media like we do?", 5th Dec., https://sensum.co/blog/the-digital-self-why-do-we-express-ourselves-on-social-media-like-we-do

16 Securing your digital presence

What you will learn

- The importance of security in a digital presence
- The danger of social hacking and its connection to privacy issues

16.1 The importance of security

An essential aspect of a successful digital presence is having a secure digital presence. Maintaining secure lines of communication between you and your personas should be seen as "normal". Security is another way of building trust with the people you engage with on a regular basis.

Fortunately, effective security is built into the majority of channels that you will use. Security is a challenge for everyone. The greatest risk and your most focused attention should lie with the channels for which you have taken the widest responsibility: your owned media, including your website and email. Making good choices early in the process of developing your presence will make the task of maintaining security a much easier proposition over the long term.

Having an SSL (secure sockets layer) certificate offered as part of your web-hosting package lets your website be accessed through addresses that are prefaced with "https://" rather than "http://". If you think of the "s" as being for "secure", your thinking is on track. (The "http" stands for hypertext transfer protocol – the original design for connecting websites to browsers.) In some cases, this feature is turned on automatically when you set up your web-hosting account. Having "https://" in front of an address tells you that the communications between a visitor's browser and your website have been encrypted. Even if there is no ecommerce set up on your website and no exchange of credit card information, the use of the more secure "https://" protocol reassures your visitors and is another facet of building trust in your presence.

Clicking on the padlock that appears on the address bar of an "https://" address indicates that the website uses a SSL certificate for secure communication and gives some additional details about the SSL certificate, including the name of the owner.

SSL security certificates do expire, and when they do, they will produce warnings in your visitors' browsers. These messages diminish trust and need to be avoided. Checking the details for how to renew certificates is advisable within the first year of using a web-hosting company.

Personal security practice is of pivotal importance for your owned media as well as your social media channels. The key – literally and metaphorically – to these services are your

DOI: 10.4324/9781003026587-16

passwords. This sentence is consciously phrased in the plural to reflect the most common error that is made in securing a digital presence: using a single password for every different channel. While your website and social media channels are intended to be part of your single integrated presence, these channels are all technically separate systems. Using a single password across this network means that your security is built on the weakest of all these systems. If hackers manage to compromise one of these systems and can determine your password, you have effectively opened up access to all of your channels. There are services such as haveibeenpwned(.com) that provide a checking service to determine if your email has been involved in a data breach.

Good management practice says that passwords should always be stored as encrypted data. The principle is that when you then try to log in again, the password you type in is first encrypted and then compared against the already-encrypted but previously stored version of your password. The process means that even if someone accessed your password, they could not do very much with this data. That is in theory. As recently as 2019, Facebook revealed that hundreds of millions of passwords had been stored as plain text – and were not encrypted in this way (Abbruzzese 2019).

You should also be cautious of any service that can email you your original password when you forget it. Secure practice is that you should be forced to reset your password when you forget it. There are two reasons for this. If your email becomes compromised and can be accessed by a third party, then that third party can also gain access to any service that emails a password in response to a "forgotten password" request. But a hacker does not need to have accessed your email account directly. More significantly, you should not treat email as secure. The original concepts behind the design of email paid minimal attention to security – it was designed in a more innocent time. The result is that email may be handed between multiple servers before reaching its destination, and these exchanges between servers may themselves not be encrypted or secured in any way. This all means that emails containing a username and a password can be intercepted and used without the hacker needing to access your email account directly.

Similar caution should be exercised with social media channels that do not lock out requests after a small number of failed attempts. Some services also delay the opportunity to do a new request after a number of failed attempts. Other services present a visual challenge to confirm that there is a person requesting access (rather than a robot). These tactics all prevent robots from attempting to log in thousands of times in a short period of time. This handbrake to access is not to prevent a robot attempting every single possible password combination but to slow down more sophisticated attempts that may already be aware of a previous password for a username. For example, if a password for one channel has been captured by a hacker as "CleverPassword12", then the robot may start trying to log in with this option on another channel and then try "CleverPassword13" and upwards until it finds success, or it is blocked entirely from any further attempts. The key principle that is being applied by a hacker is that humans usually choose their passwords, and humans are very often predictable with their choice of passwords.

While these scenarios may sound unlikely, ignoring this possibility is naive. There is software that can apply this logic without requiring a hacker to have extensive knowledge. Lists of illegally gathered passwords are traded through illicit digital market channels. The rise of "script kiddies" – inexperienced computer users who take advantage of existing tools and known exploits to attempt hacks – means that your website and digital presence are at as much risk as larger and better known websites. Script kiddies may even test their newly acquired hacking tools on a personal presence in the hope of going unnoticed and avoiding the consequences of tackling bigger corporations (and being caught).

Script kiddies and professional hackers take advantage of the double edged sword of security. When a security risk is identified in the WordPress system, in an operating system or on a social media channel, it is important that this is shared widely and publicly so that it can be fixed and actions taken to repair any issues that may have already been caused. At the same time, hackers may get early awareness of the security risk and exploit it before any fix can be applied. This is known as a zero-day exploit and can cause significant disruption before a solution can be designed and deployed.

While you cannot immunise yourself fully against zero-day exploits, the fundamentals of good security practice can help reduce the impact of any danger. Digital security uses the analogy of the onion to encourage good practice. By building up layers of secure practice, you make it harder for real harm to occur. Keeping your owned media updated (§15.1) is one of the ways to create an "onion layer" that helps avoid unexpected issues.

Maintaining strong password practices is another layer to your onion. There has been a lot of debate about how to create the best passwords. There is always a balance between a random string of letters and numbers (such as those used by default on Wi-Fi routers and usually printed on a label on the side of the box or sometimes the suggested option made by some systems, including Office365 and browsers) or a phrase of recognisable words. Random strings will inevitably be written down and present an immediate risk while phrases and words expose the risk of an automated dictionary attack. The optimum solution is found somewhere in between these two extremes with a memorable phrase sprinkled with random characters. Random capitalisation and the substitution of letters with similarly shaped numbers or characters are common practice – which also means they are predictable by hackers if you stick to the most obvious associations of the letter "o" with zero or the letter "l" with the number one.

Your security onion is made even stronger when you break it up into multiple onions. By using a different password for each channel in your presence, it makes each channel a separate and different problem for a hacker to crack. This is important because, unfortunately, you are encouraged to use the same or related username for your different channels to create a coherent presence. This means that the username of your various accounts that lets you access your different channels is well exposed publicly. However, for accounts for which only an email address is used as the username, there is some value in setting up a different email address for usernames than the one you share publicly for engaging your personas. This will not prevent attempts at accessing your account, but it is a further layer in the onion that will deter and slow down some script kiddie software.

Some debate has occurred in recent years about the frequency that a password should be changed. The haveibeenpwned(.com) site is evidence that this practice has value as data breaches can take some time before they are shared and the data sold widely through channels in the underground market. Some systems enforce a regular change to a password, which again brings the risk that you will continue to use a predictable and guessable pattern of passwords anyway. But many systems do not enforce any form of regular change and rely upon your own awareness of secure practice to take the initiative.

Another layer in the security onion is to ensure you are deploying the security features offered by your different channels. Many web-hosting services have filters that block suspicious requests before they even get to your website. Some web-hosting services will also include security options in the control panel. Do not turn off a security feature unless you are absolutely sure of the consequences and are convinced of the additional value that this action will bring. Some social media channels have a similar feature that will warn you if what you are doing will make your account less secure. These features are included and turned on by default for a definite reason, and making your presence less secure is rarely – if ever – an advisable course of action.

16.2 Social hacking (and other types of risk)

Social hacking is a wider and less technical form of risk that can often be harder to identify. An unintentional social hack is a suitable vignette that displays the many risks involved.

In 2020, just as former President Trump was in the final throes of his unsuccessful bid for a second term, an ethical hacker revealed that he had accessed the president's personal Twitter account (Modderkolk 2020). The issue was reported immediately but temporarily gave the hacker access to the account and a channel with 87 million followers. A number of factors made this hack more extraordinary. The hacker successfully guessed the password after the fifth attempt, indicating that Twitter was not limiting or blocking requests after multiple failed attempts. It was evident to the hacker that Twitter's two-factor authentication had been switched off by the president and that the password itself was the short and highly guessable "maga2020!". The moral of the story is compounded not just by the fact that the president was effectively wearing his Twitter password on a baseball hat but that in 2016, the same hacker had guessed Trump's previous Twitter password "yourefired" and that this had been his stock phrase as the host of the US television programme *The Apprentice* for a number of years up until 2016. In some reports, following the 2016 discovery of Trump's "yourefired" password, the hacker suggested "maga2020!" as a better alternative because of the use of numbers and a punctuation mark without ever expecting his advice to be taken so literally.

Social hacking can happen anywhere. In the workplace, a request to borrow a pen may involve opening a drawer that also reveals a Post-it note containing a password. Through email messages, a hacker will say that they have your password and compromising pictures with threats to release this information unless they are paid in bitcoin. Other emails will appear to be the login screen for a bank, a social media channel or a tax return. The link will point to a long and complex domain name that is simply an attempt to capture your username and password for that service. Even on the telephone, a hacker posing as a call centre operator will ask to authenticate details of your bank account when, in fact, they are doing the reverse and gathering your details. These attempts at getting access to your data are collectively described as phishing, and it has become a major issue. Charities such as Age UK now track and document current scams (AgeUK n.d.) as a warning for the elderly, who are among the most vulnerable to these types of crimes. More disturbing than the need for such a list is the length of the list, which documents dozens of different tactics currently being employed by criminals.

The ability to share information across platforms is both a feature and a risk. Allowing people to log into a new site using an existing social media login and password is a convenience. One of the key reasons that Microsoft bought LinkedIn was to exchange data between Microsoft cloud applications and LinkedIn social profiles. This type of seamless integration now lets an Outlook email recipient easily retrieve the LinkedIn profile of the sender of an email. At the same time, LinkedIn captures the regular contacts in an Outlook user's address book. The ability to transfer large amounts of content between social media platforms can also make a user vulnerable to serious breaches of privacy and security (Rose 2011).

A common feature of social media channels is the ability to share posts that contain links to other websites. When these are shared, others in a person's network will often like, open and share the link. Without even checking the links, multiple people sharing content acts to give a link authenticity and authority. In the vast majority of cases, this is exactly the behaviour that the creator of content wants. It is also the behaviour that provides opportunities for a hacker who can pose as a seemingly trustworthy source but then points to a link that is an insecure web page that downloads and installs malware on a visitor's devices for the purpose of collecting their personal data. There have also been instances when these malware scripts have been embedded in promoted YouTube videos and used to skim personal information (Kunwar and Sharma 2016; Zhang and Gupta 2018).

From the point of view of your own digital presence, you should be conscious that you are not enabling activities of this type. It is a question of trust and ethics. The biggest risk within your presence is your website and particularly any free plugins that you have chosen to use (§15.3). In some cases, plugins can share data with a third party without your knowledge (§5.2). Markup's Blacklight system (themarkup.org/blacklight) examines a website to expose this type of third-party sharing. It documents the use of Google Analytics – which you have set up yourself – but there are other forms of third-party sharing that may be surprising to you and even more so to your visitors. Even UK university websites, which might be presumed to be relatively free of this type of data sharing, reveal a significant number of cookies (§14.2) being set with large commercial organisations such as Warner Media. Cookies shared with a third party enable a visitor to be tracked across multiple websites, building up a wider picture of overall behaviour and preferences. The value of this cookie to the host of the website may be minimal but sufficiently useful to justify its use. However, the value of this one cookie – through its aggregation with the actions of millions of users across thousands of websites – will be noticeably greater to the third-party corporation.

There is value in using other online tools for checking your website. Tools such as the Ionos checker (ionos.com/tools/website-checker), the Ryte checker (ryte.com/website-checker) and the Alexa service (alexa.com/siteinfo) all provide more insight about your website from the point of view of a visitor.

TL;DR

Ensure that your digital presence is secured with layers of precautions. Use unique passwords across your channels and regularly update them. Ensure that your website is using up-to-date software in its CMS and plugins. Do not let your digital presence unwittingly become a vehicle that enables hackers to access personal information from others.

Callout 16.1: Case Study – Celeste Barber

Australian comedian

Born in Australia in 1982, Celeste Barber is a comedian who uses domestic situations and everyday observations as the basis for their material. Celeste's husband, Api Robin, often appears in the content as a collaborator but also as the target of the joke.

Celeste began and trained as an actor, appearing as characters in a number of Australian television shows before focusing on comedy. In 2015 Celeste started using Instagram and began imitating the poses and clothing styles of models and famous people. The focus of the humour was on how impractical the clothing was in an everyday context.

Celeste has also authored two books, *Challenge Accepted* and, for children, *Celeste the Giraffe Loves to Laugh*. Through their influence, Celeste raised $50 million AUD for the Rural Fire Station following the 2019–2020 Australian bushfires. It was the largest amount raised for a charity through Facebook.

In 2019 Celeste also started a podcast featuring some famous friends on the new service Luminary.

Celeste's website uses WordPress as the CMS with plugins such as Font Awesome, Instagram Feed for WordPress, Yoast, Formidable Pro Form and WooCommerce.

Channel	Link	Followers	Likes	Content
Instagram	www.instagram.com/celestebarber/	7.5m		1.3k posts
Facebook	www.facebook.com/ officialcelestebarber/	3m		2.3m posts
Twitter	https://twitter.com/celestebarber_	112k		1.5k tweets
Website	https://celestebarber.com/		Ranked 3,821,000th globally	

Callout 16.2: Your action – being secure

Consider the security across all your channels. Your passwords should be strong and distinct for each different channel. You should use separate passwords for your web hosting and for any email accounts that are part of your web-hosting service.

Check that your website is using "https://" for all your visitors requests. The most straightforward approach is to use a plugin designed for the purpose. Easy SSL or Really Simple SSL are two options to consider.

Use the tools suggested in the chapter to view your website from a technical but visitor-orientated perspective. Address the recommended changes by incorporating these actions as part of your Theory of Change.

References cited

Abbruzzese, J. (2019) "Facebook says it left 'hundreds of millions' of user passwords unencrypted", *NBC News*, 21st Mar., www.nbcnews.com/tech/tech-news/facebook-left-hundreds-millions-user-passwords-unencrypted-n985876

AgeUK (n.d.) "Latest scams", www.ageuk.org.uk/barnet/our-services/latest-scams/

Kunwar, R. and Sharma, P. (2016) "Social media: A new vector for cyber attack", *International Conference on Advances in Computing, Communication, & Automation (ICACCA)*, Spring, pp. 1–5, https://doi.org/10.1109/ICACCA.2016.7578896

Modderkolk, H. (2020) "Dutch ethical hacker logs into Trump's Twitter account", *de Volkskrant*, 22nd Oct., www.volkskrant.nl/nieuws-achtergrond/dutch-ethical-hacker-logs-into-trump-s-twitter-account~badaa815/

Rose, C. (2011) "The security implications of ubiquitous social media", *International Journal of Management & Information Systems*, 15(1), https://doi.org/10.19030/ijmis.v15i1.1593

Zhang, Z. and Gupta, B. (2018) "Social media security and trustworthiness: Overview and new direction", *Future Generation Computer Systems*, 86, Sept., pp. 914–925, https://doi.org/10.1016/j.future.2016.10.007

Further reading

Cernica, I., Popescu, N. and Tiganoaia, B. (2019) "Security evaluation of WordPress backup plugins", *22nd International Conference on Control Systems and Computer Science (CSCS)*, Bucharest, pp. 312–316, https://doi.org/10.1109/CSCS.2019.00056

Part V

Extending

17 Extend your value proposition

What you will learn

- Iterating over your presence
- Monetising your presence
- Extending your presence

17.1 The value of iteration

We have already established that you want a digital presence to achieve some form of change (Chapter 2). You have been inspired by the case studies presented throughout this book that a successful presence comes from being passionate about your skills or knowledge and communicating them genuinely and openly. You understand the value and purpose of thinking strategically. But without seeing your presence as a single integrated system, your efforts may begin well but will soon drift away from your desired goal. We have seen dozens of students and clients who have started with promising developments but abandoned their projects because they became too onerous, too muddled or too complex.

The Theory of Change is based on common sense. The focus of this approach is on revealing the assumptions and the intermediate outcomes required to reach your planned goal. These are aspects of project planning that are often overlooked with other approaches. The Theory of Change also encourages you to think of your actions, output and outcomes all interconnected and working together as a single system. A systems-based view of what you are endeavouring to achieve is also invaluable to ensure longer-term and overall success.

A systems perspective is what ties the steps described in the previous chapters together. The consequences for not accounting for the discussions in any one of the previous chapters are not fatal to the overall project. You will still build a digital presence, and it may be successful. In fact, many people start the development of their digital presence every day. However, the question is not about starting the project but rather about bringing the work to satisfactory versions of the planned result – an outcome that is less commonly realised.

This is the benefit of taking an iterative overview of your digital presence. By viewing your digital presence as a system, you can start small with only one or two social media channels combined with a website. Learning from this small system will then give you the confidence and knowledge to extend and build a wider presence.

DOI: 10.4324/9781003026587-17

Iterative development is a common concept among developers, who aim to create and release their minimum viable product (MVP) as soon as possible. This is the version of their product that delivers the minimum value to their personas and sets down a public intent for the future iterations of the product. Even when Google was one of the world's largest corporations and its search engine predominant in the English-speaking world (and beyond), many of its products were labelled "beta". The traditional concept of a beta release is that it is the first time a developer is prepared to share software or a service outside their organisation (or their closest circle of friends). The "beta" tag acknowledges that the release will contain bugs, may not respond correctly or, in some situations, may fail completely. Google and many of the other large organisations offering large-scale digital services extended this idea with a "perpetual beta". This label marks a digital service as being in a constant state of flux and has included email, search engines, mapping and collaborative editing tools. This form of soft-touch warning is despite the services being intended for a mass market and already used by millions. By not necessarily being guaranteed safe for critical operations (a key meaning of "beta" software), a perpetual beta development has agility, fluidity and flexibility that is appealing for many people as it responds to their needs more readily than other forms of more traditional software.

Google's resources and its commitment of setting aside 20% of its staff time for "maker time" are also part of this iterative perspective towards development. In order to reach "perpetual beta", Google ideas have to come from somewhere (they have to become "alpha" somewhere), and this was represented with the now retired Google Labs. Features that are in Google's search, such as similar images as well as Gmail labels, all graduated from the alpha state of Google Labs. For many years, the experiments in Google Labs were also accessible (which breaks the concept of "alpha" as an internal testing phase). Google now has its experiments site (experiments.withgoogle.com), where ideas generated by developers using Google products share their work.

Google and its activities present the example of an organisation with significant size and resources. However, the underlying thinking applies to organisations of any size as well as individuals. The principle is to create the environment for iterative development and growth. Starting modestly and building incrementally (one social media channel or WordPress plugin at a time) ensures that each step you take is sustainable and useful. If one step forward does not deliver the right results, you can easily step back to the previous situation that was working and was sustainable in order to explore alternative pathways. This is also arguably a miniature version of the "fail fast; learn faster" mindset. The Theory of Change is a useful tool for this type of iterative thinking because it is constantly asking you to think about the logic and purpose of your current actions in relation to longer-term outcomes and your goal.

In contrast to the iterative and incremental approach of Google, the history of Yahoo! provides a case study in taking a reactive outlook. After emerging as a curated directory of web resources, each addition to the service was a case of catching up with other services. When Yahoo! Mail did attempt to step ahead of the emerging Gmail service by offering 1Gb of storage, this technical advantage was easily matched by the greater resources of the search engine giant. The attempted takeover of Yahoo! by Microsoft was ultimately rejected because the company's directors claimed that the offer undervalued its worth. After a quarter of a century, Yahoo! is now primarily a news aggregator, with an email service and a Bing search form competing with the many much newer services that have a similar set of offerings (and without the burden of Yahoo!'s history and multinational corporate ownership).

17.2 Monetising your presence

Throughout this book, the question of monetising your presence has been somewhat overlooked. Many of the case studies presented through the chapters are individuals who earn significant annual incomes with their successful presence. We have taken the view that very few of the examples shown in the case studies created this presence with the express goal of creating a career in this manner but rather started the much vaguer intention of sharing their interests, skills, knowledge, desires and hopes. This perspective is an admittedly idealistic authorial vanity.

Because earning an income through social media channels or your website is primarily based on the volume of traffic you are generating; the metrics relating to visibility are also relevant to monetising your presence. Monetising primarily involves mixing commercial advertising with your content, although there are other routes to consider also. One of the reasons that YouTube figures heavily in the profiles of the various case studies throughout this book is because of the relatively clear route to monetisation.

For YouTube, having 1,000 subscribers, 4,000 hours of viewed video and agreeing to abide by the terms of service sets you on the path to monetising your presence with the YouTube Partner Programme. Payment rates are measured by the "cost per thousand (mille)" or CPM views charged to the advertiser and then determined by the split that goes to YouTube and the content creator. The amount does vary significantly by region, advertiser and the content itself. This means that at the lowest end of the range, the payment to you as a content creator could be $0.30 USD but rising up to $10 USD for the most successful YouTubers – known as the Google Preferred and the top 5% of all content. This means that payment ranges from $0.0003 USD to $0.01 USD per view. And using this financial perspective, you can consider the case studies presented throughout this book to identify the very approximate lifetime earnings on YouTube for each individual.

The Google Ads account that you need to set up for YouTube is also one of the routes to monetising your website. The Google Ads platform is not only an opportunity for delivering your paid media but also a way of accepting payment on your owned media. The Google Ads platform can be enabled on a website, provided there is sufficient traffic, by adding some code into your pages. Fortunately, this can be done relatively easily by adding a plugin such as Site Kit (support.google.com/adsense/answer/7527509). Google offers some indication of the potential income that can be earned by hosting advertisements depending on the locations, topic and scale of the traffic on the website (google.com/adsense/start/). For example, a beauty and fitness website based in Europe with 50,000 page visits a month would expect to earn $4,200 USD each year while a website from Asia with 252,000 monthly visits with a gaming focus would expect an income of around $22,220 USD each year.

Other social media channels also have programmes to support monetisation, such as Twitter, where video content can accept an ad to appear before the main content plays (help.twitter.com/en/using-twitter/how-to-monetize-in-media-studio). However, there are other methods of monetising content that go beyond using the advertising systems pre-built into the channels themselves. Sponsorship from an organisation is possible but will generally be premised on a significant volume of views for the content you are producing. This is an approach employed by high-profile UK-based plumber, YouTuber and maker Colin Furze, who is sponsored by eBay to deliver a project based on materials entirely sourced through the eBay portal. This relationship has resulted in full-scale replicas of a *Star Wars* Tie Silencer (colinfurze.com/tie-silencer.html) and an *Avengers* Hulkbuster. While any commercial relationship is undisclosed, there is evidence that an individual with a well-recognised presence on Instagram can earn over $1,500 USD for an image that references a sponsor. The value of the role that individuals with large followings have in a commercial sense and their ability to influence is well established. Many talent agencies worldwide now represent these influencers in the same way that film stars have been represented for nearly 100 years since the early heyday of Hollywood (Secret Agent Man 2013).

Commercial endorsements and sponsorships through your social media channels and website are controlled by laws within your own country. The specifics of the laws do vary from country to country, so you need to familiarise yourself with the requirements if this is part of a pathway outlined in your Theory of Change. A common criticism is the use of a tweet by someone with high visibility to endorse a product. Without clearly stating that the tweet is an endorsement, the practice can at least offend some followers and at worse could be illegal. Different laws and regulations can generally be found online: for example, for the UK, at tinyurl.com/UK-ASA-guidelines; for the US, at guides.loc.gov/influencer-marketing/regulations; and for Australia, at tinyurl.com/Australia-ACCC-Guidelines.

A further method for monetising your presence is through ecommerce or merchandise that extends your presence in an entirely new way and beyond the realms of the digital. In the spirit of the punk bands of the 1970s, merchandising can be done in a number of ways and can be successful with relatively small followings if your items match your personas' sentiments. The original handmade memorabilia from the punk era can now attract significant price tags (eddielock.co.uk/collections/memorabilia).

There are a number of steps for merchandising. The first step is to identify designs and content that are strong candidates for your personas. These might take the form of a strong image that you use consistently through your presence (§10.2) or a phrase that you are prone to overusing. You may choose to focus on longer forms of content. For example, this could be a selection of the best content from your website or a collection of images you have created for Instagram. The type of content that you identify clearly influences the physical form of the merchandise that you are creating.

Time invested at the design phase of your merchandising development will support a sustainable perspective (as with all aspects of your presence). You may focus on a very small number of merchandising options with a high-quality specification, such as embroidered or hand-painted rather than digital printed designs on your t-shirts. Your merchandise is part of your presence and should reflect the design sentiment you are representing in all your other channels (Chapter 10).

After identifying some candidate content or designs, you have a choice to make regarding the production. It is possible to order items in bulk from a supplier, store them and then arrange the delivery of individual items as they are ordered. The advantage of this more traditional approach is a higher financial return from each sale. It may also give you an opportunity to work with a supplier who is local to you. There are some key provisos as this is an approach that is best done at large scale and with sufficiently appealing items to be sold quickly. (Otherwise, there are then storage costs to consider.) In other words, the classic challenges that are faced by all retail businesses. These challenges are all compounded if your merchandising efforts focus on sized items such as t-shirts. Unless you know your personas very well, getting the right mix of sizes in a large order could produce a surplus of one size and a shortage in another (provoking a need to then bulk reorder).

Fortunately, there is a production method to shortcut much of this complexity. The concept of drop-shipping is well established and removes the step in the process in which all the merchandise has to pass through your hands before being sold to your followers or fans. Most drop-shipping companies produce an item on demand as it is ordered, meaning that for items such as t-shirts, there is never a shortage of the most in-demand sizes. Drop-shipping companies can also add different items to their inventory that you can then customise. For example, drop-shippers responded to the massive increase in demand for face masks during the COVID-19 pandemic (Case Study 7.2) and let customers add a customised design to these items as easily as anything else in their inventory. Services such as Vistaprint and Zazzle offer a wide range of items that can be customised and shipped directly to your customers through their corporate portals (for example, Vistaprint's Pro-Advantage). Some companies focus more tightly on a specific product like t-shirts (for example, tshirtstudio.com). An added advantage to this approach is its scalability. You can start off very small, but the system behind these suppliers can (and does) handle thousands of orders a month.

Before committing to a drop-shipping approach, you should check that the company ships to at least the majority of locations where your personas are found. Given the ethical concerns about the source and labour associated with items such as t-shirts, you should also satisfy yourself that the ethics of the company align with your own (§5.1 and §12.1). A further consideration for your choice of supplier will be the amount of design support that is offered. This type of support costs money and will reduce the amount of income that you will receive initially. In the longer term, strong designs will help give your merchandise longevity and wider appeal. Alternatively, working collaboratively with a local designer with a supplier chosen for their ethical stance and the quality of their items can produce a more satisfying arrangement that aligns closely with your own perspectives.

Books can also be created with the drop-shipping approach. Amazon offers Kindle Direct Publishing (kdp.amazon.com), which uses Amazon's own printing resources to produce your book on demand as it is ordered. This approach can enable an author to respond quickly to current affairs and circumstances (for example, Connock 2020). However, if you are confident about your book idea and the content has a timelessness, the value of a traditional publisher should be considered. The process of pitching an idea and having it reviewed by the publisher can be valuable in tightening up your ideas and really focusing on the intended persona for your work. The financial return from this form of publishing may be less to you personally, but the marketing reach that this type of collaboration provides can bring in a global audience and noticeably widen the audience for your digital presence.

Once you have determined the production process, there is the final stage of enabling your personas to buy your merchandise. Adding an ecommerce plugin such as Shopify or Odoo to your WordPress website is one approach to merchandising. If you have already taken this approach to curating content (§11.2), adding some merchandise may be a natural and logical extension that complements the development of your presence. If you are using a drop-shipper, there are plugins (such as SC Simple Zazzle and the more generic Printful) that let you easily drop links into your content that then connect directly to a product you have created. Others, such as Vistaprint, let you create a shop front through their site. If you consider this approach as an additional channel for your presence, you can then add links from your own website, in an email newsletter and on other channels.

If you have aspirations to founding a startup based around physical items, then monetisation is an immediate concern and would be built into your Theory of Change as a longer-term outcome. Drop-shippers supplying your merchandise to your customers are then primary channels to develop within your presence.

17.3 Extending your presence

If you search for "Tiger", "Grogu" or "Alkane" using Google on your mobile device, you get a response that moves a digital presence beyond flat text or images. The 3D search results arguably challenge the original four forms of content that we have described (§8.1). Although the results are images, they are lifted beyond the page and offer an additional dimension to existing content. Although limited in utility now, there is the real potential of being able to explore an entirely virtual space with a mobile device. The prospect of this form of navigation and linking together of digital spaces makes a compelling case for considering how to extend your presence in different and unexpected ways.

The development of the Oculus Quest into a relatively accessible consumer device supporting 3D content is one direction of travel for the technology (Kohn 2020). 3D virtual reality is also a direction being pursued actively by large companies such as Microsoft to reinvent the business meeting. The COVID-19 pandemic provided impetus to move away from physical face-to-face meetings and necessitated reconsideration of the value of travelling long distances for these meetings. The impetus led to long-term development and a persistent change in practice. 3D virtual meetings offer new prospects for your own digital presence to include small group meetings and workshops as a different way of engaging with your personas (and to get to know them better). Virtual workshops can help showcase your ideas in a newly engaging way that is also ethically sustainable as your guests avoid the need for long plane flights or car journeys.

The release of Apple's iPhone 12 with its built in lidar scanner offers another trajectory for new forms of content (Stein 2020). The scanner enables software on the phone to calculate its position within a physical space. The same technology is used in autonomous vehicles to avoid collisions, and its purpose in a phone is not dissimilar. By positioning the phone inside a room, it is possible to map the room itself as a digital twin. This means your phone can record the details of the room as well as the position of its contents. With the right software, real estate agents could build a virtual mockup of a property on their itinerary very quickly and enable clients to visit virtual versions of houses they are interested in purchasing. For your own presence, a lidar scan of a location could help your personas understand the location in new ways. This level of detail could even help create richer engagement by, for example, asking about objects they can see in the digital twin. The application to games is also readily apparent. It could be possible to customise an already-available generic game engine with your own location data, allowing you to create a game built around your own presence. The high-profile augmented reality game Pokémon Go and its parent company, Niantic, are already exploring the use of lidar to enable the creatures in the game to hide behind physical objects (such as trees and fences) that are between the player and the location of the Pokémon. The game is also the engine to build a crowd-sourced lidar-mapped digital twin of the physical world that players can engage with globally (Matney 2020).

A more immediate technology that can be explored as a new channel for your presence is voice. The popularity of digital personal assistance devices such as Amazon's Alexa, Google Home Assistant and Apple's Siri, as well as independent open-source developments such as Mycroft(.ai), already makes a voice channel a viable option. At the simplest level, a podcast that you produce can be listened to through one of these assistants already and without intervention from you. But if the idea is right and your personas are the sort of people who use digital assistants, it may be possible to go one step further and create content that interacts through an assistant. On Alexa, these are called "skills" (Amazon n.d.); Google calls these "smart actions" (Google n.d.); and for Siri, these are "commands" (Apple n.d.). However, distributing these interactions beyond your own personal devices does enter the realm of more complex technical developments for the moment (although you could explore this opportunity now by hiring expertise sourced through Fiverr.com).

In contrast to digital voice assistants that sit in the home or on the phones of your personas, sitting on the web are the new wave of chatbots. Already used regularly by large service organisations, a chatbot attempts to create a human conversation with visitors to a website by answering questions that are asked by visitors. There is some variability between chatbots in terms of their capability, and this form of technology benefits from being "trained" with previous conversations that have happened between humans about the same (or very similar) topics. Good chatbots can convince many people that they are speaking to a human, but poorly trained and designed chatbots can be spotted straight away. The technology behind chatbots is constantly improving, and there will be increasingly more "good" and far fewer "poor" chatbots. There are already chatbot plugins for WordPress, such as Chatbot for WordPress, Tidio Live, IBM Watson and Chatra to explore. As with all plugins, though, consider the purpose and value of the plugin for your personas and judge the candidates based on clear systematic criteria (§8.2).

All these potential extensions to your presence dip into the world of technical development and coding. However, there is a final development that may not push you towards learning this skill set (although see §18.2), but rather the capability may come to you in the form of "no-code" or "low-code" solutions. The concept is that by using an intuitive and visual interface, it is possible to design and develop apps or applications without writing code. There has been a movement towards lowering the boundaries to application development for many years, and many attempts have been made to achieve this goal, most notably with Microsoft's Visual Basic in 1991. Technology has developed significantly since this earlier product was retired in 2008, and there are now a number of companies pushing this boundary of possibility once again. Bubble(.io) and glideapps(.com) attempt to simplify the process for anyone. Glideapps, as an example, attempts to take a Google Sheet (a spreadsheet) and automate the process of turning it into a mobile app. Depending on the complexity of purpose, the outcomes can be high quality and as compelling as an app handcrafted by professional developers.

New technology developments emerge constantly. Some are fads while others are the third or fourth attempt to introduce a technology. As with so much of your presence, the first question should not be "How can I use this?" but rather "How would my personas benefit from this?"

TL;DR

Start small with your digital presence and build up iteratively. Learn rapidly from little mistakes and take pursue alternative options to achieve your outcomes. Monetising your presence is possible in a number of different ways. YouTube requires an existing large following, but you can already explore merchandise and sponsorship with a smaller audience. Be conscious of new developments in technology that would enhance your presence. Not every new technology will be a valuable option for every presence.

Callout 17.1: Case Study – Jeffrey Lynn Steininger Jr. (aka Jeffree Star)

Challenging assumptions and earning a significant income

Born in California, USA, in 1985, Jeffree Star is one of the most high-profile YouTube personalities and one of its highest earners. Although known primarily as a makeup artist (and heavy eye makeup), Jeffree is also a singer, DJ and fashion designer with the debut EP *Plastic Surgery Slumber Party* going to number one on the iTunes dance chart.

Jeffree used their life savings to launch a make-up brand (a notoriously tough market to break into as a new brand) but through the use of social media recognition has built the project into a multimillion-dollar company. Jeffree's estimated earnings from YouTube in 2020 were $15 million USD, reckoned to be the tenth-highest income from YouTube (Haasch 2020).

Before Jeffree became high profile on social media, their father died when they were six. Later, they discovered an interest in makeup at age 13 and worked at makeup counters in Los Angeles once they finished school. Jeffree had previously made several racist comments through social media but in 2017 apologised for previous behaviour and acknowledged that this form of comment was not acceptable from anyone.

Jeffree's website is created with Shopify and a number of add-ons such as MailChimp and Facebook Pixel.

Channel	Link	Followers	Likes	Content
YouTube	www.instagram.com/ jeffreestarcosmetics/	16.9m	2.4bn views	387 videos
Facebook	www.facebook.com/ JeffreeStar	3m	3m likes	
Twitter	https://twitter.com/ jeffreestar	7.1m		39.9k tweets
Instagram	www.instagram.com/ jeffreestarcosmetics/	7m		6.2k
Website	https:// jeffreestarcosmetics. com/		Ranked 25,200th website globally	

References cited

Amazon (n.d.) "Build skills with the Alexa skills kit", https://developer.amazon.com/en-US/docs/alexa/ask-overviews/build-skills-with-the-alexa-skills-kit.html

Apple (n.d.) "How to customize voice control commands on your iPhone, iPad, and iPod touch", https://support.apple.com/en-us/HT210418

Connock, A. (2020) *You're on Mute!: Optimal Online Video Conferencing – In Business, Education & Media*, Goring: Bite-Sized Public Affairs Book.

Google (n.d.) "Create a smart home action", https://developers.google.com/assistant/smarthome/develop/create

Haasch, P. (2020) "These were the highest paid YouTubers of 2020, according to Forbes estimates", *Insider*, 19th Dec., www.insider.com/youtuber-money-rich-richest-top-jeffree-star-mr-beast-paid-2020-12

Kohn, E. (2020) "VR can be the film industry's future, but the barriers to entry are surreal", *IndieWire*, 7th June, www.indiewire.com/2020/06/virtual-reality-could-save-film-industry-1202234384/

Matney, E. (2020) "To own an AR future, Niantic wants to build a smarter map of the world", *TechCrunch*, 11th Nov., https://techcrunch.com/2020/11/11/to-own-an-ar-future-niantic-wants-to-build-a-smarter-map-of-the-world/

Secret Agent Man (2013) "The history of Hollywood agents", *Backstage*, 26th Aug., www.backstage.com/magazine/article/history-hollywood-agents-12929/

Stein, S. (2020) "Lidar on the iPhone 12 Pro: What it can do now, and why it matters for the future", *CNet*, 27th Dec., www.cnet.com/how-to/lidar-sensor-on-iphone-12-pro-and-ipad-pro-2020-what-it-can-do-now-and-future/

Further reading

Bland, D. and Osterwalder, A. (2019) *Testing Business Ideas: A Field Guide for Rapid Experimentation*, Hoboken, NJ: Wiley.

18 Digital by default – future tools and opportunities

What you will learn

- Exploring the value of creativity
- Exploring the value of technical skills
- The parameters of the future

18.1 Creativity

Throughout this book, you have stepped through a series of actions and read examples of people creating a strong digital presence. Throughout this book, its guidance has emphasised the skills that are most valuable to you for creating a digital presence. Discussing content and consistency has hinted at a skill that is valuable and sometimes overlooked in a digital context; that skill is creativity.

As a content creator, you have to continuously come up with ideas that are engaging. That is a hard task. The task is still harder because the standard for what is considered engaging is always shifting. Content that would have been regarded as compelling five years ago is just seen as average today. Creating content can become an exhausting process if you do not harness your own creativity. The idea of an eccentric inventor, rogue programmer or disheveled artist painting in a basement is the typical Hollywood caricature of a creative individual. As with so many Hollywood portrayals, the truth is much more mundane but fortunately more inclusive. "Creativity is commonly defined as the production of something that is both original and useful" (Bronson and Merryman 2010). We are all creative in different ways, but so often our channels to express this side of our skills are progressively shut down as we progress through the years of our formal education. Developing a digital presence provides so many opportunities to open new channels for the expression of your creativity.

Sometimes being creative requires a technique to get your ideas going. At the very least, having a regular routine for producing content and putting it on your website will help this happen. A routine places the pressure of a deadline on you, and this itself will always force some creativity out of you.

More systematic techniques can drive your creativity even further. The principle is similar across the many techniques. By posing a challenge question, your creativity is pushed to discover a solution. The best challenge questions are "big" questions that help reduce pain for your personas. But smaller-scale questions such as "How can I best represent this data?" can also work. Because you are in control of your content, the response to the challenge question does not have to deliver the actual solution, but it could be a description of the

DOI: 10.4324/9781003026587-18

solution, a sketch of the solution or, failing that, a discussion about possible solutions. It may even be that your content is a prompt for someone else to fully develop a solution. But even this is a story and an opportunity for further creative content.

The SCAMPER technique is an example of ways that existing products and services can be changed. This technique reimagines an existing product and services and tries to substitute, combine, adjust, modify (or magnify or minify), put to another use, eliminate or reverse (or rearrange) in ways that can bring new value and opportunities. Perhaps the most effective example of this technique was Amazon's reinvention of the ecommerce customer journey. Previously, someone shopping online would need to create an account and login before they could make a purchase. By reversing the process so that the selection of goods happened before any credentials were entered by a customer meant that greater investment in the purchase had already occurred, and there was a much greater likelihood of completing a payment. Considering other ways that existing goods or services could be redesigned through SCAMPER is a rich vein for content and encourages high levels of creative thinking.

LEGO Serious Play or using LEGO more generally is another method of generating creative thinking. The technique can be used to generate data for academic papers (Fletcher et al. 2016), create new products, reimagine an organisation's structure or plan a community project. Because LEGO are tangible items, using them can become a content opportunity for creating images and descriptions, as well as documenting any solutions that come out of the activity. As with many creative techniques, the opportunities for content are not just found in the final outputs but the entire process of creation, as well as any subsequent usage and application – the outcomes.

Even more creative techniques are documented through Gamestorming(.com) (Gray et al. 2010) and Tinkertoys (Michalko 2006). Although aimed at getting corporate teams thinking and engaged, the same principles can be used for groups of friends or between you and people who are representative of your personas.

Creativity is not a case of "being creative" or learning how to become creative – it is about trying ideas and "doing" creativity by setting aside concerns about being right or wrong.

18.2 Technical skills

The number one difficulty that small and medium-size businesses identify is finding qualified people with technical skills. The underlying problem that they less regularly recognise is finding people with an understanding of technology who can translate this into the vocabulary of business and management. Technical skills and technical translation skills are both incredibly valuable. The range of abilities covered by technical skills is also very large. Programming, different facets of web design and database administration, as well as querying and representing data, all fall into these wide categories of skills.

Having any one of these skills would also be an advantage for your own digital presence. Having some technical capability would enable you to expand your presence with more customised and unique features on your website (even if this was solely a unique WordPress theme that you created) as well as your social media channels.

Technical skills would also assist in making sense of the vast array of technical terms (and acronyms) that this book has consciously shielded you from being confronted with. We have specifically talked about links when technical literature would say URLs (uniform resource locators). Using SSL (secure sockets layer) was reduced to the clear statement that you should use it without delving deeply into why this is so important. We have presented how to create a website as being a case of using a content management system called WordPress. Extending this website is then discussed by adding the building blocks of individual plugins. We have hidden the underlying technologies that this system (and all of the web) is built upon: HTML (hypertext markup language), CSS (cascading style sheets) and JavaScript. This is not to say that this is the wrong approach. Using a CMS will save significant amounts of time, will be more robust and secure than trying to create your own website, and you will benefit from innovations in website development as soon as they are introduced into the CMS itself.

Creating a website should be analogous to the actions of driving a car, not building one from components. But if you want to take your website further, understanding the underlying technologies will help you to make better-informed decisions. If you need to, you can also make tweaks "under the hood" with enough confidence to reverse anything you might break. A simple example: If you have found the perfect theme but your preference is for hot pink borders rather than the boring navy blue that is built into the theme, you might edit the CSS files by replacing every reference to "#000080" with "#FF69B4". (For completeness, these are what are known as the hexadecimal codes for the respective colours.) This is a relatively straightforward find-and-replace operation, but understanding CSS and its relationship to what you see on the screen will definitely make things easier.

Technical skills or the ability to translate technical actions into more understandable descriptions can also help support the development of the technologies that your digital presence is now using. You may not have already considered the costs associated with WordPress, but effectively, the underlying CMS is available entirely for free. It is likely that the plugins you are using are also free. The open-source philosophy that underlies these developments was also mentioned in relation to the use of Creative Commons licenses by Wikipedia (§10.3). The community-oriented aspect of open-source development might be another inspiration for developing greater technical skills. The potential contribution is not restricted to writing code either. Open-source projects also require other roles, including translators to ensure that the user experience can be optimised in multiple languages and writers who can support the documentation of the project. "Giving back" may be enough motivation for contributing to a project with your existing skills. But in becoming involved with an open-source community, you are also exposed to the full set of activities involved in bringing a technical project to fruition.

Improving your technical skills will also support the other skills that we have emphasised throughout the book. Technical skills encourage a greater degree of self-reflection, employing critical perspectives, applying project management techniques and using systems thinking. All these skills in combination provide a robust skill set for being a good manager.

From this point of view, this book is only the starting point. You have a reason for setting a goal, and creating a digital presence supports this achievement. But your digital presence is an ongoing project, and it will lead you to new opportunities and new goals. Having a rationale for developing technical skills provides a key element to drive your learning. This is often the missing inspiration for learning in the classroom and formal learning environments. Now, with a digital presence, you have that motivation and a reason for exploring other resources and books that go deeper and explore in depth some of the underlying technologies that make the web, including some of the books that we critiqued in the Preface.

18.3 The future

The future is incredibly difficult to predict, and we are conscious of the Maes-Garreau law. This eponymous law says, "Most favorable predictions about future technology will fall [just before the death of the person making that prediction]" (KK 2007). The challenge is not to slip into this trap while still reaching beyond the scope of current technologies.

We have already seen rapid development of machine learning and artificial intelligence (AI) in a handful of years. This technology is already creeping into mainstream web technology and websites through chatbots (§17.3) as well as sites such as Bookmark(.com), Impress(.ly) and Leia (heyleia.com), which all attempt to build a website through AI technologies. Many specialised AI tools are finding their way online. The ability for anyone to isolate vocal and instrument tracks from a song can be found at sites such as lalal(.ai). AI can be used to generate a completely unique face (thispersondoesnotexist.com), CVs (thisresumedoesnotexist.com), song lyrics (theselyricsdonotexist.com), memes (imgflip.com/ai-meme) or anything (thisxdoesnotexist.com). These tools reinforce the importance of building reputation and trust in your own presence because so much content can be authored without human intervention. While results from these existing tools can vary, this automated future is clearly imminent in so many facets of life. You may even get the inspiration for your first business venture through an AI-generated suggestion (thisstartupdoesnotexist.com).

AI has also faced significant criticism for its flaws (aiweirdness.com) and its bias (Silberg and Manyika 2019). These concerns should force you to consider the ethical implications of using these tools, whether they are evident or not (§5.1). AI and any tools of technology should never be assumed to be ethically neutral or able to be deployed without ethical consequences.

More speculatively, direct neural linkages between humans and computers are being experimented with and trialled. Some early attempts at this technology used a cheap EEG monitor that was converted into a mechanical force. In 2009, Uncle Milton Star Wars Force Trainer was marketed to children as a game (although it was subsequently withdrawn). However, since 2016, Elon Musk's Neuralink has been developing a more serious brain-implant device. Testing has been done on pigs, and Musk's enthusiasm for the project is pressing for commencing a human-trial programme (BBC News 2020). A separate programme of research has used EEG monitoring to record dreams and then play them back (Nelson 2020). The more recent development appears to have been built on the findings of earlier research that recorded images of faces that people were thinking about (BEC 2016). The link between humans and computers is not science fiction, but its reaching the realm of everyday application is still some years of development away. The opportunities could be significant. Consider the ability to "dream" a website into existence, "smell" a tweet or "download" a book without the need to read it directly (the ultimate response to our concluding TL;DR sections in each chapter).

We have already observed the increasingly low bar between the concepts of online or offline, and the future will only continue to efface this distinction. From the point of view of this book, future editions will focus on creating a "successful presence" – any further clarification will be redundant. A presence will be as important in the future as it is now. You will need to be visible, and the focus of our discussions around ethical behaviour and being transparent and open will be even more emphasised.

The future has to be more sustainable than the present is now. Your presence will need to acknowledge and be fully conscious of the carbon footprint that it creates – and perhaps it should do that now (websitecarbon.com).

The future will be crowdsourced and so will predictions of the future (2050.earth).

TL;DR

Technology creates visibility. People create your reputation. Develop skills that enhance your reputation and will have value in the future.

Callout 18.1: Felix Arvid Ulf Kjellberg (aka PewDiePie)

The benchmark for personal presence

Born in Gothenberg, Sweden, in 1989 and currently living in Brighton in the UK, PewDiePie is one of the best known influencers, "YouTubers" and social media personalities. As one measure of this fame, PewDiePie's followers have a collective noun (Pewds) that mimics the practice of the fans of more traditional pop stars.

PewDiePie has won awards such as Teen Choice, been listed among *Time's* 100 most influential people in the world, championed charities such as the World Wildlife Foundation, appeared in a variety of films, written a parody self-help book and released a video for their song, "Bitch Lasagna". All this recent activity is based on the success and continued popularity of videos that were first created in 2010 (with Swedish commentary), based on the "Let's Play" format: an informed narrative walkthrough of a game. PewDiePie dropped out of a Chalmers University course to pursue a more creative pathway. With their parents refusing to support them outside university, PewDiePie supported themselves by selling artwork and working temporary jobs before monetising their YouTube presence.

PewDiePie has attracted criticism for sexist comments and statements apparently advocating sexual violence made early in their career and later lost sponsors when they made racist, ablest and homophobic comments. The format of Let's Play videos has also attracted some controversy as YouTube's ContentID system flags this type of content as a copyright violation.

PewDiePie is married to Italian Marzia Bisognin (aka CutiePie), and they chose to live in Brighton because of its reliable internet connectivity.

PewDiePie's presence is built entirely around YouTube, with the website being a vehicle for selling merchandise. The Twitter account is a placeholder to avoid squatters, and despite having no tweets, there are more followers than many Twitter users will ever gain.

PewDiePie's website is made with WordPress and uses WooCommerce, WPBakery, WP Rocket and Contact Form 7.

Channel	Link	Followers	Views	Content
YouTube	www.youtube.com/user/ PewDiePie	108m	26bn views	4.2k videos
Twitter	https://twitter.com/pewdiepie	382.2k		0 tweets
Website	https://pewdipiemerch.com/		Ranked 1.8mth website globally	

References cited

BBC News (2020) "Neuralink: Elon Musk unveils pig with chip in its brain", 29th Aug., www.bbc.co.uk/news/world-us-canada-53956683

BEC (2016) "Scientists have invented a mind-reading machine that visualises your thoughts", *Science Alert*, 23rd June, www.sciencealert.com/scientists-have-invented-a-mind-reading-machine-that-can-visualise-your-thoughts-kind-of

Bronson, P. and Merryman, A. (2010) "Creativity in America: The creativity crisis", *Newsweek*, 10th July, www.newsweek.com/2010/07/10/the-creativity-crisis.html

Fletcher, G., Greenhill, A., Griffiths, M., Holmes, K. and McLean, R. (2016) "Creatively prototyping the future high street", *Production Planning & Control*, 27(6), https://doi.org/10.1080/09537287.2016.1147094

Gray, D., Brown, S. and Macanufo, J. (2010) *Gamestorming: A Playbook for Innovators, Rulebreakers, and Changemakers*, Sebastopol, CA: O'Reilly Media.

Michalko, M. (2006) *Thinkertoys: A Handbook of Creative-Thinking Techniques*, Berkeley, CA: Ten Speed Press.

Nelson, B. (2020) "Scientists learn how to record your dreams and play them back to you", *Treehugger*, 8th May, www.treehugger.com/scientists-learn-how-to-record-your-dreams-and-play-them-4864047

Silberg, J. and Manyika, J. (2019) "Notes from the AI frontier: Tackling bias in AI (and in humans)", *McKinsey Global Institute*, June, www.mckinsey.com/~/media/McKinsey/Featured%20Insights/Artificial%20Intelligence/Tackling%20bias%20in%20artificial%20intelligence%20and%20in%20humans/MGI-Tackling-bias-in-AI-June-2019.pdf

The Technium (2007) "The Maes-Garreau point", *KK*, 14th Mar., https://kk.org/thetechnium/the-maesgarreau/

Further reading

Fry, H. (2019) *"Hello Word": How to Be Human in the Age of the Machine*, New York: W.W. Norton & Company.

Raymond, E. (2008) *The Cathedral and the Bazaar*, Sebastopol, CA: O'Reilly Media, www.catb.org/~esr/writings/cathedral-bazaar/

Index

Printed in Great Britain
by Amazon

15535231R00122